MW00718169

The
CWEB System
of Structured
Documentation

The
CWEB System
of Structured
Documentation
Version 3.6

Donald E. Knuth
Stanford University

Silvio Levy
Mathematical Sciences Research Institute

ADDISON–WESLEY

Boston, Massachusetts • San Francisco • New York
Toronto • Montreal • London • Munich • Paris • Madrid
Capetown • Sydney • Tokyo • Singapore • Mexico City

Library of Congress Cataloging-in-Publication Data

Knuth, Donald Ervin, 1938-
  The CWEB system of structured documentation, version 3.6 / Donald
E. Knuth, Silvio Levy
  ii,237 p. 28 cm.
  Includes indexes.
  ISBN 0-201-57569-8
  1. Electronic data processing documentation. 2. C (Computer
program language) 3. TeX (Computer system) I. Levy, Silvio.
II. Title. QA76.9.D3K6 2001
005.1'5--dc20
                                                    93-31104
                                                        CIP

This printing includes minor revisions to version 3.6 that were released in version 3.63.

TeX is a trademark of the American Mathematical Society.
Acrobat Reader is a trademark of Adobe Systems Incorporated.

Copyright © 1994 by Addison-Wesley Publishing Company, Inc.

All rights reserved. No part of this publication may be reproduced, stored in a retrieval system, or transmitted, in any form or by any means, electronic, mechanical, photocopying, recording, or otherwise, without the prior written permission of the publisher. Printed in the United States of America.

Permission is granted to make and distribute verbatim copies of the electronic form of this document provided that the electronic copyright notice and this permission notice are preserved on all copies.

Permission is granted to copy and distribute modified versions of the electronic form of this document under the conditions for verbatim copying, provided that the entire resulting derived work is distributed under the terms of a permission notice identical to this one.

Internet page http://www-cs-faculty.stanford.edu/~knuth/cweb.html contains current information about CWEB and related topics.

ISBN 0-201-57569-8

3 4 5 6 7 8–CRS–05 04 03 02 01

The CWEB System of Structured Documentation

Donald E. Knuth and Silvio Levy

This document describes a version of Don Knuth's WEB system, adapted to C by Silvio Levy. Since its creation in 1987, CWEB has been revised and enhanced in various ways, by both Knuth and Levy. We now believe that its evolution is near an end; however, bug reports, suggestions and comments are still welcome, and should be sent to Levy (levy@math.berkeley.edu).

Readers who are familiar with Knuth's memo "The WEB System of Structured Documentation" will be able to skim this material rapidly, because CWEB and WEB share the same philosophy and (essentially) the same syntax. In some respects CWEB is a simplification of WEB: for example, CWEB does not need WEB's features for macro definition and string handling, because C and its preprocessor already take care of macros and strings. Similarly, the WEB conventions of denoting octal and hexadecimal constants by @'77 and @"3f are replaced by C's conventions 077 and 0x3f. All other features of WEB have been retained, and new features have been added.

We thank all who contributed suggestions and criticism to the development of CWEB. We are especially grateful to Steve Avery, Nelson Beebe, Hans-Hermann Bode, Klaus Guntermann, Norman Ramsey, Joachim Schnitter, and Saroj Mahapatra, who contributed code, and to Cameron Smith, who made many suggestions improving the manual. Ramsey has made literate programming accessible to users of yet other languages by means of his SPIDER system [see *Communications of the ACM* **32** (1989), 1051–1055]. The book *Literate Programming* by Knuth (1992) contains a comprehensive bibliography of related early work. Bode, Schnitter, and Mahapatra adapted CWEB so that it works for C++ as well; therefore in the text below you can read C++ for C if you so desire.

Introduction

The philosophy behind CWEB is that programmers who want to provide the best possible documentation for their programs need two things simultaneously: a language like TEX for formatting, and a language like C for programming. Neither type of language can provide the best documentation by itself. But when both are appropriately combined, we obtain a system that is much more useful than either language separately.

The structure of a software program may be thought of as a "web" that is made up of many interconnected pieces. To document such a program, we want to explain each individual part of the web and how it relates to its neighbors. The typographic tools provided by TEX give us an opportunity to explain the local structure of each part by making that structure visible, and the programming tools provided by C make it possible for us to specify the algorithms formally and unambiguously. By combining the two, we can develop a style of programming that maximizes our ability to perceive the structure of a complex piece of software, and at the same time the documented programs can be mechanically translated into a working software system that matches the documentation.

The CWEB system consists of two programs named CWEAVE and CTANGLE. When writing a CWEB program the user keeps the C code and the documentation in the same file, called the CWEB file and generally named something.w. The command 'cweave something' creates an output file something.tex, which can then be fed to TEX, yielding a "pretty printed" version of something.w that correctly handles typographic details like page layout and the use of indentation, italics, boldface, and mathematical symbols. The typeset output also includes extensive cross-index information that is gathered automatically. Similarly, if you run the command 'ctangle something' you will get a C file something.c, which can then be compiled to yield executable code.

Besides providing a documentation tool, CWEB enhances the C language by providing the ability to permute pieces of the program text, so that a large system can be understood entirely in terms of small sections and their local interrelationships. The CTANGLE program is so named because it takes a given web and moves the sections from their web structure into the order required by C; the advantage of programming in CWEB is that the algorithms can be expressed in "untangled" form, with each section explained separately. The CWEAVE program is so named because it takes a given web and intertwines the TEX and C portions contained in each section, then it knits the whole fabric into a structured document. (Get it? Wow.) Perhaps there is some deep connection here with the fact that the German word for "weave" is "*webe*", and the corresponding Latin imperative is "*texe*"!

A user of CWEB should be fairly familiar with the C programming language. A minimal amount of acquaintance with TeX is also desirable, but in fact it can be acquired as one uses CWEB, since straight text can be typeset in TeX with virtually no knowledge of that language. To someone familiar with both C and TeX the amount of effort necessary to learn the commands of CWEB is small.

Overview

Two kinds of material go into CWEB files: TeX text and C text. A programmer writing in CWEB should be thinking both of the documentation and of the C program being created; i.e., the programmer should be instinctively aware of the different actions that CWEAVE and CTANGLE will perform on the CWEB file. TeX text is essentially copied without change by CWEAVE, and it is entirely deleted by CTANGLE; the TeX text is "pure documentation." C text, on the other hand, is formatted by CWEAVE and it is shuffled around by CTANGLE, according to rules that will become clear later. For now the important point to keep in mind is that there are two kinds of text. Writing CWEB programs is something like writing TeX documents, but with an additional "C mode" that is added to TeX's horizontal mode, vertical mode, and math mode.

A CWEB file is built up from units called *sections* that are more or less self-contained. Each section has three parts:

- A TeX part, containing explanatory material about what is going on in the section.
- A middle part, containing macro definitions that serve as abbreviations for C constructions that would be less comprehensible if written out in full each time. They are turned by CTANGLE into preprocessor macro definitions.
- A C part, containing a piece of the program that CTANGLE will produce. This C code should ideally be about a dozen lines long, so that it is easily comprehensible as a unit and so that its structure is readily perceived.

The three parts of each section must appear in this order; i.e., the TeX commentary must come first, then the middle part, and finally the C code. Any of the parts may be empty.

A section begins with either of the symbols '@␣' or '@*', where '␣' denotes a blank space. A section ends at the beginning of the next section (i.e., at the next '@␣' or '@*'), or at the end of the file, whichever comes first. The CWEB file may also contain material that is not part of any section at all, namely the text (if any) that occurs before the first section. Such text is said to be "in limbo"; it is ignored by CTANGLE and copied essentially verbatim by CWEAVE, so its function is to provide any additional formatting instructions that may be desired in the TeX output. Indeed, it is customary to begin a CWEB file with TeX code in limbo that loads special fonts, defines special macros, changes the page sizes, and/or produces a title page.

Sections are numbered consecutively, starting with 1. These numbers appear at the beginning of each section of the TeX documentation output by CWEAVE, and they appear as bracketed comments at the beginning and end of the code generated by that section in the C program output by CTANGLE.

Section Names

Fortunately, you never mention these numbers yourself when you are writing in CWEB. You just say '@␣' or '@*' at the beginning of each new section, and the numbers are supplied automatically by CWEAVE and CTANGLE. As far as you are concerned, a section has a *name* instead of a number; its name is specified by writing '@<' followed by TeX text followed by '@>'. When CWEAVE outputs a section name, it replaces the '@<' and '@>' by angle brackets and inserts the section number in small type. Thus, when you read the output of CWEAVE it is easy to locate any section that is referred to in another section.

For expository purposes, a section name should be a good description of the contents of that section; i.e., it should stand for the abstraction represented by the section. Then the section can be "plugged into" one or more other sections in such a way that unimportant details of its inner workings are suppressed. A section name therefore ought to be long enough to convey the necessary meaning.

Unfortunately, it is laborious to type such long names over and over again, and it is also difficult to specify a long name twice in exactly the same way so that CWEAVE and CTANGLE will be able to match the names to the sections. To ameliorate this situation, CWEAVE and CTANGLE let you abbreviate a section name, so long as the full name appears somewhere in the CWEB file; you can type simply '@<α...@>', where α is any string that is a prefix of exactly one section name appearing in the file. For example, '@<Clear the arrays@>' can be abbreviated to '@<Clear...@>' if no other section name begins with the five letters 'Clear'. Elsewhere you might use the abbreviation '@<Clear t...@>', and so on.

Section names must otherwise match character for character, except that consecutive characters of white space (spaces, tab marks, newlines, and/or form feeds) are treated as equivalent to a single space, and such spaces are deleted at the beginning and end of the name. Thus, '`@< Clear  the arrays @>`' will also match the name in the previous example. Spaces following the ellipsis in abbreviations are ignored as well, but not those before, so that '`@<Clear t ...@>`' would not match '`@<Clear the arrays@>`'.

What CTANGLE Does

We have said that a section begins with '`@␣`' or '`@*`', but we didn't say how it gets divided up into a TeX part, a middle part, and a C part. The middle part begins with the first appearance of '`@d`' or '`@f`' in the section, and the C part begins with the first appearance of '`@c`' or '`@<section name@>=`'. In the latter case you are saying, in effect, that the section name stands for the C text that follows. Alternatively, if the C part begins with '`@c`' instead of a section name, the current section is said to be *unnamed*.

The construct '`@<section name@>`' can appear any number of times in the C part of a section: Subsequent appearances indicate that a named section is being "used" rather than "defined." In other words, the C code for the named section, presumably defined elsewhere, should be spliced in at this point in the C program. Indeed, the main idea of CTANGLE is to make a C program out of individual sections, named and unnamed. The exact way in which this is done is this: First all the macro definitions indicated by '`@d`' are turned into C preprocessor macro definitions and copied at the beginning. Then the C parts of unnamed sections are copied down, in order; this constitutes the first-order approximation to the text of the program. (There should be at least one unnamed section, otherwise there will be no program.) Then all section names that appear in the first-order approximation are replaced by the C parts of the corresponding sections, and this substitution process continues until no section names remain. All comments are removed, because the C program is intended only for the eyes of the C compiler.

If the same name has been given to more than one section, the C text for that name is obtained by putting together all of the C parts in the corresponding sections. This feature is useful, for example, in a section named 'Global variables', since one can then declare global variables in whatever sections those variables are introduced. When several sections have the same name, CWEAVE assigns the first section number as the number corresponding to that name, and it inserts a note at the bottom of that section telling the reader to 'See also sections so-and-so'; this footnote gives the numbers of all the other sections having the same name as the present one. The C text corresponding to a section is usually formatted by CWEAVE so that the output has an equivalence sign in place of the equals sign in the CWEB file; i.e., the output says '⟨ section name ⟩ ≡ C text'. However, in the case of the second and subsequent appearances of a section with the same name, this '≡' sign is replaced by '+≡', as an indication that the following C text is being appended to the C text of another section.

As CTANGLE enters and leaves sections, it inserts preprocessor `#line` commands into the C output file. This means that when the compiler gives you error messages, or when you debug your program, the messages refer to line numbers in the CWEB file, and not in the C file. In most cases you can therefore forget about the C file altogether.

What CWEAVE Does

The general idea of CWEAVE is to make a `.tex` file from the CWEB file in the following way: The first line of the `.tex` file tells TeX to input a file with macros that define CWEB's documentation conventions. The next lines of the file will be copied from whatever TeX text is in limbo before the first section. Then comes the output for each section in turn, possibly interspersed with end-of-page marks. Finally, CWEAVE will generate a cross-reference index that lists each section number in which each C identifier appears, and it will also generate an alphabetized list of the section names, as well as a table of contents that shows the page and section numbers for each "starred" section.

What is a "starred" section, you ask? A section that begins with '`@*`' instead of '`@␣`' is slightly special in that it denotes a new major group of sections. The '`@*`' should be followed by the title of this group, followed by a period. Such sections will always start on a new page in the TeX output, and the group title will appear as a running headline on all subsequent pages until the next starred section. The title will also appear in the table of contents, and in boldface type at the beginning of its section. Caution: Do not use TeX control sequences in such titles, unless you know that the cwebmac macros will do the right thing with them. The reason is that these titles are converted to uppercase when they appear as running heads, and they are converted to boldface when they appear at the beginning of their sections, and they are also written out to a table-of-contents file used for temporary storage while TEX is working; whatever control sequences you use must be meaningful in all three of these modes.

The TEX output produced by CWEAVE for each section consists of the following: First comes the section number (e.g., '\M123.' at the beginning of section 123, except that '\N' appears in place of '\M' at the beginning of a starred section). Then comes the TEX part of the section, copied almost verbatim except as noted below. Then comes the middle part and the C part, formatted so that there will be a little extra space between them if both are nonempty. The middle and C parts are obtained by inserting a bunch of funny-looking TEX macros into the C program; these macros handle typographic details about fonts and proper math spacing, as well as line breaks and indentation.

C Code in TEX Text and Vice Versa

When you are typing TEX text, you will probably want to make frequent reference to variables and other quantities in your C code, and you will want those variables to have the same typographic treatment when they appear in your text as when they appear in your program. Therefore the CWEB language allows you to get the effect of C editing within TEX text, if you place '|' marks before and after the C material. For example, suppose you want to say something like this:

If pa is declared as 'int *pa', the assignment $pa = \&a[0]$ makes pa point to the zeroth element of a.

The TEX text would look like this in your CWEB file:

```
If |pa| is declared as '|int *pa|', the
assignment |pa=&a[0]| makes |pa| point to the zeroth element of |a|.
```

And CWEAVE translates this into something you are glad you didn't have to type:

```
If \\{pa} is declared as '\&{int} ${}{*}\\{pa}$',
the assignment $\\{pa}\K{\AND}\|a[\T{0}]$
makes \\{pa} point to the zeroth element of \|a.
```

Incidentally, the cross-reference index that CWEAVE would make, in the presence of a comment like this, would include the current section number as one of the index entries for pa, even though pa might not appear in the C part of this section. Thus, the index covers references to identifiers in the explanatory comments as well as in the program itself; you will soon learn to appreciate this feature. However, the identifiers **int** and a would not be indexed, because CWEAVE does not make index entries for reserved words or single-letter identifiers. Such identifiers are felt to be so ubiquitous that it would be pointless to mention every place where they occur.

Although a section begins with TEX text and ends with C text, we have noted that the dividing line isn't sharp, since C text can be included in TEX text if it is enclosed in '|...|'. Conversely, TEX text appears frequently within C text, because everything in comments (i.e., between /* and */, or following //) is treated as TEX text. Likewise, the text of a section name consists of TEX text, but the construct @<section name@> as a whole is expected to be found in C text; thus, one typically goes back and forth between the C and TEX environments in a natural way, as in these examples:

```
if (x==0) @<Empty the |buffer| array@>
```
```
... using the algorithm in |@<Empty the |buffer| array@>|.
```

The first of these excerpts would be found in the C part of a section, into which the code from the section named "Empty the *buffer* array" is being spliced. The second excerpt would be found in the TEX part of the section, and the named section is being "cited", rather than defined or used. (Note the '|...|' surrounding the section name in this case.)

Macros

The control code @d followed by

$\qquad\qquad$ *identifier* C text $\qquad$ or by $\qquad$ *identifier* ($par_1, \ldots, par_n$) C text

(where there is no blank between the *identifier* and the parentheses in the second case) is transformed by CTANGLE into a preprocessor command, starting with #define, which is printed at the top of the C output file as explained earlier.

A '@d' macro definition can go on for several lines, and the newlines don't have to be protected by backslashes, since CTANGLE itself inserts the backslashes. If for any reason you need a #define command at a specific spot in your C file, you can treat it as C code, instead of as a CWEB macro; but then you do have to protect newlines yourself.

Strings and constants

If you want a string to appear in the C file, delimited by pairs of ' or " marks as usual, you can type it exactly so in the CWEB file, except that the character '@' should be typed '@@' (it becomes a control code, the only one that can appear in strings; see below). Strings should end on the same line as they begin, unless there's a backslash at the end of lines within them.

TEX and C have different ways to refer to octal and hex constants, because TEX is oriented to technical writing while C is oriented to computer processing. In TEX you make a constant octal or hexadecimal by prepending ' or ", respectively, to it; in C the constant should be preceded by 0 or 0x. In CWEB it seems reasonable to let each convention hold in its respective realm; so in C text you get 40_8 by typing '040', which CTANGLE faithfully copies into the C file (for the compiler's benefit) and which CWEAVE prints as $^\circ 40$. Similarly, CWEAVE prints the hexadecimal C constant '0x20' as $^\#20$. The use of italic font for octal digits and typewriter font for hexadecimal digits makes the meaning of such constants clearer in a document. For consistency, then, you should type '|040|' or '|0x20|' in the TEX part of the section.

Control codes

A CWEB *control code* is a two-character combination of which the first is '@'. We've already seen the meaning of several control codes; it's time to list them more methodically.

In the following list, the letters in brackets after a control code indicate in what contexts that code is allowed. *L* indicates that the code is allowed in limbo; *T* (for TEX), *M* (for middle), and *C* (for C) mean that the code is allowed in each of the three parts of a section, at top level—that is, outside such constructs as '|...|' and section names. An arrow → means that the control code terminates the present part of the CWEB file, and inaugurates the part indicated by the letter following the arrow. Thus $[LTMC \to T]$ next to @␣ indicates that this control code can occur in limbo, or in any of the three parts of a section, and that it starts the (possibly empty) TEX part of the following section.

Two other abbreviations can occur in these brackets: The letter *r* stands for *restricted context*, that is, material inside C comments, section names, C strings and control texts (defined below); the letter *c* stands for *inner* C *context*, that is, C material inside '|...|' (including '|...|'s inside comments, but not those occurring in other restricted contexts). An asterisk * following the brackets means that the context from this control code to the matching @> is restricted.

Control codes involving letters are case-insensitive; thus @d and @D are equivalent. Only the lowercase versions are mentioned specifically below.

@@ $[LTMCrc]$ A double @ denotes the single character '@'. This is the only control code that is legal everywhere. Note that you must use this convention if you are giving an internet email address in a CWEB file (e.g., levy@@math.berkeley.edu).

Here are the codes that introduce the TEX part of a section.

@␣ $[LTMC \to T]$ This denotes the beginning of a new (unstarred) section. A tab mark or form feed or end-of-line character is equivalent to a space when it follows an @ sign (and in most other cases).

@* $[LTMC \to T]$ This denotes the beginning of a new starred section, i.e., a section that begins a new major group. The title of the new group should appear after the @*, followed by a period. As explained above, TEX control sequences should be avoided in such titles unless they are quite simple. When CWEAVE and CTANGLE read a @*, they print an asterisk on the terminal followed by the current section number, so that the user can see some indication of progress. The very first section should be starred.

You can specify the "depth" of a starred section by typing * or a decimal number after the @*; this indicates the relative ranking of the current group of sections in the program hierarchy. Top-level portions of the program, introduced by @**, get their names typeset in boldface type in the table of contents; they are said to have depth −1. Otherwise the depth is a nonnegative number, which governs the amount of indentation on the contents page. Such indentation helps clarify the structure of a long program. The depth is assumed to be 0 if it is not specified explicitly; when your program is short, you might as well leave all depths zero. A starred section always begins a new page in the output, unless the depth is greater than 1.

The middle part of each section consists of any number of macro definitions (beginning with @d) and format definitions (beginning with @f or @s), intermixed in any order.

@d $[TM \to M]$ Macro definitions begin with @d, followed by an identifier and optional parameters and C text as explained earlier.

@f $[TM \to M]$ Format definitions begin with @f; they cause CWEAVE to treat identifiers in a special way when they appear in C text. The general form of a format definition is '@f l r', followed by an optional comment enclosed between /* and */, where l and r are identifiers; CWEAVE will subsequently treat identifier l as it currently treats r. This feature allows a CWEB programmer to invent new reserved words and/or to unreserve some of C's reserved identifiers. For example, the common words 'error' and 'line' have been given a special meaning in the C preprocessor, so CWEAVE is set up to format them specially; if you want a variable named *error* or *line*, you should say

@f error normal   @f line normal

somewhere in your program.

If r is the special identifier '*TeX*', identifier l will be formatted as a TeX control sequence; for example, '@f foo TeX' in the CWEB file will cause identifier *foo* to be output as \foo by CWEAVE. The programmer should define \foo to have whatever custom format is desired, assuming TeX math mode. (Each underline character is converted to x when making the TeX control sequence, and each dollar sign is converted to X; thus *foo_bar* becomes \fooxbar. Other characters, including digits, are left untranslated, so TeX will consider them as macro parameters, not as part of the control sequence itself. For example,

\def\x#1{x_{#1}} @f x1 TeX @f x2 TeX

will format x1 and x2 not as *x1* and *x2* but as x_1 and x_2.)

If r is the special identifier '*make_pair*', identifier l will be treated as a C++ function template. For example, after @f convert make_pair one can say 'convert<int>(2.5)' without having < and > misunderstood as less-than and greater-than signs.

CWEAVE knows that identifiers being defined with a **typedef** should become reserved words; thus you don't need format definitions very often.

@s $[TM \to M;\ L]$ Same as @f, but CWEAVE does not show the format definition in the output, and the optional C comment is not allowed. This is used mostly in @i files.

Next come the codes that govern the C part of a section.

@c @p $[TM \to C]$ The C part of an unnamed section begins with @c (or with @p for "program"; both control codes do the same thing). This causes CTANGLE to append the following C code to the first-order program text, as explained on page 3. Note that CWEAVE does not print a '@c' in the TeX output, so if you are creating a CWEB file based on a TeX-printed CWEB documentation you have to remember to insert @c in the appropriate places of the unnamed sections.

@< $[TM \to C;\ C;\ c]$ * This control code introduces a section name (or unambiguous prefix, as discussed above), which consists of TeX text and extends to the matching @>. The whole construct @<...@> is conceptually a C element. The behavior is different depending on the context:

A @< appearing in contexts T and M attaches the following section name to the current section, and inaugurates the C part of the section. The closing @> should be followed by = or +=.

In context C, @< indicates that the named section is being used—its C definition is spliced in by CTANGLE, as explained on page 3. As an error-detection measure, CTANGLE and CWEAVE complain if such a section name is followed by =, because most likely this is meant as the definition of a new section, and so should be preceded by @␣. If you really want to say ⟨foo⟩ = *bar*, where ⟨foo⟩ is being used and not defined, put a newline before the =.

Finally, in inner C context (that is, within '|...|' in the TeX part of a section or in a comment), @<...@> means that the named section is being cited. Such an occurrence is ignored by CTANGLE. Note that even here we think of the section name as being a C element, hence the |...|.

@($[TM \to C;\ C;\ c]$ * A section name can begin with @(. Everything works just as for @<, except that the C code of the section named @(foo@> is written by CTANGLE to file foo. In this way you can get multiple-file output from a single CWEB file. (The @d definitions are not output to such files, only to the master .c file.) One use of this feature is to produce header files for other program modules that will be loaded with the present one. Another use is to produce a test routine that goes with your program. By keeping the sources for a program and its header and test routine together, you are more likely to keep all three consistent with each other. Notice that the output of a named section can be incorporated in several different output files, because you can mention @<foo@> in both @(bar1@> and @(bar2@>.

@h [Cc]   Causes CTANGLE to insert at the current spot the #define statements from the middle parts of all sections, and *not* to write them at the beginning of the C file. Useful when you want the macro definitions to come after the include files, say. (Ignored by CTANGLE inside '|...|'.)

The next several control codes introduce "control texts," which end with the next '@>'. The closing '@>' must be on the same line of the CWEB file as the line where the control text began. The context from each of these control codes to the matching @> is restricted.

@^ [TMCc]   * The control text that follows, up to the next '@>', will be entered into the index together with the identifiers of the C program; this text will appear in roman type. For example, to put the phrase "system dependencies" into the index that is output by CWEAVE, type '@^system dependencies@>' in each section that you want to index as system dependent.

@. [TMCc]   * The control text that follows will be entered into the index in typewriter type.

@: [TMCc]   * The control text that follows will be entered into the index in a format controlled by the TEX macro '\9', which you should define as desired.

@t [MCc]   * The control text that follows will be put into a TEX \hbox and formatted along with the neighboring C program. This text is ignored by CTANGLE, but it can be used for various purposes within CWEAVE. For example, you can make comments that mix C and classical mathematics, as in '$size < 2^{15}$', by typing '|size < 2@t^{15}@>|'.

@= [MCc]   * The control text that follows will be passed verbatim to the C program.

@q [LTMCc]   * The control text that follows will be totally ignored—it's a comment for readers of the CWEB file only. A file intended to be included in limbo, with @i, can identify itself with @q comments. Another use is to balance unbalanced parentheses in C strings, so that your text editor's parenthesis matcher doesn't go into a tailspin.

@! [TMCc]   * The section number in an index entry will be underlined if '@!' immediately precedes the identifier or control text being indexed. This convention is used to distinguish the sections where an identifier is defined, or where it is explained in some special way, from the sections where it is used. A reserved word or an identifier of length one will not be indexed except for underlined entries. An '@!' is implicitly inserted by CWEAVE when an identifier is being defined or declared in C code; for example, the definition

$$\textbf{int } array[\mathit{max\_dim}], \mathit{count} = \mathit{old\_count};$$

makes the names *array* and *count* get an underlined entry in the index. Statement labels, function definitions like *main*(**int** *argc*, **char** **argv*[]), and **typedef** definitions also imply underlining. An old-style function definition (without prototyping) doesn't define its arguments; the arguments will, however, be considered to be defined (i.e., their index entries will be underlined) if their types are declared before the body of the function in the usual way (e.g., '**int** *argc*; **char** **argv*[]; {...}'). Thus @! is not needed very often, except in unusual constructions or in cases like

```
enum boolean {@!false, @!true};
```

here @! gives the best results because individual constants enumerated by **enum** are not automatically underlined in the index at their point of definition.

We now turn to control codes that affect only the operation of CTANGLE.

@' [MCc]   This control code is dangerous because it has quite different meanings in CWEB and the original WEB. In CWEB it produces the decimal constant corresponding to the ASCII code for a string of length 1 (e.g., @'a' is CTANGLEd into 97 and @'\t' into 9). You might want to use this if you need to work in ASCII on a non-ASCII machine; but in most cases the C conventions of <ctype.h> are adequate for character-set-independent programming.

@& [*MCc*]   The @& operation causes whatever is on its left to be adjacent to whatever is on its right, in the
C output. No spaces or line breaks will separate these two items.

@l [*L*]   CWEB programmers have the option of using any 8-bit character code from the often-forbidden range
128–255 within TEX text; such characters are also permitted in strings and even in identifiers of the C
program. Under various extensions of the basic ASCII standard, the higher 8-bit codes correspond to
accented letters, letters from non-Latin alphabets, and so on. When such characters occur in identifiers,
CTANGLE must replace them by standard ASCII alphanumeric characters or _, in order to generate
legal C code. It does this by means of a transliteration table, which by default associates the string
Xab to the character with ASCII code #*ab* (where *a* and *b* are hexadecimal digits, and $a \geq 8$). By
placing the construction @l␣ab␣newstring in limbo, you are telling CTANGLE to replace this character
by newstring instead. For example, the ISO Latin-1 code for the letter 'ü' is #FC (or '\374'), and
CTANGLE will normally change this code to the three-character sequence XFC if it appears in an identifier.
If you say @l fc ue, the code will be transliterated into ue instead.

   CWEAVE passes 8-bit characters straight through to TEX without transliteration; therefore TEX must
be prepared to receive them. If you are formatting all your nonstandard identifiers as "custom" control
sequences, you should make TEX treat all their characters as letters. Otherwise you should either make
your 8-bit codes "active" in TEX, or load fonts that contain the special characters you need in the correct
positions. (The font selected by TEX control sequence \it is used for identifiers.) Look for special macro
packages designed for CWEB users in your language; or, if you are brave, write one yourself.

The next eight control codes (namely '@,', '@/', '@|', '@#', '@+', '@;', '@[', and '@]') have no effect on the
C program output by CTANGLE; they merely help to improve the readability of the TEX-formatted C that
is output by CWEAVE, in unusual circumstances. CWEAVE's built-in formatting method is fairly good when
dealing with syntactically correct C text, but it is incapable of handling all possible cases, because it must
deal with fragments of text involving macros and section names; these fragments do not necessarily obey C's
syntax. Although CWEB allows you to override the automatic formatting, your best strategy is not to worry
about such things until you have seen what CWEAVE produces automatically, since you will probably need to
make only a few corrections when you are touching up your documentation.

@, [*MCc*]   This control code inserts a thin space in CWEAVE's output. Sometimes you need this extra space
if you are using macros in an unusual way, e.g., if two identifiers are adjacent.

@/ [*MC*]   This control code causes a line break to occur within a C program formatted by CWEAVE. Line
breaks are chosen automatically by TEX according to a scheme that works 99% of the time, but sometimes
you will prefer to force a line break so that the program is segmented according to logical rather than
visual criteria. If a comment follows, say '@/@,' to break the line before the comment.

@| [*MC*]   This control code specifies an optional line break in the midst of an expression. For example,
if you have a long expression on the right-hand side of an assignment statement, you can use '@|' to
specify breakpoints more logical than the ones that TEX might choose on visual grounds.

@# [*MC*]   This control code forces a line break, like @/ does, and it also causes a little extra white space
to appear between the lines at this break. You might use it, for example, between groups of macro
definitions that are logically separate but within the same section. CWEB automatically inserts this extra
space between functions, between external declarations and functions, and between declarations and
statements within a function.

@+ [*MC*]   This control code cancels a line break that might otherwise be inserted by CWEAVE, e.g., before
the word '**else**', if you want to put a short if–else construction on a single line. If you say '{@+' at the
beginning of a compound statement that is the body of a function, the first declaration or statement of
the function will appear on the same line as the left brace, and it will be indented by the same amount
as the second declaration or statement on the next line.

@; [*MC*]   This control code is treated like a semicolon, for formatting purposes, except that it is invisible.
You can use it, for example, after a section name or macro when the C text represented by that section
or macro is a compound statement or ends with a semicolon. Consider constructions like

```
            if (condition) macro @;
            else break;
```

where *macro* is defined to be a compound statement (enclosed in braces). This is a well-known infelicity
of C syntax.

@[[*MC*]   See @].

@] [*MC*]   Place @[...@] brackets around program text that CWEAVE is supposed to format as an expression, if it doesn't already do so. (This occasionally applies to unusual macro arguments.) Also insert '@[@]' between a simple type name and a left parenthesis when declaring a pointer to a function, as in

int @[@] (*f)();

otherwise CWEAVE will confuse the first part of that declaration with the C++ expression '**int**(*f*)'. Another example, for people who want to use low-level #define commands in the midst of C code and the definition begins with a cast:

#define foo @[(int)(bar)@]

The remaining control codes govern the input that CWEB sees.

@x @y @z [*change_file*]   CWEAVE and CTANGLE are designed to work with two input files, called *web_file* and *change_file*, where *change_file* contains data that overrides selected portions of *web_file*. The resulting merged text is actually what has been called the CWEB file elsewhere in this report.

    Here's how it works: The change file consists of zero or more "changes," where a change has the form '@x⟨old lines⟩@y⟨new lines⟩@z'. The special control codes @x, @y, @z, which are allowed only in change files, must appear at the beginning of a line; the remainder of such a line is ignored. The ⟨old lines⟩ represent material that exactly matches consecutive lines of the *web_file*; the ⟨new lines⟩ represent zero or more lines that are supposed to replace the old. Whenever the first "old line" of a change is found to match a line in the *web_file*, all the other lines in that change must match too.

    Between changes, before the first change, and after the last change, the change file can have any number of lines that do not begin with '@x', '@y', or '@z'. Such lines are bypassed and not used for matching purposes.

    This dual-input feature is useful when working with a master CWEB file that has been received from elsewhere (e.g., tangle.w or weave.w or tex.web), when changes are desirable to customize the program for your local computer system. You will be able to debug your system-dependent changes without clobbering the master web file; and once your changes are working, you will be able to incorporate them readily into new releases of the master web file that you might receive from time to time.

@i [*web_file*]   Furthermore the *web_file* itself can be a combination of several files. When either CWEAVE or CTANGLE is reading a file and encounters the control code @i at the beginning of a line, it interrupts normal reading and starts looking at the file named after the @i, much as the C preprocessor does when it encounters an #include line. After the included file has been entirely read, the program goes back to the next line of the original file. The file name following @i can be surrounded by " characters, but such delimiters are optional. Include files can nest.

    Change files can have lines starting with @i. In this way you can replace one included file with another. Conceptually, the replacement mechanism described above does its work first, and its output is then checked for @i lines. If @i foo occurs between @y and @z in a change file, individual lines of file foo and files it includes are not changeable; but changes can be made to lines from files that were included by unchanged input.

    On UNIX systems (and others that support environment variables), if the environment variable CWEBINPUTS is set, or if the compiler flag of the same name was defined at compile time, CWEB will look for include files in the directory thus named, if it cannot find them in the current directory.

Additional features and caveats

1. In certain installations of CWEB that have an extended character set, the characters '↑', '↓', '→', '≠', '≤', '≥', '≡', '∨', '∧', '⊂', and '⊃' can be typed as abbreviations for '++', '--', '->', '!=', '<=', '>=', '==', '||', '&&', '<<', and '>>', respectively.

    2. If you have an extended character set, you can use it with only minimal restrictions, as discussed under the rules for @l above. But you should stick to standard ASCII characters if you want to write programs that will be useful to all the poor souls out there who don't have extended character sets.

    3. The TEX file output by CWEAVE is broken into lines having at most 80 characters each. When TEX text is being copied, the existing line breaks are copied as well. If you aren't doing anything too tricky, CWEAVE

will recognize when a TEX comment is being split across two or more lines, and it will append '%' to the beginning of such continued comments.

4. C text is translated by a "bottom up" procedure that identifies each token as a "part of speech" and combines parts of speech into larger and larger phrases as much as possible according to a special grammar that is explained in the documentation of CWEAVE. It is easy to learn the translation scheme for simple constructions like single identifiers and short expressions, just by looking at a few examples of what CWEAVE does, but the general mechanism is somewhat complex because it must handle much more than C itself. Furthermore the output contains embedded codes that cause TEX to indent and break lines as necessary, depending on the fonts used and the desired page width. For best results it is wise to avoid enclosing long C texts in |...|, since the indentation and line breaking codes are omitted when the |...| text is translated from C to TEX. Stick to simple expressions or statements. If a C preprocessor command is enclosed in |...|, the # that introduces it must be at the beginning of a line, or CWEAVE won't print it correctly.

5. Comments are not permitted in |...| text. After a '|' signals the change from TEX text to C text, the next '|' that is not part of a string or control text or section name ends the C text.

6. A comment must have properly nested occurrences of left and right braces, otherwise CWEAVE will complain. But it does try to balance the braces, so that TEX won't foul up too much.

7. When you're debugging a program and decide to omit some of your C code, do NOT simply "comment it out." Such comments are not in the spirit of CWEB documentation; they will appear to readers as if they were explanations of the uncommented-out instructions. Furthermore, comments of a program must be valid TEX text; hence CWEAVE will get confused if you enclose C statements in /*...*/ instead of in /*|...|*/. If you must comment out C code, you can surround it with preprocessor commands like #if 0==1 and #endif.

8. The @f feature allows you to define one identifier to act like another, and these format definitions are carried out sequentially. In general, a given identifier has only one printed format throughout the entire document, and this format is used even before the @f that defines it. The reason is that CWEAVE operates in two passes; it processes @f's and cross-references on the first pass and it does the output on the second. (However, identifiers that implicitly get a boldface format, thanks to a typedef declaration, don't obey this rule; they are printed differently before and after the relevant typedef. This is unfortunate, but hard to fix. You can get around the restriction by saying, say, '@s foo int', before or after the typedef.)

9. Sometimes it is desirable to insert spacing into formatted C code that is more general than the thin space provided by '@,'. The @t feature can be used for this purpose; e.g., '@t\hskip 1in@>' will leave one inch of blank space. Furthermore, '@t\4@>' can be used to backspace by one unit of indentation, since the control sequence \4 is defined in cwebmac to be such a backspace. (This control sequence is used, for example, at the beginning of lines that contain labeled statements, so that the label will stick out a little at the left.) You can also use '@t\3{-5@>' to force a break in the middle of an expression.

10. Each identifier in CWEB has a single formatting convention. Therefore you shouldn't use the same identifier to denote, say, both a type name and part of a struct, even though C does allow this.

Running the programs

The UNIX command line for CTANGLE is

        ctangle [options] web_file[.w] [{change_file[.ch]|-} [out_file]]

and the same conventions apply to CWEAVE. If '-' or no change file is specified, the change file is null. The extensions .w and .ch are appended only if the given file names contain no dot. If the web file defined in this way cannot be found, the extension .web will be tried. For example, 'cweave cob' will try to read cob.w; failing that, it will try cob.web before giving up. If no output file name is specified, the name of the C file output by CTANGLE is obtained by appending the extension .c; the name of the TEX file output by CWEAVE gets the extension .tex. Index files output by CWEAVE replace .tex by .idx and .scn.

Programmers who like terseness might choose to set up their operating shell so that 'wv' expands to 'cweave -bhp'; this will suppress most terminal output from CWEAVE except for error messages.

Options are introduced either by a - sign, to turn an option off, or by a + sign to turn one on. For example, '-fb' turns off options f and b; '+s' turns on option s. Options can be specified before the file names, after the file names, or both. The following options are currently implemented:

b Print a banner line at the beginning of execution. (On by default.)

e Enclose C material formatted by CWEAVE in brackets \PB{...}, so that special hooks can be used. (Off by default; has no effect on CTANGLE.)

f Force line breaks after each C statement formatted by CWEAVE. (On by default; -f saves paper but looks less C-like to some people.) (Has no effect on CTANGLE.)

h Print a happy message at the conclusion of a successful run. (On by default.)

p Give progress reports as the program runs. (On by default.)

s Show statistics about memory usage after the program runs to completion. (Off by default.) If you have large CWEB files or sections, you may need to see how close you come to exceeding the capacity of CTANGLE and/or CWEAVE.

x Include indexes and a table of contents in the TEX file output by CWEAVE. (On by default.) (Has no effect on CTANGLE.)

Further details about formatting

You may not like the way CWEAVE handles certain situations. If you're desperate, you can customize CWEAVE by changing its grammar. This means changing the source code, a task that you might find amusing. A table of grammar rules appears in the CWEAVE source listing, and you can make a separate copy of that table by copying the file prod.w found in the CWEB sources and saying 'cweave -x prod', followed by 'tex prod'.

You can see exactly how CWEAVE is parsing your C code by preceding it with the line '@ @c @2'. (The control code '@2' turns on a "peeping" mode, and '@0' turns it off.) For example, if you run CWEAVE on the file

```
@ @c @2
main (argc,argv)
char **argv;
{ for (;argc>0;argc--) printf("%s\n",argv[argc-1]); }
```

you get the following gibberish on your screen:

```
[...]
4:*exp ( +exp+ )...
11:*exp +exp+ int...
5:*+exp+ int +unorbinop+...
[...]
60: +fn_decl+*+{+ -stmt- +}-
55:*+fn_decl+ -stmt-
52:*+function-
[...]
```

The first line says that grammar rule 4 has just been applied, and CWEAVE currently has in its memory a sequence of chunks of TEX code (called "scraps") that are respectively of type *exp* (for expression), open-parenthesis, *exp* again, close-parenthesis, and further scraps that haven't yet been considered by the parser. (The + and - signs stipulate that TEX should be in or out of math mode at the scrap boundaries. The * shows the parser's current position.) Then rule 11 is applied, and the sequence (*exp*) becomes an *exp* and so on. In the end the whole C text has become one big scrap of type *function*.

Sometimes things don't work as smoothly, and you get a bunch of lines lumped together. This means that CWEAVE could not digest something in your C code. For instance, suppose '@<Argument definitions@>' had appeared instead of 'char **argv;' in the program above. Then CWEAVE would have been somewhat mystified, since it thinks that section names are just *exp*s. Thus it would tell TEX to format '⟨Argument declarations 2⟩' on the same line as '*main*(*argc*, *argv*)'. In this case you should help CWEAVE by putting '@/' after '*main*(*argc*, *argv*)'.

CWEAVE automatically inserts a bit of extra space between declarations and the first apparent statement of a block. One way to defeat this spacing locally is

```
int x;@+@t}\6{@>
@<Other locals@>@;@#
```

the '@#' will put extra space after '⟨Other locals⟩'.

Hypertext and hyperdocumentation

Many people have of course noticed analogies between CWEB and the World Wide Web. The CWEB macros are in fact set up so that the output of CWEAVE can be converted easily into Portable Document Format, with clickable hyperlinks that can be read with Adobe's Acrobat Reader, using a widely available open-source program called `dvipdfm` developed by Mark A. Wicks. After using CWEAVE to convert `cob.w` into `cob.tex`, you can prepare and view a hypertext version of the program by giving the commands

```
tex "\let\pdf+ \input cob"
dvipdfm cob
acroread cob.pdf
```

instead of invoking TeX in the normal way. (Thanks to Hans Hagen and César Augusto Rorato Crusius for the macros that make this work.) Alternatively, thanks to Hàn Thế Thành and Andreas Scherer, you can generate `cob.pdf` in one step by simply saying 'pdftex cob'.

A more elaborate system called CTWILL, which extends the usual cross references of CWEAVE by preparing links from the uses of identifiers to their definitions, is also available—provided that you are willing to work a bit harder in cases where an identifier is multiply defined. CTWILL is intended primarily for hardcopy output, but its principles could be used for hypertext as well. See Chapter 11 of *Digital Typography* by D. E. Knuth (1999), and the program sources at `ftp://labrea.stanford.edu/pub/ctwill`.

Appendices

As an example of a real program written in CWEB, Appendix A contains an excerpt from the CWEB program itself. The reader who examines the listings in this appendix carefully will get a good feeling for the basic ideas of CWEB.

Appendix B is the file that sets TeX up to accept the output of CWEAVE, and Appendix C discusses how to use some of those macros to vary the output formats.

A "long" version of this manual, which can be produced from the CWEB sources via the UNIX command `make fullmanual`, also contains appendices D, E, and F, which exhibit the complete source code for CTANGLE and CWEAVE.

Appendix A: Excerpts from a CWEB Program

This appendix consists of four listings. The first shows the CWEB input that generated sections 12–15 of the file `common.w`, which contains routines common to CWEAVE and CTANGLE. Note that some of the lines are indented to show the program structure; the indentation is ignored by CWEAVE and CTANGLE, but users find that CWEB files are quite readable if they have some such indentation.

The second and third listings show corresponding parts of the C code output by CTANGLE and of the corresponding TEX code output by CWEAVE, when run on `common.w`. The fourth listing shows how that output looks when printed out.

```
@ Procedure |prime_the_change_buffer|
sets |change_buffer| in preparation for the next matching operation.
Since blank lines in the change file are not used for matching, we have
|(change_limit==change_buffer && !changing)| if and only if
the change file is exhausted. This procedure is called only when
|changing| is 1; hence error messages will be reported correctly.

@c
void
prime_the_change_buffer()
{
  change_limit=change_buffer; /* this value is used if the change file ends */
  @<Skip over comment lines in the change file; |return| if end of file@>;
  @<Skip to the next nonblank line; |return| if end of file@>;
  @<Move |buffer| and |limit| to |change_buffer| and |change_limit|@>;
}

@ While looking for a line that begins with \.{@@x} in the change file, we
allow lines that begin with \.{@@}, as long as they don't begin with \.{@@y},
\.{@@z}, or \.{@@i} (which would probably mean that the change file is fouled up).

@<Skip over comment lines in the change file...@>=
while(1) {
  change_line++;
  if (!input_ln(change_file)) return;
  if (limit<buffer+2) continue;
  if (buffer[0]!='@@') continue;
  if (xisupper(buffer[1])) buffer[1]=tolower(buffer[1]);
  if (buffer[1]=='x') break;
  if (buffer[1]=='y' || buffer[1]=='z' || buffer[1]=='i') {
    loc=buffer+2;
    err_print("! Missing @@x in change file");
@.Missing @@x...@>
  }
}

@ Here we are looking at lines following the \.{@@x}.

@<Skip to the next nonblank line...@>=
do {
  change_line++;
  if (!input_ln(change_file)) {
    err_print("! Change file ended after @@x");
@.Change file ended...@>
    return;
  }
} while (limit==buffer);

@ @<Move |buffer| and |limit| to |change_buffer| and |change_limit|@>=
{
  change_limit=change_buffer-buffer+limit;
  strncpy(change_buffer,buffer,limit-buffer+1);
}
```

Here's the portion of the C code generated by **CTANGLE** that corresponds to the source on the preceding page. Notice that sections 13, 14 and 15 have been tangled into section 12.

```
/*:9*//*12:*/
#line 247 "common.w"

void
prime_the_change_buffer()
{
change_limit= change_buffer;
/*13:*/
#line 261 "common.w"

while(1){
change_line++;
if(!input_ln(change_file))return;
if(limit<buffer+2)continue;
if(buffer[0]!='@')continue;
if(xisupper(buffer[1]))buffer[1]= tolower(buffer[1]);
if(buffer[1]=='x')break;
if(buffer[1]=='y'||buffer[1]=='z'||buffer[1]=='i'){
loc= buffer+2;
err_print("! Missing @x in change file");

}
}

/*:13*/
#line 252 "common.w"
;
/*14:*/
#line 278 "common.w"

do{
change_line++;
if(!input_ln(change_file)){
err_print("! Change file ended after @x");

return;
}
}while(limit==buffer);

/*:14*/
#line 253 "common.w"
;
/*15:*/
#line 288 "common.w"

{
change_limit= change_buffer-buffer+limit;
strncpy(change_buffer,buffer,limit-buffer+1);
}

/*:15*/
#line 254 "common.w"
;
}

/*:12*//*16:*/
```

Here is the corresponding excerpt from `common.tex`.

```
\M{12}Procedure \PB{\\{prime\_the\_change\_buffer}}
sets \PB{\\{change\_buffer}} in preparation for the next matching operation.
Since blank lines in the change file are not used for matching, we have
\PB{$(\\{change\_limit}\E\\{change\_buffer}\W\R\\{changing})$} if and only if
the change file is exhausted. This procedure is called only when
\PB{\\{changing}} is 1; hence error messages will be reported correctly.

\Y\B\&{void} \\{prime\_the\_change\_buffer}(\,)\1\1\2\2\6
${}\{{}$\1\6
${}\\{change\_limit}\K\\{change\_buffer}{}$;\C{ this value is used if the
change file ends }\6
\X13:Skip over comment lines in the change file; \PB{\&{return}} if end of file%
\X;\6
\X14:Skip to the next nonblank line; \PB{\&{return}} if end of file\X;\6
\X15:Move \PB{\\{buffer}} and \PB{\\{limit}} to \PB{\\{change\_buffer}} and %
\PB{\\{change\_limit}}\X;\6
\4${}\}{}$\2\par
\fi

\M{13}While looking for a line that begins with \.{@x} in the change file, we
allow lines that begin with \.{@}, as long as they don't begin with \.{@y},
\.{@z}, or \.{@i} (which would probably mean that the change file is fouled
up).

\Y\B\4\X13:Skip over comment lines in the change file; \PB{\&{return}} if end
of file\X${}\E{}$\6
\&{while} (\T{1})\5
${}\{{}$\1\6
${}\\{change\_line}\PP;{}$\6
\&{if} ${}(\R\\{input\_ln}(\\{change\_file})){}$\1\5
\&{return};\2\6
\&{if} ${}(\\{limit}<\\{buffer}+\T{2}){}$\1\5
\&{continue};\2\6
\&{if} ${}(\\{buffer}[\T{0}]\I\.{'@'}){}$\1\5
\&{continue};\2\6
\&{if} (\\{xisupper}(\\{buffer}[\T{1}]))\1\5
${}\\{buffer}[\T{1}]\K\\{tolower}(\\{buffer}[\T{1}]);{}$\2\6
\&{if} ${}(\\{buffer}[\T{1}]\E\.{'x'}){}$\1\5
\&{break};\2\6
\&{if} ${}(\\{buffer}[\T{1}]\E\.{'y'}\V\\{buffer}[\T{1}]\E\.{'z'}\V\\{buffer}[%
\T{1}]\E\.{'i'}){}$\5
${}\{{}$\1\6
${}\\{loc}\K\\{buffer}+\T{2};{}$\6
\\{err\_print}(\.{"!\ Missing\ @x\ in\ cha}\)\.{nge\ file"});\6
\4${}\}{}$\2\6
\4${}\}{}$\2\par
\U12.\fi

\M{14}Here we are looking at lines following the \.{@x}.

\Y\B\4\X14:Skip to the next nonblank line; \PB{\&{return}} if end of file\X${}%
\E{}$\6
\&{do}\5
${}\{{}$\1\6
${}\\{change\_line}\PP;{}$\6
\&{if} ${}(\R\\{input\_ln}(\\{change\_file})){}$\5
${}\{{}$\1\6
\\{err\_print}(\.{"!\ Change\ file\ ended}\)\.{\ after\ @x"});\6
\&{return};\6
\4${}\}{}$\2\6
\4${}\}{}$\2\5
\&{while} ${}(\\{limit}\E\\{buffer}){}$;\par
\U12.\fi

\M{15}\B\X15:Move \PB{\\{buffer}} and \PB{\\{limit}} to \PB{\\{change\_buffer}}
and \PB{\\{change\_limit}}\X${}\E{}$\6
${}\{{}$\1\6
${}\\{change\_limit}\K\\{change\_buffer}-\\{buffer}+\\{limit};{}$\6
${}\\{strncpy}(\\{change\_buffer},\39\\{buffer},\39\\{limit}-\\{buffer}+%
\T{1});{}$\6
\4${}\}{}$\2\par
\Us12\ET16.\fi
```

And here's what the same excerpt looks like when typeset.

12.   Procedure *prime_the_change_buffer* sets *change_buffer* in preparation for the next matching operation. Since blank lines in the change file are not used for matching, we have (*change_limit* $\equiv$ *change_buffer* $\wedge$ $\neg changing$) if and only if the change file is exhausted. This procedure is called only when *changing* is 1; hence error messages will be reported correctly.

> **void** *prime_the_change_buffer* ( )
> {
>   *change_limit* $=$ *change_buffer*;   /* this value is used if the change file ends */
> $\langle$ Skip over comment lines in the change file; **return** if end of file 13 $\rangle$;
> $\langle$ Skip to the next nonblank line; **return** if end of file 14 $\rangle$;
> $\langle$ Move *buffer* and *limit* to *change_buffer* and *change_limit* 15 $\rangle$;
> }

13.   While looking for a line that begins with @x in the change file, we allow lines that begin with @, as long as they don't begin with @y, @z, or @i (which would probably mean that the change file is fouled up).

$\langle$ Skip over comment lines in the change file; **return** if end of file 13 $\rangle$ $\equiv$
> **while** (1) {
>   *change_line* ++;
>   **if** ($\neg input\_ln$(*change_file*)) **return**;
>   **if** (*limit* $<$ *buffer* $+ 2$) **continue**;
>   **if** (*buffer*[0] $\neq$ '@') **continue**;
>   **if** ($xisupper$(*buffer*[1])) *buffer*[1] $=$ *tolower*(*buffer*[1]);
>   **if** (*buffer*[1] $\equiv$ 'x') **break**;
>   **if** (*buffer*[1] $\equiv$ 'y' $\vee$ *buffer*[1] $\equiv$ 'z' $\vee$ *buffer*[1] $\equiv$ 'i') {
>   *loc* $=$ *buffer* $+ 2$;
> err_print("!␣Missing␣@x␣in␣change␣file");
>   }
> }

This code is used in section 12.

14.   Here we are looking at lines following the @x.

$\langle$ Skip to the next nonblank line; **return** if end of file 14 $\rangle$ $\equiv$
> **do** {
>   *change_line* ++;
>   **if** ($\neg input\_ln$(*change_file*)) {
> err_print("!␣Change␣file␣ended␣after␣@x");
>   **return**;
>   }
> } **while** (*limit* $\equiv$ *buffer*);

This code is used in section 12.

15. $\langle$ Move *buffer* and *limit* to *change_buffer* and *change_limit* 15 $\rangle$ $\equiv$
> {
>   *change_limit* $=$ *change_buffer* $-$ *buffer* $+$ *limit*;
>   *strncpy*(*change_buffer*, *buffer*, *limit* $-$ *buffer* $+ 1$);
> }

This code is used in sections 12 and 16.

Appendix B: The `cwebmac.tex` file

This is the file that extends "plain TEX" format in order to support the features needed by the output of
CWEAVE.

```
% standard macros for CWEB listings (in addition to plain.tex)
% Version 3.63 --- January 2001
\ifx\documentstyle\undefined\else\endinput\fi % LaTeX will use other macros
\xdef\fmtversion{\fmtversion+CWEB3.63}
\newif\ifpdf
\ifx\pdf+\pdftrue\fi
% Uncomment the following line if you want PDF goodies to be the default
%\ifx\pdf-\else\pdftrue\fi
\def\pdflinkcolor{0 0 1} % the RGB values for hyperlink color
\newif\ifpdftex
\ifx\pdfoutput\undefined \pdftexfalse
\else \pdftextrue \pdfoutput=1 \pdfcompresslevel=9 \input pdfcolor \fi
\newif\ifacro \ifpdf\acrotrue\fi \ifpdftex\acrotrue\fi

\let\:=\. % preserve a way to get the dot accent
 % (all other accents will still work as usual)

\parskip 0pt % no stretch between paragraphs
\parindent 1em % for paragraphs and for the first line of C text

\font\ninerm=cmr9
\let\mc=\ninerm % medium caps
\def\CEE/{{\mc C\spacefactor1000}}
\def\UNIX/{{\mc U\kern-.05emNIX\spacefactor1000}}
\def\TEX/{\TeX}
\def\CPLUSPLUS/{{\mc C\PP\spacefactor1000}}
\def\Cee{\CEE/} % for backward compatibility
\def\9#1{}
 % with this definition of \9 you can say @:sort key}{TeX code@>
 % to alphabetize an index entry by the sort key but format with the TeX code
\font\eightrm=cmr8
\let\sc=\eightrm % for smallish caps (NOT a caps-and-small-caps font)
\let\mainfont=\tenrm
\let\cmntfont\tenrm
%\font\tenss=cmss10 \let\cmntfont\tenss % alternative comment font
\font\titlefont=cmr7 scaled\magstep4 % title on the contents page
\font\ttitlefont=cmtt10 scaled\magstep2 % typewriter type in title
\font\tentex=cmtex10 % TeX extended character set (used in strings)
\fontdimen7\tentex=0pt % no double space after sentences

\def\\#1{\leavevmode\hbox{\it#1\/\kern.05em}} % italic type for identifiers
\def\|#1{\leavevmode\hbox{$#1$}} % one-letter identifiers look better this way
\def\&#1{\leavevmode\hbox{\bf
  \def\_{\kern.04em\vbox{\hrule width.3em height .6pt}\kern.08em}%
  #1\/\kern.05em}} % boldface type for reserved words
\def\.#1{\leavevmode\hbox{\tentex % typewriter type for strings
  \let\\=\BS % backslash in a string
  \let\{=\LB % left brace in a string
  \let\}=\RB % right brace in a string
  \let\~=\TL % tilde in a string
  \let\ =\SP % space in a string
  \let\_=\UL % underline in a string
  \let\&=\AM % ampersand in a string
  \let\^=\CF % circumflex in a string
  #1\kern.05em}}
\def\){{\tentex\kern-.05em\discretionary{\hbox{\tentex\BS}}{}{}}
\def\AT{@} % at sign for control text (not needed in versions >= 2.9)
\def\ATL{\par\noindent\bgroup\catcode`\_=12 \postATL} % print @l in limbo
\def\postATL#1 #2 {\bf letter \\{\uppercase{\char"#1}}
   tangles as \tentex "#2"\egroup\par}
\def\noATL#1 #2 {}
\def\noatl{\let\ATL=\noATL} % suppress output from @l
\def\ATH{{\acrofalse\X\kern-.5em:Preprocessor definitions\X}}
\let\PB=\relax % hook for program brackets |...| in TeX part or section name

\chardef\AM=`\& % ampersand character in a string
```

```
\chardef\BS=`\\ % backslash in a string
\chardef\LB=`\{ % left brace in a string
\chardef\RB=`\} % right brace in a string
\def\SP{{\tt\char` }} % (visible) space in a string
\chardef\TL=`\~ % tilde in a string
\chardef\UL=`\_ % underline character in a string
\chardef\CF=`\^ % circumflex character in a string

\newbox\PPbox % symbol for ++
\setbox\PPbox=\hbox{\kern.5pt\raise1pt\hbox{\sevenrm+\kern-1pt+}\kern.5pt}
\def\PP{\copy\PPbox}
\newbox\MMbox \setbox\MMbox=\hbox{\kern.5pt\raise1pt\hbox{\sevensy\char0
 \kern-1pt\char0}\kern.5pt}
\def\MM{\copy\MMbox}
\newbox\MGbox % symbol for ->
\setbox\MGbox=\hbox{\kern-2pt\lower3pt\hbox{\teni\char'176}\kern1pt}
\def\MG{\copy\MGbox}
\def\MRL#1{\mathrel{\let\K==#1}}
%\def\MRL#1{\KK#1}\def\KK#1#2{\buildrel\;#1\over{#2}}
\let\GG=\gg
\let\LL=\ll
\let\NULL=\Lambda
\mathchardef\AND="2026 % bitwise and; also \& (unary operator)
\let\OR=\mid % bitwise or
\let\XOR=\oplus % bitwise exclusive or
\def\CM{{\sim}} % bitwise complement
\newbox\MODbox \setbox\MODbox=\hbox{\eightrm\%}
\def\MOD{\mathbin{\copy\MODbox}}
\def\DC{\kern.1em{::}\kern.1em} % symbol for ::
\def\PA{\mathbin{.*}} % symbol for .*
\def\MGA{\mathbin{\MG*}} % symbol for ->*
\def\this{\&{this}}

\newbox\bak \setbox\bak=\hbox to -1em{} % backspace one em
\newbox\bakk\setbox\bakk=\hbox to -2em{} % backspace two ems

\newcount\ind % current indentation in ems
\def\1{\global\advance\ind by1\hangindent\ind em} % indent one more notch
\def\2{\global\advance\ind by-1} % indent one less notch
\def\3#1{\hfil\penalty#10\hfilneg} % optional break within a statement
\def\4{\copy\bak} % backspace one notch
\def\5{\hfil\penalty-1\hfilneg\kern2.5em\copy\bakk\ignorespaces}% optional break
\def\6{\ifmmode\else\par % forced break
  \hangindent\ind em\noindent\kern\ind em\copy\bakk\ignorespaces\fi}
\def\7{\Y\6} % forced break and a little extra space
\def\8{\hskip-\ind em\hskip 2em} % no indentation

\newcount\gdepth % depth of current major group, plus one
\newcount\secpagedepth
\secpagedepth=3 % page breaks will occur for depths -1, 0, and 1
\newtoks\gtitle % title of current major group
\newskip\intersecskip \intersecskip=12pt minus 3pt % space between sections
\let\yskip=\smallskip
\def\?{\mathrel?}
\def\note#1#2.{\Y\noindent{\hangindent2em%
    \baselineskip10pt\eightrm#1~\ifacro{\pdfnote#2.}\else#2\fi.\par}}
% The following are pdf macros
\newtoks\toksA \newtoks\toksB \newtoks\toksC \newtoks\toksD
\newcount\countA \countA=0 \newcount\countB \countB=0
\def\thewidth{\the\wd0\space}
\def\theheight{\the\ht0\space}
\def\thedepth{\the\dp0\space}
\ifpdftex
 \ifx\pdfannotlink\undefined\let\pdfannotlink\pdfstartlink\fi% for pdfTeX 0.14
 \def\pdflink#1#2{\hbox{\pdfannotlink attr{/Border [0 0 0]} goto num #1
   \BlueGreen #1\Black\pdfendlink}}
\else\def\pdflink#1#2{\setbox0=\hbox{\special{pdf: bc [ \pdflinkcolor ]}{#1}%
    \special{pdf: ec}}\special{pdf: ann width \thewidth\space height \theheight
     \space depth \thedepth\space << /Type /Annot /Subtype /Link
    /Border [0 0 0] /A << /S /GoTo /D (#2) >> >>}\box0\relax}\fi
\def\pdfnote#1.{\setbox0=\hbox{\toksA={#1.}\toksB={}\maketoks}\the\toksA}
```

```
\def\firstsecno#1.{\setbox0=\hbox{\toksA={#1.}\toksB={}
    \def\makenote{\addtokens{\toksB}{\the\toksC}\def\makenote{\toksD={}
      \toksC={}\let\space\empty}\makenote}\maketoks}}
\def\addtokens#1#2{\edef\addtoks{\noexpand#1={\the#1#2}}\addtoks}
\def\adn#1{\addtokens{\toksC}{#1}\global\countA=1\let\next=\maketoks}
\def\poptoks#1#2|ENDTOKS|{\let\first=#1\toksD={#1}\toksA={#2}}
\def\maketoks{%
    \expandafter\poptoks\the\toksA|ENDTOKS|
    \ifx\first0\adn0
    \else\ifx\first1\adn1 \else\ifx\first2\adn2 \else\ifx\first3\adn3
    \else\ifx\first4\adn4 \else\ifx\first5\adn5 \else\ifx\first6\adn6
    \else\ifx\first7\adn7 \else\ifx\first8\adn8 \else\ifx\first9\adn9
    \else
        \ifnum0=\countA\else\makenote\fi
        \ifx\first.\let\next=\done\else
            \let\next=\maketoks
            \addtokens{\toksB}{\the\toksD}
            \ifx\first,\addtokens{\toksB}{\space}\fi
        \fi
    \fi\fi\fi\fi\fi\fi\fi\fi\fi\fi
    \next
}
\def\makenote{\addtokens{\toksB}%
    {\noexpand\pdflink{\the\toksC}{\romannumeral\the\toksC}}\toksC={}\global\countA=0}
\def\done{\edef\st{\global\noexpand\toksA={\the\toksB}}\st}
\def\pdfURL#1#2{\ifpdftex\pdfannotlink attr {/Border [0 0 0]} user {
    /Type /Action /Subtype /Link /A << /S /URI /URI (#2) >>
    }\BlueGreen #1\Black \pdfendlink
  \else \ifpdf{\setbox0=\hbox{\special{pdf: bc [ \pdflinkcolor ]}{#1}%
    \special{pdf: ec}}\special{pdf: ann width \thewidth\space height \theheight
      \space depth \thedepth\space << /Border [0 0 0]
      /Type /Action /Subtype /Link /A << /S /URI /URI (#2) >> >>}\box0\relax}%
  \else #1 ({\tt#2})\fi\fi}
{\catcode`\~=12 \gdef\TILDE/{~}} % ~ in a URL
{\catcode`\_=12 \gdef\UNDER/{_}} % _ in a URL
% End of pdf macros
\def\lapstar{\rlap{*}}
\def\stsec{\rightskip=0pt % get out of C mode (cf. \B)
  \sfcode`;=1500 \pretolerance 200 \hyphenpenalty 50 \exhyphenpenalty 50
  \noindent{\let\*=\lapstar\bf\secstar.\quad}%
  \ifpdftex\smash{\raise\baselineskip\hbox to0pt{%
      \let\*=\empty\pdfdest num \secstar fith}}
  \else\ifpdf\smash{\raise\baselineskip\hbox to0pt{%
      \let\*=\empty\special{%
        pdf: dest (\romannumeral\secstar) [ @thispage /FitH @ypos ]}}}\fi\fi}
\let\startsection=\stsec
\def\defin#1{\global\advance\ind by 2 \1\&{#1 } } % begin `define' or `format'
\def\A{\note{See also section}} % xref for doubly defined section name
\def\As{\note{See also sections}} % xref for multiply defined section name
\def\B{\rightskip=0pt plus 100pt minus 10pt % go into C mode
  \sfcode`;=3000
  \pretolerance 10000
  \hyphenpenalty 1000 % so strings can be broken (discretionary \ is inserted)
  \exhyphenpenalty 10000
  \global\ind=2 \1\ \unskip}
\def\C#1{\5\5\quad$/\ast\,${\cmntfont #1}$\,\ast/$}
\let\SHC\C % "// short comments" treated like "/* ordinary comments */"
%\def\C#1{\5\5\quad$\triangleright\,${\cmntfont#1}$\,\triangleleft$}
%\def\SHC#1{\5\5\quad$\diamond\,${\cmntfont#1}}
\def\D{\defin{\#define}} % macro definition
\let\E=\equiv % equivalence sign
\def\ET{ and~} % conjunction between two section numbers
\def\ETs{, and~} % conjunction between the last two of several section numbers
\def\F{\defin{format}} % format definition
\let\G=\ge % greater than or equal sign
% \H is long Hungarian umlaut accent
\let\I=\ne % unequal sign
\def\J{\.{@\&}} % TANGLE's join operation
\let\K== % assignment operator
%\let\K=\leftarrow % "honest" alternative to standard assignment operator
% \L is Polish letter suppressed-L
```

```
\outer\def\M#1{\MN{#1}\ifon\vfil\penalty-100\vfilneg % beginning of section
  \vskip\intersecskip\startsection\ignorespaces}
\outer\def\N#1#2#3.{\gdepth=#1\gtitle={#3}\MN{#2}% beginning of starred section
  \ifon\ifnum#1<\secpagedepth \vfil\eject % force page break if depth is small
    \else\vfil\penalty-100\vfilneg\vskip\intersecskip\fi\fi
  \message{*\secno} % progress report
  \edef\next{\write\cont{\ZZ{#3}{#1}{\secno}% write to contents file
                   {\noexpand\the\pageno}}}\next % \ZZ{title}{depth}{sec}{page}
  \ifpdf\special{pdf: outline #1 << /Title (#3) /Dest
    [ @thispage /FitH @ypos ] >>}\fi
  \ifon\startsection{\bf#3.\quad}\ignorespaces}
\def\MN#1{\par % common code for \M, \N
  {\xdef\secstar{#1}\let\*=\empty\xdef\secno{#1}}% remove \* from section name
  \ifx\secno\secstar \onmaybe \else\ontrue \fi
  \mark{{{\tensy x}\secno}{\the\gdepth}{\the\gtitle}}}
% each \mark is {section reference or null}{depth plus 1}{group title}
% \O is Scandinavian letter O-with-slash
% \P is paragraph sign
\def\Q{\note{This code is cited in section}} % xref for mention of a section
\def\Qs{\note{This code is cited in sections}} % xref for mentions of a section
\let\R=\lnot % logical not
% \S is section sign
\def\T#1{\leavevmode % octal, hex or decimal constant
  \hbox{$\def\?{\kern.2em}%
    \def\$##1{\egroup_{\,\rm##1}\bgroup}% suffix to constant
    \def\_{\cdot 10^{\aftergroup}}% power of ten (via dirty trick)
    \let\~=\oct \let\^=\hex {#1}$}}
\def\U{\note{This code is used in section}} % xref for use of a section
\def\Us{\note{This code is used in sections}} % xref for uses of a section
\let\V=\lor % logical or
\let\W=\land % logical and
\def\X#1:#2X{\ifmmode\gdef\XX{\null$\null}\else\gdef\XX{}\fi %$% section name
  \XX$\langle\,${\let\I=\ne#2\eightrm\kern.5em
    \ifacro{\pdfnote#1.}\else#1\fi}$\,\rangle$\XX}
\def\Y{\par\yskip}
\let\Z=\le
\let\ZZ=\let % now you can \write the control sequence \ZZ
\let\*=*

\let\Xand=\W
\def\Xandxeq{\MRL{{\W}{\K}}}
\let\Xbitand=\AND
\let\Xbitor=\OR
\let\Xcompl=\CM
\let\Xnot=\R
\let\Xnotxeq=\I
\let\Xor=\V
\def\Xorxeq{\MRL{{\OR}{\K}}}
\let\Xxor=\XOR
\def\Xxorxeq{\MRL{{\XOR}{\K}}}

%\def\oct{\hbox{\rm\char'23\kern-.2em\it\aftergroup\?\aftergroup}} % WEB style
%\def\hex{\hbox{\rm\char"7D\tt\aftergroup}} % WEB style
\def\oct{\hbox{$^\circ$\kern-.1em\it\aftergroup\?\aftergroup}}% CWEB style
\def\hex{\hbox{$^{\scriptscriptstyle\#}$\tt\aftergroup}} % CWEB style
\def\vb#1{\leavevmode\hbox{\kern2pt\vrule\vtop{\vbox{\hrule
      \hbox{\strut\kern2pt\.{#1}\kern2pt}}
    \hrule}\vrule\kern2pt}} % verbatim string

\def\onmaybe{\let\ifon=\maybe} \let\maybe=\iftrue
\newif\ifon \newif\iftitle \newif\ifpagesaved

\def\lheader{\mainfont\the\pageno\eightrm\qquad\grouptitle\hfill\title\qquad
  \mainfont\topsecno} % top line on left-hand pages
\def\rheader{\mainfont\topsecno\eightrm\qquad\title\hfill\grouptitle
  \qquad\mainfont\the\pageno} % top line on right-hand pages
\def\grouptitle{\let\i=I\let\j=J\uppercase\expandafter{\expandafter
                  \takethree\topmark}}
\def\topsecno{\expandafter\takeone\topmark}
\def\takeone#1#2#3{#1}
\def\taketwo#1#2#3{#2}
```

```
\def\takethree#1#2#3{#3}
\def\nullsec{\eightrm\kern-2em} % the \kern-2em cancels \qquad in headers

\let\page=\pagebody \raggedbottom
% \def\page{\box255 }\normalbottom % faster, but loses plain TeX footnotes
\def\normaloutput#1#2#3{\ifodd\pageno\hoffset=\pageshift\fi
 \shipout\vbox{
  \vbox to\fullpageheight{
  \iftitle\global\titlefalse
  \else\hbox to\pagewidth{\vbox to10pt{}\ifodd\pageno #3\else#2\fi}\fi
  \vfill#1}} % parameter #1 is the page itself
  \global\advance\pageno by1}

\gtitle={\.{CWEB} output} % this running head is reset by starred sections
\mark{\noexpand\nullsec0{\the\gtitle}}
\def\title{\expandafter\uppercase\expandafter{\jobname}}
\def\topofcontents{\centerline{\titlefont\title}\vskip.7in
  \vfill} % this material will start the table of contents page
\def\startpdf{\ifpdftex\pdfcatalog{/PageMode /UseOutlines}\else
    \ifpdf{\special{pdf: docview << /PageMode /UseOutlines >>}}\fi\fi}
\def\botofcontents{\vfill
  \centerline{\covernote}} % this material will end the table of contents page
\def\covernote{}
\def\contentspagenumber{0} % default page number for table of contents
\newdimen\pagewidth \pagewidth=6.5in % the width of each page
\newdimen\pageheight \pageheight=8.7in % the height of each page
\newdimen\fullpageheight \fullpageheight=9in % page height including headlines
\newdimen\pageshift \pageshift=0in % shift righthand pages wrt lefthand ones
\def\magnify#1{\mag=#1\pagewidth=6.5truein\pageheight=8.7truein
  \fullpageheight=9truein\setpage}
\def\setpage{\hsize\pagewidth\vsize\pageheight} % use after changing page size
\def\contentsfile{\jobname.toc} % file that gets table of contents info
\def\readcontents{\input \contentsfile}
\def\readindex{\input \jobname.idx}
\def\readsections{\input \jobname.scn}

\newwrite\cont
\output{\setbox0=\page % the first page is garbage
  \openout\cont=\contentsfile
      \write\cont{\catcode `\noexpand\@=11\relax}   % \makeatletter
  \global\output{\normaloutput\page\lheader\rheader}}
\setpage
\vbox to \vsize{} % the first \topmark won't be null

\def\ch{\note{The following sections were changed by the change file:}
  \let\*=\relax}
\newbox\sbox % saved box preceding the index
\newbox\lbox % lefthand column in the index
\def\inx{\par\vskip6pt plus 1fil % we are beginning the index
  \def\page{\box255 } \normalbottom
  \write\cont{} % ensure that the contents file isn't empty
      \write\cont{\catcode `\noexpand\@=12\relax}   % \makeatother
  \closeout\cont % the contents information has been fully gathered
  \output{\ifpagesaved\normaloutput{\box\sbox}\lheader\rheader\fi
    \global\setbox\sbox=\page \global\pagesavedtrue}
  \pagesavedfalse \eject % eject the page-so-far and predecessors
  \setbox\sbox\vbox{\unvbox\sbox} % take it out of its box
  \vsize=\pageheight \advance\vsize by -\ht\sbox % the remaining height
  \hsize=.5\pagewidth \advance\hsize by -10pt
    % column width for the index (20pt between cols)
  \parfillskip 0pt plus .6\hsize % try to avoid almost empty lines
  \def\lr{L} % this tells whether the left or right column is next
  \output{\if L\lr\global\setbox\lbox=\page \gdef\lr{R}
    \else\normaloutput{\vbox to\pageheight{\box\sbox\vss
        \hbox to\pagewidth{\box\lbox\hfil\page}}}\lheader\rheader
    \global\vsize\pageheight\gdef\lr{L}\global\pagesavedfalse\fi}
  \message{Index:}
  \parskip 0pt plus .5pt
  \outer\def\I##1, ##2.{\par\hangindent2em\noindent##1:\kern1em
    \ifacro\pdfnote##2.\else##2\fi.} % index entry
  \def\[##1]{$\underline{##1}$} % underlined index item
```

```
    \rm \rightskip0pt plus 2.5em \tolerance 10000 \let\*=\lapstar
    \hyphenpenalty 10000 \parindent0pt
    \readindex}
\def\fin{\par\vfill\eject % this is done when we are ending the index
    \ifpagesaved\null\vfill\eject\fi % output a null index column
    \if L\lr\else\null\vfill\eject\fi % finish the current page
    \parfillskip 0pt plus 1fil
    \def\grouptitle{NAMES OF THE SECTIONS}
    \ifacro \def\outsecname{Names of the sections} \let\Xpdf\X \fi
    \ifpdftex \makebookmarks \pdfdest name {NOS} fitb
      \pdfoutline goto name {NOS} count -\secno {\outsecname}
      \def\X##1:##2\X{\Xpdf##1:##2\X
        \firstsecno##1.\toks0{##2}\pdfoutline goto num \the\toksA {\the\toks0}}
    \else\ifpdf
      \special{pdf: outline -1 << /Title (\outsecname)
        /Dest [ @thispage /FitH @ypos ] >>}
      \def\X##1:##2\X{\Xpdf##1:##2\X
        \firstsecno##1.\toks0{##2} \special{pdf: outline 0 << /Title
          (\the\toks0) /A << /S /GoTo /D (\romannumeral\the\toksA) >> >>}}
    \fi\fi
    \let\topsecno=\nullsec
    \message{Section names:}
    \output={\normaloutput\page\lheader\rheader}
    \setpage
    \def\note##1##2.{\quad{\eightrm##1~\ifacro{\pdfnote##2.}\else{##2}\fi.}}
    \def\Q{\note{Cited in section}} % crossref for mention of a section
    \def\Qs{\note{Cited in sections}} % crossref for mentions of a section
    \def\U{\note{Used in section}} % crossref for use of a section
    \def\Us{\note{Used in sections}} % crossref for uses of a section
    \def\I{\par\hangindent 2em}\let\*=*
    \readsections}
\def\makebookmarks{% read contents info for PDF outlines (twice)
    \let\ZZ=\scanbookmarkline \readcontents\relax
    \let\ZZ=\writebookmarkline \readcontents\relax}
\def\expnumber#1{\expandafter\ifx\csname#1\endcsname\relax 0%
    \else \csname#1\endcsname \fi} % Petr Olsak's macros from texinfo.tex
\def\advancenumber#1{\countA=\expnumber{#1}\relax \advance\countA by1
    \expandafter\xdef\csname#1\endcsname{\the\countA}}
\def\scanbookmarkline#1#2#3#4{% remember last level item and add to parent
    \expandafter\xdef\csname curr#2\endcsname{#3}
    \ifnum#2>0\countB=#2 \advance\countB by-1
      \advancenumber{chunk\the\countB.\expnumber{curr\the\countB}}\fi}
\def\writebookmarkline#1#2#3#4{\pdfoutline goto num #3
    count -\expnumber{chunk#2.#3}{#1}}
\def\con{\par\vfill\eject % finish the section names
% \ifodd\pageno\else\titletrue\null\vfill\eject\fi % for duplex printers
    \rightskip 0pt \hyphenpenalty 50 \tolerance 200
    \setpage \output={\normaloutput\page\lheader\rheader}
    \titletrue % prepare to output the table of contents
    \pageno=\contentspagenumber
    \def\grouptitle{TABLE OF CONTENTS}
    \message{Table of contents:}
    \topofcontents \startpdf
    \line{\hfil Section\hbox to3em{\hss Page}}
    \let\ZZ=\contentsline
    \readcontents\relax % read the contents info
    \botofcontents \end} % print the contents page(s) and terminate
\def\contentsline#1#2#3#4{\ifnum#2=0 \smallbreak\fi
    \line{\consetup{#2}#1
      \rm\leaders\hbox to .5em{.\hfil}\hfil
      \ \ifacro\pdflink{#3}{\romannumeral#3}\else#3\fi\hbox to3em{\hss#4}}}
\def\consetup#1{\ifcase#1 \bf % depth -1 (@**)
    \or % depth 0 (@*)
    \or \hskip2em % depth 1 (@*1)
    \or \hskip4em \or \hskip6em \or \hskip8em \or \hskip10em % depth 2,3,4,5
    \else \hskip12em \fi} % depth 6 or more
\def\noinx{\let\inx=\end} % no indexes or table of contents
\def\nosecs{\let\FIN=\fin \def\fin{\let\parfillskip=\end \FIN}}
    % no index of section names or table of contents
\def\nocon{\let\con=\end} % no table of contents
\def\today{\ifcase\month\or
```

```
    January\or February\or March\or April\or May\or June\or
    July\or August\or September\or October\or November\or December\fi
  \space\number\day, \number\year}
\newcount\twodigits
\def\hours{\twodigits=\time \divide\twodigits by 60 \printtwodigits
  \multiply\twodigits by-60 \advance\twodigits by\time :\printtwodigits}
\def\gobbleone1{}
\def\printtwodigits{\advance\twodigits100
  \expandafter\gobbleone\number\twodigits
  \advance\twodigits-100 }
\def\TeX{{\ifmmode\it\fi
  \leavevmode\hbox{T\kern-.1667em\lower.424ex\hbox{E}\hskip-.125em X}}}
\def\,{\relax\ifmmode\mskip\thinmuskip\else\thinspace\fi}
\def\datethis{\def\startsection{\leftline{\sc\today\ at \hours}\bigskip
  \let\startsection=\stsec\stsec}}
  % say '\datethis' in limbo, to get your listing timestamped before section 1
\def\datecontentspage{%
  \def\topofcontents{\leftline{\sc\today\ at \hours}\bigskip
  \centerline{\titlefont\title}\vfill}} % timestamps the contents page
```

Appendix C: How to use CWEB macros

The macros in `cwebmac` make it possible to produce a variety of formats without editing the output of CWEAVE, and the purpose of this appendix is to explain some of the possibilities.

1. Four fonts have been declared in addition to the standard fonts of PLAIN format: You can say '{\mc UNIX}' to get UNIX in medium-size caps; you can say '{\sc STUFF}' to get STUFF in small caps; and you can select the largish fonts \titlefont and \ttitlefont in the title of your document, where \ttitlefont is a typewriter style of type. There are macros \UNIX/ and \CEE/ to refer to UNIX and C with medium-size caps.

2. When you mention an identifier in TEX text, you normally call it '|identifier|'. But you can also say '\\{identifier}'. The output will look the same in both cases, but the second alternative doesn't put *identifier* into the index, since it bypasses CWEAVE's translation from C mode. In the second case you have to put a backslash before each underline character in the identifier.

3. To get typewriter-like type, as when referring to 'CWEB', you can use the '\.' macro (e.g., '\.{CWEB}'). In the argument to this macro you should insert an additional backslash before the symbols listed as 'special string characters' in the index to CWEAVE, i.e., before backslashes and dollar signs and the like. A '\␣' here will result in the visible space symbol; to get an invisible space following a control sequence you can say '{␣}'. If the string is long, you can break it up into substrings that are separated by '\)'; the latter gives a discretionary backslash if TEX has to break a line here.

4. The three control sequences \pagewidth, \pageheight, and \fullpageheight can be redefined in the limbo section at the beginning of your CWEB file, to change the dimensions of each page. The default settings

```
\pagewidth=6.5in
\pageheight=8.7in
\fullpageheight=9in
```

were used to prepare this manual; \fullpageheight is \pageheight plus room for the additional heading and page numbers at the top of each page. If you change any of these quantities, you should call the macro \setpage immediately after making the change.

5. The \pageshift macro defines an amount by which right-hand pages (i.e., odd-numbered pages) are shifted right with respect to left-hand (even-numbered) ones. By adjusting this amount you may be able to get two-sided output in which the page numbers line up on opposite sides of each sheet.

6. The \title macro will appear at the top of each page in small caps; it is the job name unless redefined.

7. The first page usually is assigned page number 1. To start on page 16, with contents on page 15, say this: '\def\contentspagenumber{15} \pageno=\contentspagenumber \advance\pageno by 1'.

8. The macro \iftitle will suppress the header line if it is defined by '\titletrue'. The normal value is \titlefalse except for the table of contents; thus, the contents page is usually unnumbered.

Two macros are provided to give flexibility to the table of contents: \topofcontents is invoked just before the contents info is read, and \botofcontents is invoked just after. Here's a typical definition:

```
\def\topofcontents{\null\vfill
  \titlefalse % include headline on the contents page
  \def\rheader{\mainfont The {\tt CWEAVE} processor\hfil}
  \centerline{\titlefont The {\ttitlefont CWEAVE} processor}
  \vskip 15pt \centerline{(Version 3.61)} \vfill}
```

Redefining \rheader, which is the headline for right-hand pages, suffices in this case to put the desired information at the top of the contents page.

9. Data for the table of contents is written to a file that is read after the indexes have been TEXed; there's one line of data for every starred section. The file `common.toc` might look like this:

```
\ZZ {Introduction}{0}{1}{26}
\ZZ {The character set}{2}{5}{27}
```

and so on. The \topofcontents macro could redefine \ZZ so that the information appears in any desired format.

10. Sometimes it is necessary or desirable to divide the output of **CWEAVE** into subfiles that can be processed separately. For example, the listing of TEX runs to more than 500 pages, and that is enough to exceed the capacity of many printing devices and/or their software. When an extremely large job isn't cut into smaller pieces, the entire process might be spoiled by a single error of some sort, making it necessary to start everything over.

Here's a safe way to break a woven file into three parts: Say the pieces are α, β, and γ, where each piece begins with a starred section. All macros should be defined in the opening limbo section of α, and copies of this TEX code should be placed at the beginning of β and of γ. In order to process the parts separately, we need to take care of two things: The starting page numbers of β and γ need to be set up properly, and the table of contents data from all three runs needs to be accumulated.

The **cwebmac** macros include two control sequences \contentsfile and \readcontents that facilitate the necessary processing. We include '\def\contentsfile{cont1}' in the limbo section of α, and we include '\def\contentsfile{cont2}' in the limbo section of β; this causes TEX to write the contents data for α and β into cont1.tex and cont2.tex. Now in γ we say

        \def\readcontents{\input cont1 \input cont2 \input \contentsfile} ;

this brings in the data from all three pieces, in the proper order.

However, we still need to solve the page-numbering problem. One way to do it is to include the following in the limbo material for β:

        \message{Please type the last page number of part 1: }
        \read -1 to \temp \pageno=\temp \advance\pageno by 1

Then you simply provide the necessary data when TEX requests it; a similar construction is used at the beginning of γ.

This method can, of course, be used to divide a woven file into any number of pieces.

11. Sometimes it is nice to include things in the index that are typeset in a special way. For example, we might want to have an index entry for 'TEX'. **CWEAVE** provides two simple ways to typeset an index entry (unless the entry is an identifier or a reserved word): '@^' gives roman type, and '@.' gives typewriter type. But if we try to typeset 'TEX' in roman type by saying, e.g., '@^\TeX@>', the backslash character gets in the way, and this entry wouldn't appear in the index with the T's.

The solution is to use the '@:' feature, declaring a macro that simply removes a sort key as follows:

                                \def\9#1{}

Now you can say, e.g., '@:TeX}{\TeX@>' in your CWEB file; **CWEAVE** puts it into the index alphabetically, based on the sort key, and produces the macro call '\9{TeX}{\TeX}' which will ensure that the sort key isn't printed.

A similar idea can be used to insert hidden material into section names so that they are alphabetized in whatever way you might wish. Some people call these tricks "special refinements"; others call them "kludges."

12. The control sequence \secno is set to the number of the section being typeset.

13. If you want to list only the sections that have changed, together with the index, put the command '\let\maybe=\iffalse' in the limbo section before the first section of your CWEB file. It's customary to make this the first change in your change file.

This feature has a TEXnical limitation, however: You cannot use it together with control sequences like \proclaim or \+ or \newcount that plain TEX has declared to be '\outer', because TEX refuses to skip silently over such control sequences. One way to work around this limitation is to say

                \fi \let\proclaim\relax \def\proclaim{...} \ifon

where \proclaim is redefined to be the same as usual but without an \outer qualification. (The \fi here stops the conditional skipping, and the \ifon turns it back on again.) Similarly,

                                \fi \newcount\n \ifon

is a safe way to use \newcount. Plain TEX already provides a non-outer macro \tabalign that does the work of \+; you can say

$$\text{\\fi \\let\\+\\tabalign \\ifon}$$

if you prefer the shorter notation \+.

14.   To get output in languages other than English, redefine the macros \A, \As, \ET, \ETs, \Q, \Qs, \U, \Us, \ch, \fin, \con, \today, \datethis, and \datecontentspage. CWEAVE itself need not be changed.

15.   Some output can be selectively suppressed with the macros \noatl, \noinx, \nosecs, \nocon.

16.   All accents and special text symbols of plain TEX format will work in CWEB documents just as they are described in Chapter 9 of *The TEXbook*, with one exception. The dot accent (normally \.) must be typed \: instead.

17.   Several commented-out lines in `cwebmac.tex` are suggestions that users may wish to adopt. For example, one such line inserts a blank page if you have a duplex printer. Appendices D, E, and F of the complete version of this manual are printed using a commented-out option that substitutes '←' for '=' in the program listings. Looking at those appendices might help you decide which format you like better.

18.   Andreas Scherer has contributed a macro called \pdfURL with which one can say things like the following, anywhere in the TEX parts or the C comments of a CWEB file:

```
You can send email to \pdfURL{the author}{mailto:andreas.scherer@@pobox.com}
or visit \pdfURL{his home page}{http://www.pobox.com/\TILDE/scherer}.
```

In a PDF document, the first argument will appear in blue as clickable text; the Acrobat reader, if correctly configured, will then redirect those links to the user's browser and open either the email client or the HTML viewer. In a hardcopy document, both arguments will be printed (the second in parentheses and typewriter type). Certain special characters in an Internet address need to be handled in a somewhat awkward way, so that CWEAVE and/or TEX will not confuse them with formatting controls: Use @@ for @ and \TILDE/ for ~ and \UNDER/ for _.

Common code for CTANGLE and CWEAVE

(Version 3.61)

1. Introduction. This file contains code common to both CTANGLE and CWEAVE, which roughly concerns the following problems: character uniformity, input routines, error handling and parsing of command line. We have tried to concentrate in this file all the system dependencies, so as to maximize portability.

In the texts below we will sometimes use CWEB to refer to either of the two component programs, if no confusion can arise.

The file begins with a few basic definitions.

⟨ Include files 5 ⟩
⟨ Preprocessor definitions ⟩
⟨ Definitions that should agree with CTANGLE and CWEAVE 2 ⟩
⟨ Other definitions 3 ⟩
⟨ Predeclaration of procedures 33 ⟩

2. In certain cases CTANGLE and CWEAVE should do almost, but not quite, the same thing. In these cases we've written common code for both, differentiating between the two by means of the global variable *program*.

#define *ctangle* 0
#define *cweave* 1

⟨ Definitions that should agree with CTANGLE and CWEAVE 2 ⟩ ≡
    typedef short boolean;
    boolean *program*;   /* CWEAVE or CTANGLE? */

See also sections 7, 10, 20, 27, 29, 32, 56, 67, and 77.

This code is used in section 1.

3. CWEAVE operates in three phases: First it inputs the source file and stores cross-reference data, then it inputs the source once again and produces the TEX output file, and finally it sorts and outputs the index. Similarly, CTANGLE operates in two phases. The global variable *phase* tells which phase we are in.

⟨ Other definitions 3 ⟩ ≡
    int *phase*;   /* which phase are we in? */

See also section 11.

This code is used in section 1.

4. There's an initialization procedure that gets both CTANGLE and CWEAVE off to a good start. We will fill in the details of this procedure later.

    void *common_init*( )
    {
      ⟨ Initialize pointers 30 ⟩;
      ⟨ Set the default options common to CTANGLE and CWEAVE 68 ⟩;
      ⟨ Scan arguments and open output files 78 ⟩;
    }

5.   The character set.   CWEB uses the conventions of C programs found in the standard `ctype.h` header file.

⟨ Include files 5 ⟩ ≡
#include `<ctype.h>`

See also sections 8 and 22.

This code is used in section 1.

6.   A few character pairs are encoded internally as single characters, using the definitions below. These definitions are consistent with an extension of ASCII code originally developed at MIT and explained in Appendix C of *The TeXbook*; thus, users who have such a character set can type things like ≠ and ∧ instead of != and &&. (However, their files will not be too portable until more people adopt the extended code.)

If the character set is not ASCII, the definitions given here may conflict with existing characters; in such cases, other arbitrary codes should be substituted. The indexes to CTANGLE and CWEAVE mention every case where similar codes may have to be changed in order to avoid character conflicts. Look for the entry "ASCII code dependencies" in those indexes.

#define *and_and* °4   /* '&&'; corresponds to MIT's ∧ */
#define *lt_lt* °20   /* '<<'; corresponds to MIT's ⊂ */
#define *gt_gt* °21   /* '>>'; corresponds to MIT's ⊃ */
#define *plus_plus* °13   /* '++'; corresponds to MIT's ↑ */
#define *minus_minus* °1   /* '--'; corresponds to MIT's ↓ */
#define *minus_gt* °31   /* '->'; corresponds to MIT's → */
#define *not_eq* °32   /* '!='; corresponds to MIT's ≠ */
#define *lt_eq* °34   /* '<='; corresponds to MIT's ≤ */
#define *gt_eq* °35   /* '>='; corresponds to MIT's ≥ */
#define *eq_eq* °36   /* '=='; corresponds to MIT's ≡ */
#define *or_or* °37   /* '||'; corresponds to MIT's ∨ */
#define *dot_dot_dot* °16   /* '...'; corresponds to MIT's ∞ */
#define *colon_colon* °6   /* '::'; corresponds to MIT's ∈ */
#define *period_ast* °26   /* '.*'; corresponds to MIT's ⊗ */
#define *minus_gt_ast* °27   /* '->*'; corresponds to MIT's ↹ */

7. Input routines.   The lowest level of input to the CWEB programs is performed by *input_ln*, which must be told which file to read from. The return value of *input_ln* is 1 if the read is successful and 0 if not (generally this means the file has ended). The conventions of TEX are followed; i.e., the characters of the next line of the file are copied into the *buffer* array, and the global variable *limit* is set to the first unoccupied position. Trailing blanks are ignored. The value of *limit* must be strictly less than *buf_size*, so that *buffer*[*buf_size* − 1] is never filled.

Since *buf_size* is strictly less than *long_buf_size*, some of CWEB's routines use the fact that it is safe to refer to *(*limit* + 2) without overstepping the bounds of the array.

#define *buf_size* 100   /* for CWEAVE and CTANGLE */
#define *longest_name* 1000
#define *long_buf_size* (*buf_size* + *longest_name*)   /* for CWEAVE */
#define *xisspace*(*c*) (*isspace*(*c*) ∧ ((**unsigned char**) *c* < °*200*))
#define *xisupper*(*c*) (*isupper*(*c*) ∧ ((**unsigned char**) *c* < °*200*))

⟨ Definitions that should agree with CTANGLE and CWEAVE 2 ⟩ +≡
  char *buffer*[*long_buf_size*];   /* where each line of input goes */
  char **buffer_end* ← *buffer* + *buf_size* − 2;   /* end of *buffer* */
  char **limit* ← *buffer*;   /* points to the last character in the buffer */
  char **loc* ← *buffer*;   /* points to the next character to be read from the buffer */

8.   ⟨ Include files 5 ⟩ +≡
#include <stdio.h>

9.   In the unlikely event that your standard I/O library does not support *feof*, *getc*, and *ungetc* you may have to change things here.

```
int input_ln(fp)       /* copies a line into buffer or returns 0 */
    FILE *fp;       /* what file to read from */
{
  register int c ← EOF;       /* character read; initialized so some compilers won't complain */
  register char *k;       /* where next character goes */
  if (feof(fp)) return (0);       /* we have hit end-of-file */
  limit ← k ← buffer;       /* beginning of buffer */
  while (k ≤ buffer_end ∧ (c ← getc(fp)) ≠ EOF ∧ c ≠ '\n')
    if ((*(k++) ← c) ≠ '␣') limit ← k;
  if (k > buffer_end)
    if ((c ← getc(fp)) ≠ EOF ∧ c ≠ '\n') {
      ungetc(c, fp);
      loc ← buffer;
      err_print("!␣Input␣line␣too␣long");
    }
  if (c ≡ EOF ∧ limit ≡ buffer) return (0);       /* there was nothing after the last newline */
  return (1);
}
```

10.   Now comes the problem of deciding which file to read from next. Recall that the actual text that CWEB should process comes from two streams: a *web_file*, which can contain possibly nested include commands @i, and a *change_file*, which might also contain includes. The *web_file* together with the currently open include files form a stack *file*, whose names are stored in a parallel stack *file_name*. The boolean *changing* tells whether or not we're reading from the *change_file*.

   The line number of each open file is also kept for error reporting and for the benefit of CTANGLE.

format *line*   *x*   /* make *line* an unreserved word */
#define   *max_include_depth*   10
              /* maximum number of source files open simultaneously, not counting the change file */
#define   *max_file_name_length*   60
#define   *cur_file*   *file*[*include_depth*]   /* current file */
#define   *cur_file_name*   *file_name*[*include_depth*]   /* current file name */
#define   *cur_line*   *line*[*include_depth*]   /* number of current line in current file */
#define   *web_file*   *file*[0]   /* main source file */
#define   *web_file_name*   *file_name*[0]   /* main source file name */
⟨ Definitions that should agree with CTANGLE and CWEAVE 2 ⟩ +≡
   int *include_depth*;   /* current level of nesting */
   FILE **file*[*max_include_depth*];   /* stack of non-change files */
   FILE **change_file*;   /* change file */
   char *file_name*[*max_include_depth*][*max_file_name_length*];   /* stack of non-change file names */
   char *change_file_name*[*max_file_name_length*];   /* name of change file */
   char *alt_web_file_name*[*max_file_name_length*];   /* alternate name to try */
   int *line*[*max_include_depth*];   /* number of current line in the stacked files */
   int *change_line*;   /* number of current line in change file */
   int *change_depth*;   /* where @y originated during a change */
   boolean *input_has_ended*;   /* if there is no more input */
   boolean *changing*;   /* if the current line is from *change_file* */
   boolean *web_file_open* ← 0;   /* if the web file is being read */

11.   When *changing* ≡ 0, the next line of *change_file* is kept in *change_buffer*, for purposes of comparison with the next line of *cur_file*. After the change file has been completely input, we set *change_limit* ← *change_buffer*, so that no further matches will be made.

   Here's a shorthand expression for inequality between the two lines:

#define   *lines_dont_match*
         (*change_limit* − *change_buffer* ≠ *limit* − *buffer* ∨ *strncmp*(*buffer*, *change_buffer*, *limit* − *buffer*))
⟨ Other definitions 3 ⟩ +≡
   char *change_buffer*[*buf_size*];   /* next line of *change_file* */
   char **change_limit*;   /* points to the last character in *change_buffer* */

12.   Procedure *prime_the_change_buffer* sets *change_buffer* in preparation for the next matching operation. Since blank lines in the change file are not used for matching, we have (*change_limit* ≡ *change_buffer* ∧ ¬*changing*) if and only if the change file is exhausted. This procedure is called only when *changing* is 1; hence error messages will be reported correctly.

   void *prime_the_change_buffer*()
   {
      change_limit ← *change_buffer*;   /* this value is used if the change file ends */
      ⟨ Skip over comment lines in the change file; **return** if end of file 13 ⟩;
      ⟨ Skip to the next nonblank line; **return** if end of file 14 ⟩;
      ⟨ Move *buffer* and *limit* to *change_buffer* and *change_limit* 15 ⟩;
   }

13.   While looking for a line that begins with @x in the change file, we allow lines that begin with @, as long as they don't begin with @y, @z, or @i (which would probably mean that the change file is fouled up).

⟨ Skip over comment lines in the change file; **return** if end of file 13 ⟩ ≡

```
while (1) {
  change_line ++;
  if (¬input_ln(change_file)) return;
  if (limit < buffer + 2) continue;
  if (buffer[0] ≠ '@') continue;
  if (xisupper(buffer[1])) buffer[1] ← tolower(buffer[1]);
  if (buffer[1] ≡ 'x') break;
  if (buffer[1] ≡ 'y' ∨ buffer[1] ≡ 'z' ∨ buffer[1] ≡ 'i') {
    loc ← buffer + 2;
    err_print("!␣Missing␣@x␣in␣change␣file");
  }
}
```

This code is used in section 12.

14.   Here we are looking at lines following the @x.

⟨ Skip to the next nonblank line; **return** if end of file 14 ⟩ ≡

```
do {
  change_line ++;
  if (¬input_ln(change_file)) {
    err_print("!␣Change␣file␣ended␣after␣@x");
    return;
  }
} while (limit ≡ buffer);
```

This code is used in section 12.

15.   ⟨ Move buffer and limit to change_buffer and change_limit 15 ⟩ ≡

```
{
  change_limit ← change_buffer − buffer + limit;
  strncpy(change_buffer, buffer, limit − buffer + 1);
}
```

This code is used in sections 12 and 16.

16.   The following procedure is used to see if the next change entry should go into effect; it is called only when *changing* is 0. The idea is to test whether or not the current contents of *buffer* matches the current contents of *change_buffer*. If not, there's nothing more to do; but if so, a change is called for: All of the text down to the @y is supposed to match. An error message is issued if any discrepancy is found. Then the procedure prepares to read the next line from *change_file*.

When a match is found, the current section is marked as changed unless the first line after the @x and after the @y both start with either '@*' or '@␣' (possibly preceded by whitespace).

This procedure is called only when *buffer* < *limit*, i.e., when the current line is nonempty.

#define   *if_section_start_make_pending*(b)
    { *limit* ← '!';
       for (*loc* ← *buffer*; *xisspace*(*loc*); *loc*++) ;
       limit ← '␣';
       if (*loc* ≡ '@' ∧ (*xisspace*(*(loc* + 1)) ∨ *(loc* + 1) ≡ '*')) *change_pending* ← b;
    }

void *check_change*( )   /* switches to *change_file* if the buffers match */
{
  int n ← 0;   /* the number of discrepancies found */
  if (*lines_dont_match*) **return**;
  change_pending ← 0;
  if (¬*changed_section*[*section_count*]) {
    if_section_start_make_pending(1);
    if (¬*change_pending*) *changed_section*[*section_count*] ← 1;
  }
  while (1) {
    changing ← 1;
    print_where ← 1;
    change_line++;
    if (¬*input_ln*(*change_file*)) {
      err_print("!␣Change␣file␣ended␣before␣@y");
      change_limit ← *change_buffer*;
      changing ← 0;
      return;
    }
    if (*limit* > *buffer* + 1 ∧ *buffer*[0] ≡ '@') {
      if (*xisupper*(*buffer*[1])) *buffer*[1] ← *tolower*(*buffer*[1]);
      ⟨ If the current line starts with @y, report any discrepancies and **return** 17 ⟩;
    }
    ⟨ Move *buffer* and *limit* to *change_buffer* and *change_limit* 15 ⟩;
    changing ← 0;
    cur_line++;
    while (¬*input_ln*(*cur_file*)) {   /* pop the stack or quit */
      if (*include_depth* ≡ 0) {
        err_print("!␣CWEB␣file␣ended␣during␣a␣change");
        input_has_ended ← 1;
        return;
      }
      include_depth--;
      cur_line++;
    }
    if (*lines_dont_match*) n++;
  }

}

17. ⟨ If the current line starts with @y, report any discrepancies and **return** 17 ⟩ ≡
> **if** ($buffer[1] \equiv$ 'x' $\vee$ $buffer[1] \equiv$ 'z') {
>> $loc \leftarrow buffer + 2;$
>> $err\_print(\texttt{"!\textvisiblespace Where\textvisiblespace is\textvisiblespace the\textvisiblespace matching\textvisiblespace @y?"});$
>
> }
> **else if** ($buffer[1] \equiv$ 'y') {
>> **if** ($n > 0$) {
>>> $loc \leftarrow buffer + 2;$
>>> $printf(\texttt{"\textbackslash n!\textvisiblespace Hmm...\textvisiblespace \%d\textvisiblespace "}, n);$
>>> $err\_print(\texttt{"of\textvisiblespace the\textvisiblespace preceding\textvisiblespace lines\textvisiblespace failed\textvisiblespace to\textvisiblespace match"});$
>>
>> }
>> $change\_depth \leftarrow include\_depth;$
>> **return**;
>
> }

This code is used in section 16.

18. The *reset_input* procedure, which gets CWEB ready to read the user's CWEB input, is used at the beginning of phase one of CTANGLE, phases one and two of CWEAVE.

> **void** *reset_input* ( )
> {
>> $limit \leftarrow buffer;$
>> $loc \leftarrow buffer + 1;$
>> $buffer[0] \leftarrow$ '$\textvisiblespace$';
>> ⟨ Open input files 19 ⟩;
>> $include\_depth \leftarrow 0;$
>> $cur\_line \leftarrow 0;$
>> $change\_line \leftarrow 0;$
>> $change\_depth \leftarrow include\_depth;$
>> $changing \leftarrow 1;$
>> $prime\_the\_change\_buffer( );$
>> $changing \leftarrow \neg changing;$
>> $limit \leftarrow buffer;$
>> $loc \leftarrow buffer + 1;$
>> $buffer[0] \leftarrow$ '$\textvisiblespace$';
>> $input\_has\_ended \leftarrow 0;$
>
> }

19. The following code opens the input files.
⟨ Open input files 19 ⟩ ≡
> **if** (($web\_file \leftarrow fopen(web\_file\_name, \texttt{"r"})) \equiv \Lambda$) {
>> $strcpy(web\_file\_name, alt\_web\_file\_name);$
>> **if** (($web\_file \leftarrow fopen(web\_file\_name, \texttt{"r"})) \equiv \Lambda$)
>>> $fatal(\texttt{"!\textvisiblespace Cannot\textvisiblespace open\textvisiblespace input\textvisiblespace file\textvisiblespace "}, web\_file\_name);$
>
> }
> $web\_file\_open \leftarrow 1;$
> **if** (($change\_file \leftarrow fopen(change\_file\_name, \texttt{"r"})) \equiv \Lambda$)
>> $fatal(\texttt{"!\textvisiblespace Cannot\textvisiblespace open\textvisiblespace change\textvisiblespace file\textvisiblespace "}, change\_file\_name);$

This code is used in section 18.

20. The *get_line* procedure is called when *loc* > *limit*; it puts the next line of merged input into the buffer and updates the other variables appropriately. A space is placed at the right end of the line. This procedure returns ¬*input_has_ended* because we often want to check the value of that variable after calling the procedure.

If we've just changed from the *cur_file* to the *change_file*, or if the *cur_file* has changed, we tell CTANGLE to print this information in the C file by means of the *print_where* flag.

#define *max_sections* 2000
　　　　　　/∗ number of identifiers, strings, section names; must be less than 10240 ∗/

⟨ Definitions that should agree with CTANGLE and CWEAVE 2 ⟩ +≡
　　typedef unsigned short sixteen_bits;
　　sixteen_bits *section_count*;　　　/∗ the current section number ∗/
　　boolean *changed_section*[*max_sections*];　　　/∗ is the section changed? ∗/
　　boolean *change_pending*;
　　　　/∗ if the current change is not yet recorded in *changed_section*[*section_count*] ∗/
　　boolean *print_where* ← 0;　　　/∗ should CTANGLE print line and file info? ∗/

21.　　**int** *get_line*( )　　　/∗ inputs the next line ∗/
　　{
　restart:
　　　if (*changing* ∧ *include_depth* ≡ *change_depth*)
　　　　⟨ Read from *change_file* and maybe turn off *changing* 25 ⟩;
　　　if (¬*changing* ∨ *include_depth* > *change_depth*) {
　　　　⟨ Read from *cur_file* and maybe turn on *changing* 24 ⟩;
　　　　if (*changing* ∧ *include_depth* ≡ *change_depth*) **goto** *restart*;
　　　}
　　　loc ← *buffer*;
　　　∗*limit* ← '␣';
　　　if (∗*buffer* ≡ '@' ∧ (∗(*buffer* + 1) ≡ 'i' ∨ ∗(*buffer* + 1) ≡ 'I')) {
　　　　loc ← *buffer* + 2;
　　　　while (*loc* ≤ *limit* ∧ (∗*loc* ≡ '␣' ∨ ∗*loc* ≡ '\t' ∨ ∗*loc* ≡ '"')) *loc*++;
　　　　if (*loc* ≥ *limit*) {
　　　　　err_print("!␣Include␣file␣name␣not␣given");
　　　　　goto *restart*;
　　　　}
　　　　if (*include_depth* ≥ *max_include_depth* − 1) {
　　　　　err_print("!␣Too␣many␣nested␣includes");
　　　　　goto *restart*;
　　　　}
　　　　include_depth++;　　　/∗ push input stack ∗/
　　　　⟨ Try to open include file, abort push if unsuccessful, go to *restart* 23 ⟩;
　　　}
　　　return (¬*input_has_ended*);
　　}

22.   When an @i line is found in the *cur_file*, we must temporarily stop reading it and start reading from the named include file. The @i line should give a complete file name with or without double quotes. If the environment variable CWEBINPUTS is set, or if the compiler flag of the same name was defined at compile time, CWEB will look for include files in the directory thus named, if it cannot find them in the current directory. (Colon-separated paths are not supported.) The remainder of the @i line after the file name is ignored.

#define   *too_long*( )
$$\{$$
        include_depth −−;
        err_print("!␣Include␣file␣name␣too␣long");
        goto *restart*;
$$\}$$

⟨ Include files 5 ⟩ +≡
#include <stdlib.h>   /∗ declaration of *getenv* and *exit* ∗/

23. ⟨ Try to open include file, abort push if unsuccessful, go to *restart* 23 ⟩ ≡

```
{
   char temp_file_name[max_file_name_length];
   char *cur_file_name_end ← cur_file_name + max_file_name_length − 1;
   char *k ← cur_file_name, *kk;
   int l;      /* length of file name */
   while (*loc ≠ '␣' ∧ *loc ≠ '\t' ∧ *loc ≠ '"' ∧ k ≤ cur_file_name_end) *k++ ← *loc ++;
   if (k > cur_file_name_end) too_long( );
   *k ← '\0';
   if ((cur_file ← fopen(cur_file_name, "r")) ≠ Λ) {
      cur_line ← 0;
      print_where ← 1;
      goto restart;      /* success */
   }
   kk ← getenv("CWEBINPUTS");
   if (kk ≠ Λ) {
      if ((l ← strlen(kk)) > max_file_name_length − 2) too_long( );
      strcpy(temp_file_name, kk);
   }
   else {
#ifdef CWEBINPUTS
      if ((l ← strlen(CWEBINPUTS)) > max_file_name_length − 2) too_long( );
      strcpy(temp_file_name, CWEBINPUTS);
#else
      l ← 0;
#endif    /* CWEBINPUTS */
   }
   if (l > 0) {
      if (k + l + 2 ≥ cur_file_name_end) too_long( );
      for ( ; k ≥ cur_file_name; k−−) *(k + l + 1) ← *k;
      strcpy(cur_file_name, temp_file_name);
      cur_file_name[l] ← '/';      /* UNIX pathname separator */
      if ((cur_file ← fopen(cur_file_name, "r")) ≠ Λ) {
         cur_line ← 0;
         print_where ← 1;
         goto restart;      /* success */
      }
   }
   include_depth −−;
   err_print("!␣Cannot␣open␣include␣file");
   goto restart;
}
```

This code is used in section 21.

24. ⟨ Read from *cur_file* and maybe turn on *changing* 24 ⟩ ≡
```
  {
    cur_line ++;
    while (¬input_ln(cur_file)) {        /* pop the stack or quit */
      print_where ← 1;
      if (include_depth ≡ 0) {
        input_has_ended ← 1;
        break;
      }
      else {
        fclose(cur_file);
        include_depth −−;
        if (changing ∧ include_depth ≡ change_depth) break;
        cur_line ++;
      }
    }
    if (¬changing ∧ ¬input_has_ended)
      if (limit − buffer ≡ change_limit − change_buffer)
        if (buffer[0] ≡ change_buffer[0])
          if (change_limit > change_buffer) check_change();
  }
```
This code is used in section 21.

25. ⟨ Read from *change_file* and maybe turn off *changing* 25 ⟩ ≡

```
{
    change_line ++;
    if (¬input_ln(change_file)) {
        err_print("! Change file ended without @z");
        buffer[0] ← '@';
        buffer[1] ← 'z';
        limit ← buffer + 2;
    }
    if (limit > buffer) {        /* check if the change has ended */
        if (change_pending) {
            if_section_start_make_pending(0);
            if (change_pending) {
                changed_section[section_count] ← 1;
                change_pending ← 0;
            }
        }
        *limit ← ' ';
        if (buffer[0] ≡ '@') {
            if (xisupper(buffer[1]))  buffer[1] ← tolower(buffer[1]);
            if (buffer[1] ≡ 'x' ∨ buffer[1] ≡ 'y') {
                loc ← buffer + 2;
                err_print("! Where is the matching @z?");
            }
            else if (buffer[1] ≡ 'z') {
                prime_the_change_buffer();
                changing ← ¬changing;
                print_where ← 1;
            }
        }
    }
}
```

This code is used in section 21.

26. At the end of the program, we will tell the user if the change file had a line that didn't match any relevant line in *web_file*.

```
void check_complete()
{
    if (change_limit ≠ change_buffer) {      /* changing is 0 */
        strncpy(buffer, change_buffer, change_limit − change_buffer + 1);
        limit ← buffer + (int)(change_limit − change_buffer);
        changing ← 1;
        change_depth ← include_depth;
        loc ← buffer;
        err_print("! Change file entry did not match");
    }
}
```

27. Storage of names and strings.   Both CWEAVE and CTANGLE store identifiers, section names and other strings in a large array of **char**s, called *byte_mem*. Information about the names is kept in the array *name_dir*, whose elements are structures of type *name_info*, containing a pointer into the *byte_mem* array (the address where the name begins) and other data. A *name_pointer* variable is a pointer into *name_dir*.

#**define** *max_bytes* 90000
        /* the number of bytes in identifiers, index entries, and section names; must be less than 2^{24} */
#**define** *max_names* 4000
        /* number of identifiers, strings, section names; must be less than 10240 */

⟨ Definitions that should agree with CTANGLE and CWEAVE 2 ⟩ +≡
  typedef struct name_info {
    char **byte_start*;   /* beginning of the name in *byte_mem* */
    ⟨ More elements of **name_info** structure 31 ⟩
  } **name_info**;   /* contains information about an identifier or section name */
  typedef name_info *name_pointer;   /* pointer into array of *name_info*s */
  char *byte_mem*[*max_bytes*];   /* characters of names */
  char **byte_mem_end* ← *byte_mem* + *max_bytes* − 1;   /* end of *byte_mem* */
  name_info *name_dir*[*max_names*];   /* information about names */
  name_pointer *name_dir_end* ← *name_dir* + *max_names* − 1;   /* end of *name_dir* */

28.   The actual sequence of characters in the name pointed to by a **name_pointer** p appears in positions p‑*byte_start* to $(p+1)$‑*byte_start* − 1, inclusive. The *print_id* macro prints this text on the user's terminal.

#**define** *length*(*c*) (*c*+1)‑*byte_start* − (*c*)‑*byte_start*   /* the length of a name */
#**define** *print_id*(*c*) *term_write*((*c*)‑*byte_start*, *length*((*c*)))   /* print identifier */

29.   The first unused position in *byte_mem* and *name_dir* is kept in *byte_ptr* and *name_ptr*, respectively. Thus we usually have *name_ptr*‑*byte_start* ≡ *byte_ptr*, and certainly we want to keep *name_ptr* ≤ *name_dir_end* and *byte_ptr* ≤ *byte_mem_end*.

⟨ Definitions that should agree with CTANGLE and CWEAVE 2 ⟩ +≡
  name_pointer *name_ptr*;   /* first unused position in *byte_start* */
  char **byte_ptr*;   /* first unused position in *byte_mem* */

30.   ⟨ Initialize pointers 30 ⟩ ≡
  name_dir‑*byte_start* ← *byte_ptr* ← *byte_mem*;   /* position zero in both arrays */
  name_ptr ← *name_dir* + 1;   /* *name_dir*[0] will be used only for error recovery */
  name_ptr‑*byte_start* ← *byte_mem*;   /* this makes name 0 of length zero */

See also sections 34 and 41.

This code is used in section 4.

31.   The names of identifiers are found by computing a hash address h and then looking at strings of bytes signified by the **name_pointer**s *hash*[*h*], *hash*[*h*]‑*link*, *hash*[*h*]‑*link*‑*link*, . . . , until either finding the desired name or encountering the null pointer.

⟨ More elements of **name_info** structure 31 ⟩ ≡
  struct name_info **link*;

See also sections 40 and 55.

This code is used in section 27.

32.   The hash table itself consists of *hash_size* entries of type **name_pointer**, and is updated by the *id_lookup* procedure, which finds a given identifier and returns the appropriate **name_pointer**. The matching is done by the function *names_match*, which is slightly different in CWEAVE and CTANGLE. If there is no match for the identifier, it is inserted into the table.

#**define** *hash_size*   353   /* should be prime */

⟨ Definitions that should agree with CTANGLE and CWEAVE 2 ⟩ +≡
    typedef name_pointer *∗**hash_pointer**;
    name_pointer *hash*[*hash_size*];   /* heads of hash lists */
    hash_pointer *hash_end* ← *hash* + *hash_size* − 1;   /* end of *hash* */
    hash_pointer *h*;   /* index into hash-head array */

33.   ⟨ Predeclaration of procedures 33 ⟩ ≡
    extern int *names_match*( );

See also sections 38, 46, 53, 57, 60, 63, 69, and 81.

This code is used in section 1.

34.   Initially all the hash lists are empty.

⟨ Initialize pointers 30 ⟩ +≡
    for (*h* ← *hash*; *h* ≤ *hash_end*; *∗h*++ ← Λ) ;

35.   Here is the main procedure for finding identifiers:

    name_pointer *id_lookup*(*first*, *last*, *t*)   /* looks up a string in the identifier table */
        char *∗first*;   /* first character of string */
        char *∗last*;   /* last character of string plus one */
        char *t*;   /* the *ilk*; used by CWEAVE only */
    {
      char *∗i* ← *first*;   /* position in *buffer* */
      int *h*;   /* hash code */
      int *l*;   /* length of the given identifier */
      name_pointer *p*;   /* where the identifier is being sought */
      if (*last* ≡ Λ)
        for (*last* ← *first*; *∗last* ≠ '\0'; *last*++) ;
      l ← *last* − *first*;   /* compute the length */
      ⟨ Compute the hash code *h* 36 ⟩;
      ⟨ Compute the name location *p* 37 ⟩;
      if (*p* ≡ *name_ptr*) ⟨ Enter a new name into the table at position *p* 39 ⟩;
      return (*p*);
    }

36.   A simple hash code is used: If the sequence of character codes is $c_1 c_2 \ldots c_n$, its hash value will be

$$(2^{n-1} c_1 + 2^{n-2} c_2 + \cdots + c_n) \bmod hash\_size.$$

⟨ Compute the hash code *h* 36 ⟩ ≡
    h ← (**unsigned char**) *∗i*;
    while (++*i* < *last*) *h* ← (*h* + *h* + (**int**)((**unsigned char**) *∗i*)) % *hash_size*;

This code is used in section 35.

37.   If the identifier is new, it will be placed in position $p \leftarrow name\_ptr$, otherwise p will point to its existing location.

$\langle$ Compute the name location p 37 $\rangle \equiv$
  $p \leftarrow hash[h]$;
  while $(p \wedge \neg names\_match(p, first, l, t))$ $p \leftarrow p\text{-}link$;
  if $(p \equiv \Lambda)$ {
    $p \leftarrow name\_ptr$;   /* the current identifier is new */
    $p\text{-}link \leftarrow hash[h]$;
    $hash[h] \leftarrow p$;   /* insert p at beginning of hash list */
  }
This code is used in section 35.

38.   The information associated with a new identifier must be initialized in a slightly different way in **CWEAVE** than in **CTANGLE**; hence the $init\_p$ procedure.

$\langle$ Predeclaration of procedures 33 $\rangle$ $+\equiv$
  void $init\_p(\ )$;

39. $\langle$ Enter a new name into the table at position p 39 $\rangle \equiv$
  {
    if $(byte\_ptr + l > byte\_mem\_end)$ $overflow("byte_\sqcup memory")$;
    if $(name\_ptr \geq name\_dir\_end)$ $overflow("name")$;
    $strncpy(byte\_ptr, first, l)$;
    $(++name\_ptr)\text{-}byte\_start \leftarrow byte\_ptr += l$;
    if $(program \equiv cweave)$ $init\_p(p, t)$;
  }
This code is used in section 35.

40.   The names of sections are stored in $byte\_mem$ together with the identifier names, but a hash table is not used for them because **CTANGLE** needs to be able to recognize a section name when given a prefix of that name. A conventional binary search tree is used to retrieve section names, with fields called $llink$ and $rlink$ (where $llink$ takes the place of $link$). The root of this tree is stored in $name\_dir\text{-}rlink$; this will be the only information in $name\_dir[0]$.

    Since the space used by $rlink$ has a different function for identifiers than for section names, we declare it as a **union**.

#define $llink$ $link$ /* left link in binary search tree for section names */
#define $rlink$ $dummy.Rlink$ /* right link in binary search tree for section names */
#define $root$ $name\_dir\text{-}rlink$ /* the root of the binary search tree for section names */
$\langle$ More elements of **name_info** structure 31 $\rangle$ $+\equiv$
  union {
    struct name_info *$Rlink$;   /* right link in binary search tree for section names */
    char Ilk;   /* used by identifiers in **CWEAVE** only */
  } $dummy$;

41. $\langle$ Initialize pointers 30 $\rangle$ $+\equiv$
  $root \leftarrow \Lambda$;   /* the binary search tree starts out with nothing in it */

42.   If p is a **name_pointer** variable, as we have seen, $p\text{-}byte\_start$ is the beginning of the area where the name corresponding to p is stored. However, if p refers to a section name, the name may need to be stored in chunks, because it may "grow": a prefix of the section name may be encountered before the full name. Furthermore we need to know the length of the shortest prefix of the name that was ever encountered.

We solve this problem by inserting two extra bytes at $p\text{-}byte\_start$, representing the length of the shortest prefix, when p is a section name. Furthermore, the last byte of the name will be a blank space if p is a prefix. In the latter case, the name pointer $p + 1$ will allow us to access additional chunks of the name: The second chunk will begin at the name pointer $(p + 1)\text{-}link$, and if it too is a prefix (ending with blank) its $link$ will point to additional chunks in the same way. Null links are represented by $name\_dir$.

```
#define  first_chunk(p)   ((p)-byte_start + 2)
#define  prefix_length(p)
         (int)((unsigned char) *((p)-byte_start) * 256 + (unsigned char) *((p)-byte_start + 1))
#define  set_prefix_length(p, m)   (*((p)-byte_start) ← (m)/256, *((p)-byte_start + 1) ← (m) % 256)
  void print_section_name(p)
     name_pointer p;
  {
    char *ss, *s ← first_chunk(p);
    name_pointer q ← p + 1;
    while (p ≠ name_dir) {
      ss ← (p + 1)-byte_start - 1;
      if (*ss ≡ '␣' ∧ ss ≥ s) {
        term_write(s, ss - s);
        p ← q-link;
        q ← p;
      }
      else {
        term_write(s, ss + 1 - s);
        p ← name_dir;
        q ← Λ;
      }
      s ← p-byte_start;
    }
    if (q) term_write("...", 3);      /* complete name not yet known */
  }
```

43.   **void** *sprint_section_name*(*dest*, *p*)
   char **dest*;
   name_pointer *p*;
{
   char **ss*, **s* ← *first_chunk*(*p*);
   name_pointer *q* ← *p* + 1;
   while (*p* ≠ *name_dir*) {
      ss ← (*p* + 1)⁻*byte_start* − 1;
      if (**ss* ≡ '␣' ∧ *ss* ≥ *s*) {
         p ← *q*⁻*link*;
         q ← *p*;
      }
      else {
         ss++;
         p ← *name_dir*;
      }
      strncpy(*dest*, *s*, *ss* − *s*), *dest* += *ss* − *s*;
      s ← *p*⁻*byte_start*;
   }
   *dest ← '\0';
}

44.   **void** *print_prefix_name*(*p*)
   name_pointer *p*;
{
   char **s* ← *first_chunk*(*p*);
   int *l* ← *prefix_length*(*p*);
   term_write(*s*, *l*);
   if (*s* + *l* < (*p* + 1)⁻*byte_start*) *term_write*("...", 3);
}

45.   When we compare two section names, we'll need a function analogous to *strcmp*. But we do not assume the strings are null-terminated, and we keep an eye open for prefixes and extensions.

#define *less*   0   /* the first name is lexicographically less than the second */
#define *equal*   1   /* the first name is equal to the second */
#define *greater*   2   /* the first name is lexicographically greater than the second */
#define *prefix*   3   /* the first name is a proper prefix of the second */
#define *extension*   4   /* the first name is a proper extension of the second */
   int *web_strcmp*(*j*, *j_len*, *k*, *k_len*)   /* fuller comparison than *strcmp* */
      char **j*, **k*;   /* beginning of first and second strings */
      int *j_len*, *k_len*;   /* length of strings */
{
   char **j1* ← *j* + *j_len*, **k1* ← *k* + *k_len*;
   while (*k* < *k1* ∧ *j* < *j1* ∧ **j* ≡ **k*) *k*++, *j*++;
   if (*k* ≡ *k1*)
      if (*j* ≡ *j1*) **return** *equal*;
      else return *extension*;
   else if (*j* ≡ *j1*) **return** *prefix*;
   else if (**j* < **k*) **return** *less*;
   else return *greater*;
}

46. Adding a section name to the tree is straightforward if we know its parent and whether it's the *rlink* or *llink* of the parent. As a special case, when the name is the first section being added, we set the "parent" to Λ. When a section name is created, it has only one chunk, which however may be just a prefix; the full name will hopefully be unveiled later. Obviously, *prefix_length* starts out as the length of the first chunk, though it may decrease later.

The information associated with a new node must be initialized differently in CWEAVE and CTANGLE; hence the *init_node* procedure, which is defined differently in cweave.w and ctangle.w.

⟨ Predeclaration of procedures 33 ⟩ +≡
    extern void *init_node*( );

47.   **name_pointer** *add_section_name*(*par*, *c*, *first*, *last*, *ispref*)   /∗ install a new node in the tree ∗/
        name_pointer *par*;   /∗ parent of new node ∗/
        int *c*;   /∗ right or left? ∗/
        char ∗*first*;   /∗ first character of section name ∗/
        char ∗*last*;   /∗ last character of section name, plus one ∗/
        int *ispref*;   /∗ are we adding a prefix or a full name? ∗/
    {
        name_pointer $p \leftarrow$ *name_ptr*;   /∗ new node ∗/
        char ∗$s \leftarrow$ *first_chunk*(*p*);
        int *name_len* $\leftarrow$ *last* − *first* + *ispref*;   /∗ length of section name ∗/
        if (*s* + *name_len* > *byte_mem_end*) *overflow*("byte␣memory");
        if (*name_ptr* + 1 ≥ *name_dir_end*) *overflow*("name");
        (++*name_ptr*)→*byte_start* ← *byte_ptr* ← *s* + *name_len*;
        if (*ispref*) {
            ∗(*byte_ptr* − 1) ← '␣';
            name_len −−;
            name_ptr→*link* ← *name_dir*;
            (++*name_ptr*)→*byte_start* ← *byte_ptr*;
        }
        set_prefix_length(*p*, *name_len*);
        strncpy(*s*, *first*, *name_len*);
        p→*llink* ← Λ;
        p→*rlink* ← Λ;
        init_node(*p*);
        return *par* ≡ Λ ? (*root* ← *p*) : *c* ≡ *less* ? (*par*→*llink* ← *p*) : (*par*→*rlink* ← *p*);
    }

48.   **void** *extend_section_name* (*p*, *first*, *last*, *ispref*)
    name_pointer *p*;   /∗ name to be extended ∗/
    char ∗*first*;   /∗ beginning of extension text ∗/
    char ∗*last*;   /∗ one beyond end of extension text ∗/
    int *ispref*;   /∗ are we adding a prefix or a full name? ∗/
{
  char ∗*s*;
  name_pointer $q \leftarrow p + 1$;
  int *name_len* $\leftarrow$ *last* $-$ *first* $+$ *ispref*;

  if (*name_ptr* $\geq$ *name_dir_end*) *overflow*("name");
  while (*q*‑*link* $\neq$ *name_dir*) $q \leftarrow q$‑*link*;
  q‑*link* $\leftarrow$ *name_ptr*;
  s $\leftarrow$ *name_ptr*‑*byte_start*;
  name_ptr‑*link* $\leftarrow$ *name_dir*;
  if (*s* + *name_len* > *byte_mem_end*) *overflow*("byte␣memory");
  (++*name_ptr*)‑*byte_start* $\leftarrow$ *byte_ptr* $\leftarrow$ *s* + *name_len*;
  strncpy(*s*, *first*, *name_len*);
  if (*ispref*) ∗(*byte_ptr* $-$ 1) $\leftarrow$ '␣';
}

49.   The *section_lookup* procedure is supposed to find a section name that matches a new name, installing the new name if it doesn't match an existing one. The new name is the string between *first* and *last*; a "match" means that the new name exactly equals or is a prefix or extension of a name in the tree.

name_pointer *section_lookup* (*first*, *last*, *ispref*)   /∗ find or install section name in tree ∗/
    char ∗*first*, ∗*last*;   /∗ first and last characters of new name ∗/
    int *ispref*;   /∗ is the new name a prefix or a full name? ∗/
{
  int $c \leftarrow 0$;   /∗ comparison between two names; initialized so some compilers won't complain ∗/
  name_pointer $p \leftarrow root$;   /∗ current node of the search tree ∗/
  name_pointer $q \leftarrow \Lambda$;   /∗ another place to look in the tree ∗/
  name_pointer $r \leftarrow \Lambda$;   /∗ where a match has been found ∗/
  name_pointer *par* $\leftarrow \Lambda$;   /∗ parent of *p*, if *r* is Λ; otherwise parent of *r* ∗/
  int *name_len* $\leftarrow$ *last* $-$ *first* $+$ 1;

  ⟨ Look for matches for new name among shortest prefixes, complaining if more than one is found 50 ⟩;
  ⟨ If no match found, add new name to tree 51 ⟩;
  ⟨ If one match found, check for compatibility and return match 52 ⟩;
}

50.   A legal new name matches an existing section name if and only if it matches the shortest prefix of that section name. Therefore we can limit our search for matches to shortest prefixes, which eliminates the need for chunk-chasing at this stage.

⟨ Look for matches for new name among shortest prefixes, complaining if more than one is found 50 ⟩ ≡

```
while (p) {       /* compare shortest prefix of p with new name */
    c ← web_strcmp(first, name_len, first_chunk(p), prefix_length(p));
    if (c ≡ less ∨ c ≡ greater) {       /* new name does not match p */
        if (r ≡ Λ)       /* no previous matches have been found */
            par ← p;
        p ← (c ≡ less ? p⃗llink : p⃗rlink);
    }
    else {       /* new name matches p */
        if (r ≠ Λ) {       /* and also r: illegal */
            printf("\n!␣Ambiguous␣prefix:␣matches␣<");
            print_prefix_name(p);
            printf(">\n␣and␣<");
            print_prefix_name(r);
            err_print(">");
            return name_dir;       /* the unsection */
        }
        r ← p;       /* remember match */
        p ← p⃗llink;       /* try another */
        q ← r⃗rlink;       /* we'll get back here if the new p doesn't match */
    }
    if (p ≡ Λ)  p ← q, q ← Λ;       /* q held the other branch of r */
}
```

This code is used in section 49.

51.   ⟨ If no match found, add new name to tree 51 ⟩ ≡

```
if (r ≡ Λ)       /* no matches were found */
    return add_section_name(par, c, first, last + 1, ispref);
```

This code is used in section 49.

52. Although error messages are given in anomalous cases, we do return the unique best match when a discrepancy is found, because users often change a title in one place while forgetting to change it elsewhere.

⟨ If one match found, check for compatibility and return match 52 ⟩ ≡

```
  switch (section_name_cmp(&first, name_len, r)) {        /* compare all of r with new name */
  case prefix:
    if (¬ispref) {
      printf("\n!␣New␣name␣is␣a␣prefix␣of␣<");
      print_section_name(r);
      err_print(">");
    }
    else if (name_len < prefix_length(r)) set_prefix_length(r, name_len);      /* fall through */
  case equal: return r;
  case extension:
    if (¬ispref ∨ first ≤ last) extend_section_name(r, first, last + 1, ispref);
    return r;
  case bad_extension: printf("\n!␣New␣name␣extends␣<");
    print_section_name(r);
    err_print(">");
    return r;
  default:        /* no match: illegal */
    printf("\n!␣Section␣name␣incompatible␣with␣<");
    print_prefix_name(r);
    printf(">,\n␣which␣abbreviates␣<");
    print_section_name(r);
    err_print(">");
    return r;
  }
```

This code is used in section 49.

53. The return codes of *section_name_cmp*, which compares a string with the full name of a section, are those of *web_strcmp* plus *bad_extension*, used when the string is an extension of a supposedly already complete section name. This function has a side effect when the comparison string is an extension: It advances the address of the first character of the string by an amount equal to the length of the known part of the section name.

The name `@<foo...@>` should be an acceptable "abbreviation" for `@<foo@>`. If such an abbreviation comes after the complete name, there's no trouble recognizing it. If it comes before the complete name, we simply append a null chunk. This logic requires us to regard `@<foo...@>` as an "extension" of itself.

#define *bad_extension* 5

⟨ Predeclaration of procedures 33 ⟩ +≡

```
  int section_name_cmp();
```

54.   **int** $section\_name\_cmp(pfirst, len, r)$
    char $**pfirst$;   /* pointer to beginning of comparison string */
    int len;   /* length of string */
    name_pointer r;   /* section name being compared */
 {
   char $*first \leftarrow *pfirst$;   /* beginning of comparison string */
   name_pointer $q \leftarrow r + 1$;   /* access to subsequent chunks */
   char $*ss, *s \leftarrow first\_chunk(r)$;
   int c;   /* comparison */
   int $ispref$;   /* is chunk r a prefix? */
   while (1) {
     $ss \leftarrow (r + 1)\text{-}byte\_start - 1$;
     if $(*ss \equiv '\sqcup' \wedge ss \geq r\text{-}byte\_start)$ $ispref \leftarrow 1, q \leftarrow q\text{-}link$;
     else $ispref \leftarrow 0, ss \mathbin{++}, q \leftarrow name\_dir$;
     switch $(c \leftarrow web\_strcmp(first, len, s, ss - s))$ {
     case $equal$:
      if $(q \equiv name\_dir)$
       if $(ispref)$ {
        $*pfirst \leftarrow first + (ss - s)$;
        return $extension$;   /* null extension */
       }
       else return $equal$;
      else return $(q\text{-}byte\_start \equiv (q + 1)\text{-}byte\_start)\ ?\ equal : prefix$;
     case $extension$:
      if $(\neg ispref)$ **return** $bad\_extension$;
      $first \mathrel{+}= ss - s$;
      if $(q \neq name\_dir)$ {
       $len \mathrel{-}= ss - s$;
       $s \leftarrow q\text{-}byte\_start$;
       $r \leftarrow q$;
       continue;
      }
      $*pfirst \leftarrow first$;
      return $extension$;
     default: **return** c;
     }
   }
 }

55.   The last component of **name_info** is different for CTANGLE and CWEAVE. In CTANGLE, if p is a pointer to a section name, $p\text{-}equiv$ is a pointer to its replacement text, an element of the array $text\_info$. In CWEAVE, on the other hand, if p points to an identifier, $p\text{-}xref$ is a pointer to its list of cross-references, an element of the array $xmem$. The make-up of $text\_info$ and $xmem$ is discussed in the CTANGLE and CWEAVE source files, respectively; here we just declare a common field $equiv\_or\_xref$ as a pointer to a **char**.

⟨ More elements of **name_info** structure 31 ⟩ $+\equiv$
   char $*equiv\_or\_xref$;   /* info corresponding to names */

56. Reporting errors to the user. A global variable called *history* will contain one of four values at the end of every run: *spotless* means that no unusual messages were printed; *harmless_message* means that a message of possible interest was printed but no serious errors were detected; *error_message* means that at least one error was found; *fatal_message* means that the program terminated abnormally. The value of *history* does not influence the behavior of the program; it is simply computed for the convenience of systems that might want to use such information.

#define *spotless* 0   /* *history* value for normal jobs */
#define *harmless_message* 1   /* *history* value when non-serious info was printed */
#define *error_message* 2   /* *history* value when an error was noted */
#define *fatal_message* 3   /* *history* value when we had to stop prematurely */
#define *mark_harmless*
  {
   if (*history* ≡ *spotless*) *history* ← *harmless_message*;
  }
#define *mark_error*   *history* ← *error_message*
⟨ Definitions that should agree with CTANGLE and CWEAVE 2 ⟩ +≡
 int *history* ← *spotless*;   /* indicates how bad this run was */

57. The command '*err_print*("!␣Error␣message")' will report a syntax error to the user, by printing the error message at the beginning of a new line and then giving an indication of where the error was spotted in the source file. Note that no period follows the error message, since the error routine will automatically supply a period. A newline is automatically supplied if the string begins with "!".
⟨ Predeclaration of procedures 33 ⟩ +≡
 void *err_print*( );

58. **void** *err_print*(*s*)   /* prints '.' and location of error message */
  char *s;
 {
  char *k, *l;   /* pointers into *buffer* */
  printf(*s* ≡ '!' ? "\n%s" : "%s", *s*);
  if (*web_file_open*) ⟨ Print error location based on input buffer 59 ⟩;
  update_terminal;
  mark_error;
 }

59.   The error locations can be indicated by using the global variables *loc*, *cur_line*, *cur_file_name* and *changing*, which tell respectively the first unlooked-at position in *buffer*, the current line number, the current file, and whether the current line is from *change_file* or *cur_file*. This routine should be modified on systems whose standard text editor has special line-numbering conventions.

⟨ Print error location based on input buffer 59 ⟩ ≡
```
{
    if (changing ∧ include_depth ≡ change_depth) printf(".␣(l.␣%d␣of␣change␣file)\n", change_line);
    else if (include_depth ≡ 0) printf(".␣(l.␣%d)\n", cur_line);
    else printf(".␣(l.␣%d␣of␣include␣file␣%s)\n", cur_line, cur_file_name);
    l ← (loc ≥ limit ? limit : loc);
    if (l > buffer) {
        for (k ← buffer; k < l; k++)
            if (*k ≡ '\t') putchar('␣');
            else putchar(*k);      /* print the characters already read */
        putchar('\n');
        for (k ← buffer; k < l; k++) putchar('␣');      /* space out the next line */
    }
    for (k ← l; k < limit; k++) putchar(*k);      /* print the part not yet read */
    if (*limit ≡ '|') putchar('|');      /* end of C text in section names */
    putchar('␣');      /* to separate the message from future asterisks */
}
```
This code is used in section 58.

60.   When no recovery from some error has been provided, we have to wrap up and quit as graciously as possible. This is done by calling the function *wrap_up* at the end of the code.

   CTANGLE and CWEAVE have their own notions about how to print the job statistics.

⟨ Predeclaration of procedures 33 ⟩ +≡
```
    int wrap_up();
    extern void print_stats();
```

61.   Some implementations may wish to pass the *history* value to the operating system so that it can be used to govern whether or not other programs are started. Here, for instance, we pass the operating system a status of 0 if and only if only harmless messages were printed.
```
    int wrap_up()
    {
        putchar('\n');
        if (show_stats) print_stats();      /* print statistics about memory usage */
        ⟨ Print the job history 62 ⟩;
        if (history > harmless_message) return (1);
        else return (0);
    }
```

62. ⟨ Print the job *history* 62 ⟩ ≡
  switch (*history*) {
  case *spotless*:
    if (*show_happiness*) *printf* (" (No␣errors␣were␣found.)\n");
    break;
  case *harmless_message*: *printf* (" (Did␣you␣see␣the␣warning␣message␣above?)\n");
    break;
  case *error_message*: *printf* (" (Pardon␣me,␣but␣I␣think␣I␣spotted␣something␣wrong.)\n");
    break;
  case *fatal_message*: *printf* (" (That␣was␣a␣fatal␣error,␣my␣friend.)\n");
  }   /* there are no other cases */
This code is used in section 61.

63. When there is no way to recover from an error, the *fatal* subroutine is invoked. This happens most often when *overflow* occurs.

⟨ Predeclaration of procedures 33 ⟩ +≡
  void *fatal* ( ), *overflow* ( );

64. The two parameters to *fatal* are strings that are essentially concatenated to print the final error message.

  void *fatal* (*s, t*)
      char *∗s, ∗t*;
  {
    if (*∗s*) *printf* (*s*);
    err_print (*t*);
    history ← *fatal_message*;
    exit (*wrap_up* ( ));
  }

65. An overflow stop occurs if CWEB's tables aren't large enough.
  void *overflow* (*t*)
      char *∗t*;
  {
    printf ("\n!␣Sorry,␣%s␣capacity␣exceeded", *t*);
    fatal ("", "");
  }

66. Sometimes the program's behavior is far different from what it should be, and CWEB prints an error message that is really for the CWEB maintenance person, not the user. In such cases the program says *confusion* ("indication␣of␣where␣we␣are").

#define *confusion* (*s*) *fatal* ("!␣This␣can't␣happen:␣", *s*)

67.   Command line arguments.   The user calls CWEAVE and CTANGLE with arguments on the command line. These are either file names or flags to be turned off (beginning with "-") or flags to be turned on (beginning with "+"). The following globals are for communicating the user's desires to the rest of the program. The various file name variables contain strings with the names of those files. Most of the 128 flags are undefined but available for future extensions.

#define *show_banner* *flags*['b']   /* should the banner line be printed? */
#define *show_progress* *flags*['p']   /* should progress reports be printed? */
#define *show_stats* *flags*['s']   /* should statistics be printed at end of run? */
#define *show_happiness* *flags*['h']   /* should lack of errors be announced? */
⟨ Definitions that should agree with CTANGLE and CWEAVE 2 ⟩ +≡
    int *argc*;   /* copy of *ac* parameter to *main* */
    char **argv;   /* copy of *av* parameter to *main* */
    char *C_file_name*[*max_file_name_length*];   /* name of *C_file* */
    char *tex_file_name*[*max_file_name_length*];   /* name of *tex_file* */
    char *idx_file_name*[*max_file_name_length*];   /* name of *idx_file* */
    char *scn_file_name*[*max_file_name_length*];   /* name of *scn_file* */
    boolean *flags*[128];   /* an option for each 7-bit code */

68.   The *flags* will be initially zero. Some of them are set to 1 before scanning the arguments; if additional flags are 1 by default they should be set before calling *common_init*.
⟨ Set the default options common to CTANGLE and CWEAVE 68 ⟩ ≡
    show_banner ← *show_happiness* ← *show_progress* ← 1;
This code is used in section 4.

69.   We now must look at the command line arguments and set the file names accordingly. At least one file name must be present: the CWEB file. It may have an extension, or it may omit the extension to get ".w" or ".web" added. The TEX output file name is formed by replacing the CWEB file name extension by ".tex", and the C file name by replacing the extension by ".c", after removing the directory name (if any).

If there is a second file name present among the arguments, it is the change file, again either with an extension or without one to get ".ch". An omitted change file argument means that "/dev/null" should be used, when no changes are desired.

If there's a third file name, it will be the output file.
⟨ Predeclaration of procedures 33 ⟩ +≡
    void *scan_args*( );

70.   **void** *scan_args*( )
  {
    char $*dot\_pos$;   /* position of '.' in the argument */
    char $*name\_pos$;   /* file name beginning, sans directory */
    register char $*s$;   /* register for scanning strings */
    boolean $found\_web \leftarrow 0$, $found\_change \leftarrow 0$, $found\_out \leftarrow 0$;   /* have these names been seen? */
    boolean $flag\_change$;
    while $(-\!\!-argc > 0)$ {
      if $((**(+\!\!+argv) \equiv \,'\text{-}' \lor **argv \equiv \,'\text{+}') \land *(*argv + 1))$ ⟨ Handle flag argument 74 ⟩
      else {
        $s \leftarrow name\_pos \leftarrow *argv$; $dot\_pos \leftarrow \Lambda$;
        while $(*s)$ {
          if $(*s \equiv \,'.')$ $dot\_pos \leftarrow s\!+\!+$;
          else if $(*s \equiv \,'/')$ $dot\_pos \leftarrow \Lambda$, $name\_pos \leftarrow +\!\!+s$;
          else $s\!+\!+$;
        }
        if $(\neg found\_web)$ ⟨ Make web_file_name, tex_file_name, and C_file_name 71 ⟩
        else if $(\neg found\_change)$ ⟨ Make $change\_file\_name$ from $fname$ 72 ⟩
        else if $(\neg found\_out)$ ⟨ Override tex_file_name and C_file_name 73 ⟩
        else ⟨ Print usage error message and quit 75 ⟩;
      }
    }
    if $(\neg found\_web)$ ⟨ Print usage error message and quit 75 ⟩;
    if $(found\_change \leq 0)$ $strcpy(change\_file\_name, \texttt{"/dev/null"})$;
  }

71.   We use all of $*argv$ for the web_file_name if there is a '.' in it, otherwise we add $\texttt{".w"}$. If this file can't be opened, we prepare an $alt\_web\_file\_name$ by adding $\texttt{"web"}$ after the dot. The other file names come from adding other things after the dot. We must check that there is enough room in web_file_name and the other arrays for the argument.

⟨ Make web_file_name, tex_file_name, and C_file_name 71 ⟩ ≡
  {
    if $(s - *argv > max\_file\_name\_length - 5)$ ⟨ Complain about argument length 76 ⟩;
    if $(dot\_pos \equiv \Lambda)$ $sprintf(web\_file\_name, \texttt{"\%s.w"}, *argv)$;
    else {
      $strcpy(web\_file\_name, *argv)$;
      $*dot\_pos \leftarrow 0$;   /* string now ends where the dot was */
    }
    $sprintf(alt\_web\_file\_name, \texttt{"\%s.web"}, *argv)$;
    $sprintf(tex\_file\_name, \texttt{"\%s.tex"}, name\_pos)$;   /* strip off directory name */
    $sprintf(idx\_file\_name, \texttt{"\%s.idx"}, name\_pos)$;
    $sprintf(scn\_file\_name, \texttt{"\%s.scn"}, name\_pos)$;
    $sprintf(C\_file\_name, \texttt{"\%s.c"}, name\_pos)$;
    $found\_web \leftarrow 1$;
  }
This code is used in section 70.

72. ⟨ Make *change_file_name* from *fname* 72 ⟩ ≡
```
  {
    if (strcmp(*argv, "-") ≡ 0) found_change ← −1;
    else {
      if (s − *argv > max_file_name_length − 4) ⟨ Complain about argument length 76 ⟩;
      if (dot_pos ≡ Λ) sprintf(change_file_name, "%s.ch", *argv);
      else strcpy(change_file_name, *argv);
      found_change ← 1;
    }
  }
```
This code is used in section 70.

73. ⟨ Override *tex_file_name* and *C_file_name* 73 ⟩ ≡
```
  {
    if (s − *argv > max_file_name_length − 5) ⟨ Complain about argument length 76 ⟩;
    if (dot_pos ≡ Λ) {
    sprintf(tex_file_name, "%s.tex", *argv);
    sprintf(idx_file_name, "%s.idx", *argv);
    sprintf(scn_file_name, "%s.scn", *argv);
    sprintf(C_file_name, "%s.c", *argv);
    }
    else {
    strcpy(tex_file_name, *argv);
    strcpy(C_file_name, *argv);
    if (flags['x']) {      /* indexes will be generated */
      *dot_pos ← 0;
      sprintf(idx_file_name, "%s.idx", *argv);
      sprintf(scn_file_name, "%s.scn", *argv);
    }
    }
    found_out ← 1;
  }
```
This code is used in section 70.

74. ⟨ Handle flag argument 74 ⟩ ≡
```
  {
    if (**argv ≡ '-') flag_change ← 0;
    else flag_change ← 1;
    for (dot_pos ← *argv + 1; *dot_pos > '\0'; dot_pos ++) flags[*dot_pos] ← flag_change;
  }
```
This code is used in section 70.

75. ⟨ Print usage error message and quit 75 ⟩ ≡
```
  {
    if (program ≡ ctangle)
      fatal("! Usage: ctangle [options] webfile[.w] [{changefile[.ch]|-} [outfile[.c]]]\n",
          "");
    else
      fatal("! Usage: cweave [options] webfile[.w] [{changefile[.ch]|-} [outfile[.tex]]]\n",
          "");
  }
```
This code is used in section 70.

76.   ⟨ Complain about argument length 76 ⟩ ≡
   fatal("!␣Filename␣too␣long\n", *argv*);

This code is used in sections 71, 72, and 73.

77. Output.   Here is the code that opens the output file:

⟨ Definitions that should agree with CTANGLE and CWEAVE 2 ⟩ +≡
   FILE $*C\_file$;   /* where output of CTANGLE goes */
   FILE $*tex\_file$;   /* where output of CWEAVE goes */
   FILE $*idx\_file$;   /* where index from CWEAVE goes */
   FILE $*scn\_file$;   /* where list of sections from CWEAVE goes */
   FILE $*active\_file$;   /* currently active file for CWEAVE output */

78.   ⟨ Scan arguments and open output files 78 ⟩ ≡
   $scan\_args(\ )$;
   if $(program \equiv ctangle)$ {
     if $((C\_file \leftarrow fopen(C\_file\_name, "\mathtt{w}")) \equiv \Lambda)$ $fatal("!\textvisiblespace Cannot\textvisiblespace open\textvisiblespace output\textvisiblespace file\textvisiblespace", C\_file\_name)$;
   }
   else {
     if $((tex\_file \leftarrow fopen(tex\_file\_name, "\mathtt{w}")) \equiv \Lambda)$ $fatal("!\textvisiblespace Cannot\textvisiblespace open\textvisiblespace output\textvisiblespace file\textvisiblespace", tex\_file\_name)$;
   }
This code is used in section 4.

79.   The $update\_terminal$ procedure is called when we want to make sure that everything we have output to the terminal so far has actually left the computer's internal buffers and been sent.

#define $update\_terminal$ $fflush(stdout)$ /* empty the terminal output buffer */

80.   Terminal output uses $putchar$ and $putc$ when we have to translate from CWEB's code into the external character code, and $printf$ when we just want to print strings. Several macros make other kinds of output convenient.

#define new_line $putchar(\mathtt{'\backslash n'})$
#define $putxchar$ $putchar$
#define $term\_write(a, b)$ $fflush(stdout), fwrite(a, \textbf{sizeof}(\textbf{char}), b, stdout)$
#define $C\_printf(c, a)$ $fprintf(C\_file, c, a)$
#define $C\_putc(c)$ $putc(c, C\_file)$ /* isn't C wonderfully consistent? */

81.   We predeclare several standard system functions here instead of including their system header files, because the names of the header files are not as standard as the names of the functions. (For example, some C environments have **<string.h>** where others have **<strings.h>**.)

⟨ Predeclaration of procedures 33 ⟩ +≡
   extern int $strlen(\ )$;   /* length of string */
   extern int $strcmp(\ )$;   /* compare strings lexicographically */
   extern char $*strcpy(\ )$;   /* copy one string to another */
   extern int $strncmp(\ )$;   /* compare up to n string characters */
   extern char $*strncpy(\ )$;   /* copy up to n string characters */

82. Index.

ac: 67.
active_file: <u>77</u>.
add_section_name: <u>47</u>, 51.
alt_web_file_name: <u>10</u>, 19, 71.
Ambiguous prefix ... : 50.
and_and: <u>6</u>.
argc: <u>67</u>, 70.
argv: <u>67</u>, 70, 71, 72, 73, 74, 76.
ASCII code dependencies: 6.
av: 67.
bad_extension: 52, <u>53</u>, 54.
boolean: <u>2</u>, 10, 20, 67, 70.
buf_size: <u>7</u>, 11.
buffer: <u>7</u>, 9, 11, 13, 14, 15, 16, 17, 18, 21, 24,
  25, 26, 35, 58, 59.
buffer_end: <u>7</u>, 9.
byte_mem: <u>27</u>, 29, 30, 40.
byte_mem_end: <u>27</u>, 29, 39, 47, 48.
byte_ptr: <u>29</u>, 30, 39, 47, 48.
byte_start: <u>27</u>, 28, 29, 30, 39, 42, 43, 44, 47, 48, 54.
c: <u>9</u>, <u>47</u>, <u>49</u>, <u>54</u>.
C_file: 67, <u>77</u>, 78, 80.
C_file_name: <u>67</u>, 71, 73, 78.
C_printf: <u>80</u>.
C_putc: <u>80</u>.
Cannot open change file: 19.
Cannot open input file: 19.
Cannot open output file: 78.
Change file ended...: 14, 16, 25.
Change file entry did not match: 26.
change_buffer: <u>11</u>, 12, 15, 16, 24, 26.
change_depth: <u>10</u>, 17, 18, 21, 24, 26, 59.
change_file: <u>10</u>, 11, 13, 14, 16, 19, 20, 25, 59.
change_file_name: <u>10</u>, 19, 70, 72.
change_limit: <u>11</u>, 12, 15, 16, 24, 26.
change_line: <u>10</u>, 13, 14, 16, 18, 25, 59.
change_pending: 16, <u>20</u>, 25.
changed_section: 16, <u>20</u>, 25.
changing: <u>10</u>, 11, 12, 16, 18, 21, 24, 25, 26, 59.
check_change: <u>16</u>, 24.
check_complete: <u>26</u>.
colon_colon: <u>6</u>.
common_init: <u>4</u>, 68.
confusion: <u>66</u>.
ctangle: <u>2</u>, 75, 78.
cur_file: <u>10</u>, 11, 16, 20, 22, 23, 24, 59.
cur_file_name: <u>10</u>, 23, 59.
cur_file_name_end: <u>23</u>.
cur_line: <u>10</u>, 16, 18, 23, 24, 59.
cweave: <u>2</u>, 39.
CWEB file ended...: 16.

CWEBINPUTS: 23.
dest: <u>43</u>.
dot_dot_dot: <u>6</u>.
dot_pos: <u>70</u>, 71, 72, 73, 74.
dummy: <u>40</u>.
EOF: 9.
eq_eq: <u>6</u>.
equal: <u>45</u>, 52, 54.
equiv: 55.
equiv_or_xref: <u>55</u>.
err_print: 9, 13, 14, 16, 17, 21, 22, 23, 25, 26,
  50, 52, <u>57</u>, 58, 64.
error_message: <u>56</u>, 62.
exit: 22, 64.
extend_section_name: <u>48</u>, 52.
extension: <u>45</u>, 52, 54.
fatal: 19, <u>63</u>, <u>64</u>, 65, 66, 75, 76, 78.
fatal_message: <u>56</u>, 62, 64.
fclose: 24.
feof: 9.
fflush: 79, 80.
file: <u>10</u>.
file_name: <u>10</u>.
Filename too long: 76.
first: <u>35</u>, 37, 39, <u>47</u>, <u>48</u>, <u>49</u>, 50, 51, 52, <u>54</u>.
first_chunk: <u>42</u>, 43, 44, 47, 50, 54.
flag_change: <u>70</u>, 74.
flags: <u>67</u>, 68, 73, 74.
fopen: 19, 23, 78.
found_change: <u>70</u>, 72.
found_out: <u>70</u>, 73.
found_web: <u>70</u>, 71.
fp: <u>9</u>.
fprintf: 80.
fwrite: 80.
get_line: 20, <u>21</u>.
getc: 9.
getenv: 22, 23.
greater: <u>45</u>, 50.
gt_eq: <u>6</u>.
gt_gt: <u>6</u>.
h: <u>32</u>, <u>35</u>.
harmless_message: <u>56</u>, 61, 62.
hash: 31, <u>32</u>, 34, 37.
hash_end: <u>32</u>, 34.
hash_pointer: <u>32</u>.
hash_size: <u>32</u>, 36.
high-bit character handling: 36.
history: <u>56</u>, 61, 62, 64.
Hmm... n of the preceding...: 17.
i: <u>35</u>.

⟨ Complain about argument length 76 ⟩   Used in sections 71, 72, and 73.

⟨ Compute the hash code *h* 36 ⟩   Used in section 35.

⟨ Compute the name location *p* 37 ⟩   Used in section 35.

⟨ Definitions that should agree with **CTANGLE** and **CWEAVE** 2, 7, 10, 20, 27, 29, 32, 56, 67, 77 ⟩   Used in section 1.

⟨ Enter a new name into the table at position *p* 39 ⟩   Used in section 35.

⟨ Handle flag argument 74 ⟩   Used in section 70.

⟨ If no match found, add new name to tree 51 ⟩   Used in section 49.

⟨ If one match found, check for compatibility and return match 52 ⟩   Used in section 49.

⟨ If the current line starts with @y, report any discrepancies and **return** 17 ⟩   Used in section 16.

⟨ Include files 5, 8, 22 ⟩   Used in section 1.

⟨ Initialize pointers 30, 34, 41 ⟩   Used in section 4.

⟨ Look for matches for new name among shortest prefixes, complaining if more than one is found 50 ⟩   Used
    in section 49.

⟨ Make *change_file_name* from *fname* 72 ⟩   Used in section 70.

⟨ Make *web_file_name*, *tex_file_name*, and *C_file_name* 71 ⟩   Used in section 70.

⟨ More elements of **name_info** structure 31, 40, 55 ⟩   Used in section 27.

⟨ Move *buffer* and *limit* to *change_buffer* and *change_limit* 15 ⟩   Used in sections 12 and 16.

⟨ Open input files 19 ⟩   Used in section 18.

⟨ Other definitions 3, 11 ⟩   Used in section 1.

⟨ Override *tex_file_name* and *C_file_name* 73 ⟩   Used in section 70.

⟨ Predeclaration of procedures 33, 38, 46, 53, 57, 60, 63, 69, 81 ⟩   Used in section 1.

⟨ Print error location based on input buffer 59 ⟩   Used in section 58.

⟨ Print the job *history* 62 ⟩   Used in section 61.

⟨ Print usage error message and quit 75 ⟩   Used in section 70.

⟨ Read from *change_file* and maybe turn off *changing* 25 ⟩   Used in section 21.

⟨ Read from *cur_file* and maybe turn on *changing* 24 ⟩   Used in section 21.

⟨ Scan arguments and open output files 78 ⟩   Used in section 4.

⟨ Set the default options common to **CTANGLE** and **CWEAVE** 68 ⟩   Used in section 4.

⟨ Skip over comment lines in the change file; **return** if end of file 13 ⟩   Used in section 12.

⟨ Skip to the next nonblank line; **return** if end of file 14 ⟩   Used in section 12.

⟨ Try to open include file, abort push if unsuccessful, go to *restart* 23 ⟩   Used in section 21.

The CTANGLE processor

(Version 3.62)

1. Introduction.   This is the **CTANGLE** program by Silvio Levy and Donald E. Knuth, based on **TANGLE** by Knuth. We are thankful to Nelson Beebe, Hans-Hermann Bode (to whom the C++ adaptation is due), Klaus Guntermann, Norman Ramsey, Tomas Rokicki, Joachim Schnitter, Joachim Schrod, Lee Wittenberg, and others who have contributed improvements.

The "banner line" defined here should be changed whenever **CTANGLE** is modified.

#define *banner*   "This␣is␣CTANGLE␣(Version␣3.62)\n"

⟨ Include files 6 ⟩
⟨ Preprocessor definitions ⟩
⟨ Common code for **CWEAVE** and **CTANGLE** 5 ⟩
⟨ Typedef declarations 16 ⟩
⟨ Global variables 17 ⟩
⟨ Predeclaration of procedures 2 ⟩

2. We predeclare several standard system functions here instead of including their system header files, because the names of the header files are not as standard as the names of the functions. (For example, some C environments have **<string.h>** where others have **<strings.h>**.)

⟨ Predeclaration of procedures 2 ⟩ ≡
    extern int *strlen*( );   /* length of string */
    extern int *strcmp*( );   /* compare strings lexicographically */
    extern char *∗strcpy*( );   /* copy one string to another */
    extern int *strncmp*( );   /* compare up to n string characters */
    extern char *∗strncpy*( );   /* copy up to n string characters */

See also sections 41, 46, 48, 90, and 92.

This code is used in section 1.

3. **CTANGLE** has a fairly straightforward outline. It operates in two phases: First it reads the source file, saving the C code in compressed form; then it shuffles and outputs the code.

Please read the documentation for **common**, the set of routines common to **CTANGLE** and **CWEAVE**, before proceeding further.

```
int main(ac, av)
    int ac;
    char **av;
{
    argc ← ac;
    argv ← av;
    program ← ctangle;
    ⟨ Set initial values 18 ⟩;
    common_init( );
    if (show_banner) printf(banner);     /* print a "banner line" */
    phase_one( );     /* read all the user's text and compress it into tok_mem */
    phase_two( );     /* output the contents of the compressed tables */
    return wrap_up( );     /* and exit gracefully */
}
```

4. The following parameters were sufficient in the original **TANGLE** to handle TEX, so they should be sufficient for most applications of **CTANGLE**. If you change max_bytes, max_names, or $hash\_size$ you should also change them in the file `"common.w"`.

#define max_bytes 90000
     /* the number of bytes in identifiers, index entries, and section names; used in `"common.w"` */
#define max_toks 270000 /* number of bytes in compressed C code */
#define max_names 4000 /* number of identifiers, strings, section names; must be less than 10240;
    used in `"common.w"` */
#define max_texts 2500 /* number of replacement texts, must be less than 10240 */
#define $hash\_size$ 353 /* should be prime; used in `"common.w"` */
#define $longest\_name$ 10000 /* section names shouldn't be longer than this */
#define $stack\_size$ 50 /* number of simultaneous levels of macro expansion */
#define buf_size 100 /* for **CWEAVE** and **CTANGLE** */

5. The next few sections contain stuff from the file `"common.w"` that must be included in both `"ctangle.w"` and `"cweave.w"`. It appears in file `"common.h"`, which needs to be updated when `"common.w"` changes.
  First comes general stuff:

#define $ctangle$ 0
#define $cweave$ 1

⟨ Common code for **CWEAVE** and **CTANGLE** 5 ⟩ ≡
 typedef short boolean;
 typedef char unsigned eight_bits;
 extern boolean $program$; /* **CWEAVE** or **CTANGLE**? */
 extern int $phase$; /* which phase are we in? */

See also sections 7, 8, 9, 10, 11, 12, 13, 14, and 15.

This code is used in section 1.

6. ⟨ Include files 6 ⟩ ≡
#include `<stdio.h>`

See also section 62.

This code is used in section 1.

7.   Code related to the character set:

#define *and_and* °4   /* '&&'; corresponds to MIT's ∧ */
#define *lt_lt* °20   /* '<<'; corresponds to MIT's ⊂ */
#define *gt_gt* °21   /* '>>'; corresponds to MIT's ⊃ */
#define *plus_plus* °13   /* '++'; corresponds to MIT's ↑ */
#define *minus_minus* °1   /* '--'; corresponds to MIT's ↓ */
#define *minus_gt* °31   /* '->'; corresponds to MIT's → */
#define *not_eq* °32   /* '!='; corresponds to MIT's ≠ */
#define *lt_eq* °34   /* '<='; corresponds to MIT's ≤ */
#define *gt_eq* °35   /* '>='; corresponds to MIT's ≥ */
#define *eq_eq* °36   /* '=='; corresponds to MIT's ≡ */
#define *or_or* °37   /* '||'; corresponds to MIT's ∨ */
#define *dot_dot_dot* °16   /* '...'; corresponds to MIT's ∞ */
#define *colon_colon* °6   /* '::'; corresponds to MIT's ∈ */
#define *period_ast* °26   /* '.*'; corresponds to MIT's ⊗ */
#define *minus_gt_ast* °27   /* '->*'; corresponds to MIT's ⇆ */

⟨ Common code for **CWEAVE** and **CTANGLE** 5 ⟩ +≡
   char *section_text*[*longest_name* + 1];   /* name being sought for */
   char **section_text_end* ← *section_text* + *longest_name*;   /* end of *section_text* */
   char **id_first*;   /* where the current identifier begins in the buffer */
   char **id_loc*;   /* just after the current identifier in the buffer */

8.   Code related to input routines:

#define *xisalpha*(*c*)   (*isalpha*(*c*) ∧ ((**eight_bits**) *c* < °200))
#define *xisdigit*(*c*)   (*isdigit*(*c*) ∧ ((**eight_bits**) *c* < °200))
#define *xisspace*(*c*)   (*isspace*(*c*) ∧ ((**eight_bits**) *c* < °200))
#define *xislower*(*c*)   (*islower*(*c*) ∧ ((**eight_bits**) *c* < °200))
#define *xisupper*(*c*)   (*isupper*(*c*) ∧ ((**eight_bits**) *c* < °200))
#define *xisxdigit*(*c*)   (*isxdigit*(*c*) ∧ ((**eight_bits**) *c* < °200))

⟨ Common code for **CWEAVE** and **CTANGLE** 5 ⟩ +≡
   extern char *buffer*[];   /* where each line of input goes */
   extern char **buffer_end*;   /* end of *buffer* */
   extern char **loc*;   /* points to the next character to be read from the buffer */
   extern char **limit*;   /* points to the last character in the buffer */

9.   Code related to identifier and section name storage:

#define $length(c)$ $(c+1) \rightarrow byte\_start - (c) \rightarrow byte\_start$ /* the length of a name */
#define $print\_id(c)$ $term\_write((c) \rightarrow byte\_start, length((c)))$ /* print identifier */
#define $llink$ $link$ /* left link in binary search tree for section names */
#define $rlink$ $dummy.Rlink$ /* right link in binary search tree for section names */
#define $root$ $name\_dir \rightarrow rlink$ /* the root of the binary search tree for section names */
#define $chunk\_marker$ 0

⟨ Common code for **CWEAVE** and **CTANGLE** 5 ⟩ +≡
  typedef struct name_info {
    char $*byte\_start$;   /* beginning of the name in $byte\_mem$ */
    struct name_info $*link$;
    union {
      struct name_info $*Rlink$;   /* right link in binary search tree for section names */
      char Ilk;   /* used by identifiers in **CWEAVE** only */
    } $dummy$;
    char $*equiv\_or\_xref$;   /* info corresponding to names */
  } **name_info**;   /* contains information about an identifier or section name */
  typedef name_info $*$**name_pointer**;   /* pointer into array of **name_info**s */
  typedef name_pointer $*$**hash_pointer**;
  extern char $byte\_mem[\,]$;   /* characters of names */
  extern char $*byte\_mem\_end$;   /* end of $byte\_mem$ */
  extern name_info $name\_dir[\,]$;   /* information about names */
  extern name_pointer $name\_dir\_end$;   /* end of $name\_dir$ */
  extern name_pointer $name\_ptr$;   /* first unused position in $byte\_start$ */
  extern char $*byte\_ptr$;   /* first unused position in $byte\_mem$ */
  extern name_pointer $hash[\,]$;   /* heads of hash lists */
  extern hash_pointer $hash\_end$;   /* end of $hash$ */
  extern hash_pointer h;   /* index into hash-head array */
  extern name_pointer $id\_lookup(\,)$;   /* looks up a string in the identifier table */
  extern name_pointer $section\_lookup(\,)$;   /* finds section name */
  extern void $print\_section\_name(\,)$, $sprint\_section\_name(\,)$;

10.   Code related to error handling:

#define $spotless$ 0 /* $history$ value for normal jobs */
#define $harmless\_message$ 1 /* $history$ value when non-serious info was printed */
#define $error\_message$ 2 /* $history$ value when an error was noted */
#define $fatal\_message$ 3 /* $history$ value when we had to stop prematurely */
#define $mark\_harmless$
    {
      if $(history \equiv spotless)$ $history \leftarrow harmless\_message$;
    }
#define $mark\_error$ $history \leftarrow error\_message$
#define $confusion(s)$ $fatal(\texttt{"!}\textvisiblespace\texttt{This}\textvisiblespace\texttt{can't}\textvisiblespace\texttt{happen:}\textvisiblespace\texttt{"}, s)$
⟨ Common code for **CWEAVE** and **CTANGLE** 5 ⟩ +≡
  extern $history$;   /* indicates how bad this run was */
  extern $err\_print(\,)$;   /* print error message and context */
  extern $wrap\_up(\,)$;   /* indicate $history$ and exit */
  extern void $fatal(\,)$;   /* issue error message and die */
  extern void $overflow(\,)$;   /* succumb because a table has overflowed */

11.   Code related to file handling:

format *line   x*   /* make *line* an unreserved word */
#define *max_file_name_length* 60
#define *cur_file*   *file*[*include_depth*]   /* current file */
#define *cur_file_name*   *file_name*[*include_depth*]   /* current file name */
#define *web_file_name*   *file_name*[0]   /* main source file name */
#define *cur_line*   *line*[*include_depth*]   /* number of current line in current file */
⟨ Common code for **CWEAVE** and **CTANGLE** 5 ⟩ +≡
  extern *include_depth*;   /* current level of nesting */
  extern FILE *file*[ ];   /* stack of non-change files */
  extern FILE *change_file*;   /* change file */
  extern char *C_file_name*[ ];   /* name of *C_file* */
  extern char *tex_file_name*[ ];   /* name of *tex_file* */
  extern char *idx_file_name*[ ];   /* name of *idx_file* */
  extern char *scn_file_name*[ ];   /* name of *scn_file* */
  extern char *file_name*[ ][*max_file_name_length*];   /* stack of non-change file names */
  extern char *change_file_name*[ ];   ·   /* name of change file */
  extern *line*[ ];   /* number of current line in the stacked files */
  extern *change_line*;   /* number of current line in change file */
  extern boolean *input_has_ended*;   /* if there is no more input */
  extern boolean *changing*;   /* if the current line is from *change_file* */
  extern boolean *web_file_open*;   /* if the web file is being read */
  extern *reset_input*( );   /* initialize to read the web file and change file */
  extern *get_line*( );   /* inputs the next line */
  extern *check_complete*( );   /* checks that all changes were picked up */

12.   Code related to section numbers:
⟨ Common code for **CWEAVE** and **CTANGLE** 5 ⟩ +≡
  typedef unsigned short sixteen_bits;
  extern sixteen_bits *section_count*;   /* the current section number */
  extern boolean *changed_section*[ ];   /* is the section changed? */
  extern boolean *change_pending*;   /* is a decision about change still unclear? */
  extern boolean *print_where*;   /* tells **CTANGLE** to print line and file info */

13.   Code related to command line arguments:

#define *show_banner*   *flags*['b']   /* should the banner line be printed? */
#define *show_progress*   *flags*['p']   /* should progress reports be printed? */
#define *show_happiness*   *flags*['h']   /* should lack of errors be announced? */
⟨ Common code for **CWEAVE** and **CTANGLE** 5 ⟩ +≡
  extern int *argc*;   /* copy of *ac* parameter to *main* */
  extern char **argv*;   /* copy of *av* parameter to *main* */
  extern boolean *flags*[ ];   /* an option for each 7-bit code */

14.   Code relating to output:

#define *update_terminal*   *fflush*(*stdout*)   /* empty the terminal output buffer */
#define *new_line*   *putchar*('\n')
#define *putxchar*   *putchar*
#define *term_write*(*a*, *b*)   *fflush*(*stdout*), *fwrite*(*a*, **sizeof**(**char**), *b*, *stdout*)
#define *C_printf*(*c*, *a*)   *fprintf*(*C_file*, *c*, *a*)
#define *C_putc*(*c*)   *putc*(*c*, *C_file*)

⟨ Common code for CWEAVE and CTANGLE 5 ⟩ +≡
   extern FILE *C_file;   /* where output of CTANGLE goes */
   extern FILE *tex_file;   /* where output of CWEAVE goes */
   extern FILE *idx_file;   /* where index from CWEAVE goes */
   extern FILE *scn_file;   /* where list of sections from CWEAVE goes */
   extern FILE *active_file;   /* currently active file for CWEAVE output */

15.   The procedure that gets everything rolling:

⟨ Common code for CWEAVE and CTANGLE 5 ⟩ +≡
   extern void *common_init*( );

16.   Data structures exclusive to CTANGLE.   We've already seen that the *byte_mem* array holds the names of identifiers, strings, and sections; the *tok_mem* array holds the replacement texts for sections. Allocation is sequential, since things are deleted only during Phase II, and only in a last-in-first-out manner.

A **text** variable is a structure containing a pointer into *tok_mem*, which tells where the corresponding text starts, and an integer *text_link*, which, as we shall see later, is used to connect pieces of text that have the same name. All the **text**s are stored in the array *text_info*, and we use a *text_pointer* variable to refer to them.

The first position of *tok_mem* that is unoccupied by replacement text is called *tok_ptr*, and the first unused location of *text_info* is called *text_ptr*. Thus we usually have the identity $text\_ptr \rightarrow tok\_start \equiv tok\_ptr$.

If your machine does not support **unsigned char** you should change the definition of **eight_bits** to **unsigned short**.

⟨ Typedef declarations 16 ⟩ ≡
   typedef struct {
     eight_bits *∗tok_start*;   /∗ pointer into *tok_mem* ∗/
     sixteen_bits *text_link*;   /∗ relates replacement texts ∗/
   } **text**;
   typedef text *∗***text_pointer**;

See also section 27.

This code is used in section 1.

17.   ⟨ Global variables 17 ⟩ ≡
   text *text_info*[*max_texts*];
   text_pointer *text_info_end* ← *text_info* + *max_texts* − 1;
   text_pointer *text_ptr*;   /∗ first unused position in *text_info* ∗/
   eight_bits *tok_mem*[*max_toks*];
   eight_bits *∗tok_mem_end* ← *tok_mem* + *max_toks* − 1;
   eight_bits *∗tok_ptr*;   /∗ first unused position in *tok_mem* ∗/

See also sections 23, 28, 32, 36, 38, 45, 51, 56, 59, 61, 75, and 82.

This code is used in section 1.

18.   ⟨ Set initial values 18 ⟩ ≡
   text_info→tok_start ← *tok_ptr* ← *tok_mem*;
   text_ptr ← *text_info* + 1;
   text_ptr→tok_start ← *tok_mem*;   /∗ this makes replacement text 0 of length zero ∗/

See also sections 20, 24, 39, 52, 57, and 71.

This code is used in section 3.

19.   If *p* is a pointer to a section name, *p→equiv* is a pointer to its replacement text, an element of the array *text_info*.

#define *equiv* *equiv_or_xref*   /∗ info corresponding to names ∗/

20.   ⟨ Set initial values 18 ⟩ +≡
   name_dir→equiv ← (**char** ∗) *text_info*;   /∗ the undefined section has no replacement text ∗/

21.   Here's the procedure that decides whether a name of length l starting at position *first* equals the identifier pointed to by p:

   int *names_match*(*p*, *first*, *l*)
      name_pointer *p*;   /* points to the proposed match */
      char *first*;   /* position of first character of string */
      int *l*;   /* length of identifier */
   {
     if ($length(p) \neq l$) **return** 0;
     return $\neg strncmp(first, p\text{-}byte\_start, l)$;
   }

22.   The common lookup routine refers to separate routines *init_node* and *init_p* when the data structure grows. Actually *init_p* is called only by **CWEAVE**, but we need to declare a dummy version so that the loader won't complain of its absence.

   void *init_node*(*node*)
      name_pointer *node*;
   {
     $node\text{-}equiv \leftarrow$ (**char** *) *text_info*;
   }
   void *init_p*( )
   { }

23.   Tokens.   Replacement texts, which represent C code in a compressed format, appear in *tok_mem* as mentioned above. The codes in these texts are called 'tokens'; some tokens occupy two consecutive eight-bit byte positions, and the others take just one byte.

If p points to a replacement text, *p⃗tok_start* is the *tok_mem* position of the first eight-bit code of that text. If *p⃗text_link* $\equiv 0$, this is the replacement text for a macro, otherwise it is the replacement text for a section. In the latter case *p⃗text_link* is either equal to *section_flag*, which means that there is no further text for this section, or *p⃗text_link* points to a continuation of this replacement text; such links are created when several sections have C texts with the same name, and they also tie together all the C texts of unnamed sections. The replacement text pointer for the first unnamed section appears in *text_info⃗text_link*, and the most recent such pointer is *last_unnamed*.

#define *section_flag*   *max_texts*   /* final *text_link* in section replacement texts */
⟨ Global variables 17 ⟩ +≡
    text_pointer *last_unnamed*;   /* most recent replacement text of unnamed section */

24.   ⟨ Set initial values 18 ⟩ +≡
    last_unnamed ← *text_info*;
    text_info⃗text_link ← 0;

25.   If the first byte of a token is less than $°200$, the token occupies a single byte. Otherwise we make a sixteen-bit token by combining two consecutive bytes a and b. If $°200 \leq a < °250$, then $(a - °200) \times 2^8 + b$ points to an identifier; if $°250 \leq a < °320$, then $(a - °250) \times 2^8 + b$ points to a section name (or, if it has the special value *output_defs_flag*, to the area where the preprocessor definitions are stored); and if $°320 \leq a < °400$, then $(a - °320) \times 2^8 + b$ is the number of the section in which the current replacement text appears.

Codes less than $°200$ are 7-bit **char** codes that represent themselves. Some of the 7-bit codes will not be present, however, so we can use them for special purposes. The following symbolic names are used:

    join denotes the concatenation of adjacent items with no space or line breaks allowed between them (the
        @& operation of CWEB).
    string denotes the beginning or end of a string, verbatim construction or numerical constant.

#define *string* $°2$ /* takes the place of extended ASCII *α* */
#define *join* $°177$ /* takes the place of ASCII delete */
#define *output_defs_flag* $(2 * °24000 - 1)$

26.   The following procedure is used to enter a two-byte value into *tok_mem* when a replacement text is being generated.

    void *store_two_bytes*(*x*)
        sixteen_bits *x*;
  {
    if (*tok_ptr* + 2 > *tok_mem_end*) *overflow*("token");
    tok_ptr ++ ← $x \gg 8$;   /* store high byte */
    tok_ptr ++ ← $x \, \& \, °377$;   /* store low byte */
  }

27. Stacks for output. The output process uses a stack to keep track of what is going on at different "levels" as the sections are being written out. Entries on this stack have five parts:

> end_field is the tok_mem location where the replacement text of a particular level will end;
> $byte\_field$ is the tok_mem location from which the next token on a particular level will be read;
> $name\_field$ points to the name corresponding to a particular level;
> $repl\_field$ points to the replacement text currently being read at a particular level;
> $section\_field$ is the section number, or zero if this is a macro.

The current values of these five quantities are referred to quite frequently, so they are stored in a separate place instead of in the $stack$ array. We call the current values cur_end, cur_byte, cur_name, cur_repl, and $cur\_section$.

The global variable $stack\_ptr$ tells how many levels of output are currently in progress. The end of all output occurs when the stack is empty, i.e., when $stack\_ptr \equiv stack$.

⟨ Typedef declarations 16 ⟩ +≡
typedef struct {
    eight_bits *end_field;   /* ending location of replacement text */
    eight_bits *$byte\_field$;   /* present location within replacement text */
    name_pointer $name\_field$;   /* $byte\_start$ index for text being output */
    text_pointer $repl\_field$;   /* tok_start index for text being output */
    sixteen_bits $section\_field$;   /* section number or zero if not a section */
} **output_state**;
typedef output_state *stack_pointer;

28. #**define** cur_end $cur\_state.end\_field$ /* current ending location in tok_mem */
#**define** cur_byte $cur\_state.byte\_field$ /* location of next output byte in tok_mem */
#**define** cur_name $cur\_state.name\_field$ /* pointer to current name being expanded */
#**define** cur_repl $cur\_state.repl\_field$ /* pointer to current replacement text */
#**define** $cur\_section$ $cur\_state.section\_field$ /* current section number being expanded */
⟨ Global variables 17 ⟩ +≡
  output_state cur_state;   /* cur_end, cur_byte, cur_name, cur_repl, and $cur\_section$ */
  output_state $stack[stack\_size + 1]$;   /* info for non-current levels */
  stack_pointer $stack\_ptr$;   /* first unused location in the output state stack */
  stack_pointer $stack\_end \leftarrow stack + stack\_size$;   /* end of $stack$ */

29. To get the output process started, we will perform the following initialization steps. We may assume that $text\_info \rightarrow text\_link$ is nonzero, since it points to the C text in the first unnamed section that generates code; if there are no such sections, there is nothing to output, and an error message will have been generated before we do any of the initialization.

⟨ Initialize the output stacks 29 ⟩ ≡
  $stack\_ptr \leftarrow stack + 1$;
  $cur\_name \leftarrow name\_dir$;
  $cur\_repl \leftarrow text\_info \rightarrow text\_link + text\_info$;
  $cur\_byte \leftarrow cur\_repl \rightarrow tok\_start$;
  $cur\_end \leftarrow (cur\_repl + 1) \rightarrow tok\_start$;
  $cur\_section \leftarrow 0$;
This code is used in section 42.

30.   When the replacement text for name p is to be inserted into the output, the following subroutine is called to save the old level of output and get the new one going.

We assume that the C compiler can copy structures.

```
void push_level(p)          /* suspends the current level */
    name_pointer p;
{
    if (stack_ptr ≡ stack_end) overflow("stack");
    *stack_ptr ← cur_state;
    stack_ptr++;
    if (p ≠ Λ) {            /* p ≡ Λ means we are in output_defs */
        cur_name ← p;
        cur_repl ← (text_pointer) p⁻equiv;
        cur_byte ← cur_repl⁻tok_start;
        cur_end ← (cur_repl + 1)⁻tok_start;
        cur_section ← 0;
    }
}
```

31.   When we come to the end of a replacement text, the *pop_level* subroutine does the right thing: It either moves to the continuation of this replacement text or returns the state to the most recently stacked level.

```
void pop_level(flag)        /* do this when cur_byte reaches cur_end */
    int flag;               /* flag ≡ 0 means we are in output_defs */
{
    if (flag ∧ cur_repl⁻text_link < section_flag) {     /* link to a continuation */
        cur_repl ← cur_repl⁻text_link + text_info;      /* stay on the same level */
        cur_byte ← cur_repl⁻tok_start;
        cur_end ← (cur_repl + 1)⁻tok_start;
        return;
    }
    stack_ptr−−;            /* go down to the previous level */
    if (stack_ptr > stack) cur_state ← *stack_ptr;
}
```

32.   The heart of the output procedure is the function *get_output*, which produces the next token of output and sends it on to the lower-level function *out_char*. The main purpose of *get_output* is to handle the necessary stacking and unstacking. It sends the value *section_number* if the next output begins or ends the replacement text of some section, in which case *cur_val* is that section's number (if beginning) or the negative of that value (if ending). (A section number of 0 indicates not the beginning or ending of a section, but a #**line** command.) And it sends the value *identifier* if the next output is an identifier, in which case *cur_val* points to that identifier name.

```
#define section_number  °201    /* code returned by get_output for section numbers */
#define identifier      °202    /* code returned by get_output for identifiers */
```

⟨ Global variables 17 ⟩ +≡
    int *cur_val*;   /* additional information corresponding to output token */

33.   If *get_output* finds that no more output remains, it returns with *stack_ptr* ≡ *stack*.

```
void get_output( )          /* sends next token to out_char */
{
  sixteen_bits a;           /* value of current byte */
restart:
  if (stack_ptr ≡ stack) return;
  if (cur_byte ≡ cur_end) {
    cur_val ← −((int) cur_section);      /* cast needed because of sign extension */
    pop_level(1);
    if (cur_val ≡ 0) goto restart;
    out_char(section_number);
    return;
  }
  a ← *cur_byte ++;
  if (out_state ≡ verbatim ∧ a ≠ string ∧ a ≠ constant ∧ a ≠ '\n')  C_putc(a);
        /* a high-bit character can occur in a string */
  else if (a < °200) out_char(a);        /* one-byte token */
  else {
    a ← (a − °200) * °400 + *cur_byte ++;
    switch (a/°24000) {      /* °24000 ≡ (°250 − °200) * °400 */
    case 0: cur_val ← a;
      out_char(identifier);
      break;
    case 1:
      if (a ≡ output_defs_flag)  output_defs( );
      else ⟨Expand section a − °24000, goto restart 34⟩;
      break;
    default: cur_val ← a − °50000;
      if (cur_val > 0)  cur_section ← cur_val;
      out_char(section_number);
    }
  }
}
```

34.   The user may have forgotten to give any C text for a section name, or the C text may have been associated with a different name by mistake.

⟨Expand section a − °24000, goto restart 34⟩ ≡
```
  {
    a −= °24000;
    if ((a + name_dir)‑equiv ≠ (char *) text_info)  push_level(a + name_dir);
    else if (a ≠ 0) {
      printf("\n!␣Not␣present:␣<");
      print_section_name(a + name_dir);
      err_print(">");
    }
    goto restart;
  }
```
This code is used in section 33.

35. Producing the output. The *get_output* routine above handles most of the complexity of output generation, but there are two further considerations that have a nontrivial effect on CTANGLE's algorithms.

36. First, we want to make sure that the output has spaces and line breaks in the right places (e.g., not in the middle of a string or a constant or an identifier, not at a '@&' position where quantities are being joined together, and certainly after an = because the C compiler thinks =- is ambiguous).

The output process can be in one of following states:

num_or_id means that the last item in the buffer is a number or identifier, hence a blank space or line break must be inserted if the next item is also a number or identifier.

unbreakable means that the last item in the buffer was followed by the @& operation that inhibits spaces between it and the next item.

verbatim means we're copying only character tokens, and that they are to be output exactly as stored. This is the case during strings, verbatim constructions and numerical constants.

post_slash means we've just output a slash.

normal means none of the above.

Furthermore, if the variable *protect* is positive, newlines are preceded by a '\'.

```
#define normal    0    /* non-unusual state */
#define num_or_id 1    /* state associated with numbers and identifiers */
#define post_slash 2   /* state following a / */
#define unbreakable 3  /* state associated with @& */
#define verbatim  4    /* state in the middle of a string */
```
⟨ Global variables 17 ⟩ +≡
  eight_bits *out_state*;   /* current status of partial output */
  boolean *protect*;   /* should newline characters be quoted? */

37. Here is a routine that is invoked when we want to output the current line. During the output process, *cur_line* equals the number of the next line to be output.

```
void flush_buffer()     /* writes one line to output file */
{
  C_putc('\n');
  if (cur_line % 100 ≡ 0 ∧ show_progress) {
    printf(".");
    if (cur_line % 500 ≡ 0) printf("%d", cur_line);
    update_terminal;     /* progress report */
  }
  cur_line ++;
}
```

38. Second, we have modified the original TANGLE so that it will write output on multiple files. If a section name is introduced in at least one place by @(instead of @<, we treat it as the name of a file. All these special sections are saved on a stack, *output_files*. We write them out after we've done the unnamed section.

```
#define max_files 256
```
⟨ Global variables 17 ⟩ +≡
  name_pointer *output_files*[*max_files*];
  name_pointer *cur_out_file*, *end_output_files*, *an_output_file*;
  char *cur_section_name_char*;   /* is it '<' or '(' */
  char *output_file_name*[*longest_name*];   /* name of the file */

39.   We make *end_output_files* point just beyond the end of *output_files*. The stack pointer *cur_out_file* starts out there. Every time we see a new file, we decrement *cur_out_file* and then write it in.

⟨ Set initial values 18 ⟩ +≡
    $cur\_out\_file \leftarrow end\_output\_files \leftarrow output\_files + max\_files;$

40.   ⟨ If it's not there, add *cur_section_name* to the output file stack, or complain we're out of room 40 ⟩ ≡
    {
        for (*an_output_file* ← *cur_out_file*; *an_output_file* < *end_output_files*; *an_output_file* ++)
            if (∗*an_output_file* ≡ *cur_section_name*) **break**;
        if (*an_output_file* ≡ *end_output_files*) {
            if (*cur_out_file* > *output_files*) ∗−−*cur_out_file* ← *cur_section_name*;
            else {
                overflow("output␣files");
            }
        }
    }

This code is used in section 70.

41. The big output switch.   Here then is the routine that does the output.

⟨ Predeclaration of procedures 2 ⟩ +≡
  void *phase_two* ( );

42.   void *phase_two* ( )
  {
    web_file_open ← 0;
    cur_line ← 1;
    ⟨ Initialize the output stacks 29 ⟩;
    ⟨ Output macro definitions if appropriate 44 ⟩;
    if (*text_info*→*text_link* ≡ 0 ∧ *cur_out_file* ≡ *end_output_files*) {
      printf ("\n!␣No␣program␣text␣was␣specified.");
      mark_harmless;
    }
    else {
      if (*cur_out_file* ≡ *end_output_files*) {
        if (*show_progress*) *printf* ("\nWriting␣the␣output␣file␣(%s):", *C_file_name*);
      }
      else {
        if (*show_progress*) {
          printf ("\nWriting␣the␣output␣files:");
          printf ("␣(%s)", *C_file_name*);
          update_terminal;
        }
        if (*text_info*→*text_link* ≡ 0) **goto** *writeloop*;
      }
      while (*stack_ptr* > *stack*) *get_output* ( );
      flush_buffer ( );
    writeloop: ⟨ Write all the named output files 43 ⟩;
      if (*show_happiness*) *printf* ("\nDone.");
    }
  }

43.   To write the named output files, we proceed as for the unnamed section. The only subtlety is that we have to open each one.

⟨ Write all the named output files 43 ⟩ ≡
 for (*an_output_file* ← *end_output_files*; *an_output_file* > *cur_out_file*;) {
  an_output_file −−;
  sprint_section_name (*output_file_name*, ∗*an_output_file*);
  fclose (*C_file*);
  C_file ← *fopen* (*output_file_name*, "w");
  if (*C_file* ≡ 0) *fatal* ("!␣Cannot␣open␣output␣file:", *output_file_name*);
  printf ("\n(%s)", *output_file_name*);
  update_terminal;
  cur_line ← 1;
  stack_ptr ← *stack* + 1;
  cur_name ← (∗*an_output_file*);
  cur_repl ← (**text_pointer**) *cur_name*→*equiv*;
  cur_byte ← *cur_repl*→*tok_start*;
  cur_end ← (*cur_repl* + 1)→*tok_start*;
  while (*stack_ptr* > *stack*) *get_output* ( );
  flush_buffer ( );
 }
This code is used in section 42.

44.   If a @h was not encountered in the input, we go through the list of replacement texts and copy the ones that refer to macros, preceded by the #define preprocessor command.

⟨ Output macro definitions if appropriate 44 ⟩ ≡
 if (¬*output_defs_seen*) *output_defs* ( );
This code is used in section 42.

45.   ⟨ Global variables 17 ⟩ +≡
 boolean *output_defs_seen* ← 0;

46.   ⟨ Predeclaration of procedures 2 ⟩ +≡
 void *output_defs* ( );

47.   **void** *output_defs*( )
{
    sixteen_bits *a*;
    push_level(Λ);
    for (*cur_text* ← *text_info* + 1; *cur_text* < *text_ptr*; *cur_text*++)
        if (*cur_text*→*text_link* ≡ 0) {   /* *cur_text* is the text for a macro */
            cur_byte ← *cur_text*→*tok_start*;
            cur_end ← (*cur_text* + 1)→*tok_start*;
            C_printf("%s", "#define␣");
            out_state ← *normal*;
            protect ← 1;   /* newlines should be preceded by '\\' */
            while (*cur_byte* < *cur_end*) {
                a ← *cur_byte*++;
                if (*cur_byte* ≡ *cur_end* ∧ *a* ≡ '\n') **break**;   /* disregard a final newline */
                if (*out_state* ≡ *verbatim* ∧ *a* ≠ *string* ∧ *a* ≠ *constant* ∧ *a* ≠ '\n') *C_putc*(*a*);
                    /* a high-bit character can occur in a string */
                else if (*a* < °*200*) *out_char*(*a*);   /* one-byte token */
                else {
                    a ← (*a* − °*200*) * °*400* + *cur_byte*++;
                    if (*a* < °*24000*) {   /* °*24000* ≡ (°*250* − °*200*) * °*400* */
                        cur_val ← *a*;
                        out_char(*identifier*);
                    }
                    else if (*a* < °*50000*) {
                        confusion("macro␣defs␣have␣strange␣char");
                    }
                    else {
                        cur_val ← *a* − °*50000*;
                        cur_section ← *cur_val*;
                        out_char(*section_number*);
                    }   /* no other cases */
                }
            }
            protect ← 0;
            flush_buffer( );
        }
    pop_level(0);
}

48.   A many-way switch is used to send the output. Note that this function is not called if *out_state* ≡ *verbatim*, except perhaps with arguments '\n' (protect the newline), *string* (end the string), or *constant* (end the constant).

⟨Predeclaration of procedures 2⟩ +≡
    static void *out_char*( );

49.   **static void** *out_char*(*cur_char*)
  eight_bits *cur_char*;
{
 char *∗j, ∗k;* /∗ pointer into *byte_mem* ∗/
restart:
 switch (*cur_char*) {
 case '\n':
  if (*protect* ∧ *out_state* ≠ *verbatim*) *C_putc*('␣');
  if (*protect* ∨ *out_state* ≡ *verbatim*) *C_putc*('\\');
  flush_buffer( );
  if (*out_state* ≠ *verbatim*) *out_state* ← *normal*;
  break;
 ⟨ Case of an identifier 53 ⟩;
 ⟨ Case of a section number 54 ⟩;
 ⟨ Cases like != 50 ⟩;
 case '=': **case** '>': *C_putc*(*cur_char*);
  C_putc('␣');
  out_state ← *normal*;
  break;
 case *join*: *out_state* ← *unbreakable*;
  break;
 case *constant*:
  if (*out_state* ≡ *verbatim*) {
   out_state ← *num_or_id*;
   break;
  }
  if (*out_state* ≡ *num_or_id*) *C_putc*('␣');
  out_state ← *verbatim*;
  break;
 case *string*:
  if (*out_state* ≡ *verbatim*) *out_state* ← *normal*;
  else *out_state* ← *verbatim*;
  break;
 case '/': *C_putc*('/');
  out_state ← *post_slash*;
  break;
 case '∗':
  if (*out_state* ≡ *post_slash*) *C_putc*('␣'); /∗ fall through ∗/
 default: *C_putc*(*cur_char*);
  out_state ← *normal*;
  break;
 }
}

50.   ⟨ Cases like != 50 ⟩ ≡

case *plus_plus*: *C_putc*(`'+'`);

  C_putc(`'+'`);

  out_state ← *normal*;

  break;

case *minus_minus*: *C_putc*(`'-'`);

  C_putc(`'-'`);

  out_state ← *normal*;

  break;

case *minus_gt*: *C_putc*(`'-'`);

  C_putc(`'>'`);

  out_state ← *normal*;

  break;

case *gt_gt*: *C_putc*(`'>'`);

  C_putc(`'>'`);

  out_state ← *normal*;

  break;

case *eq_eq*: *C_putc*(`'='`);

  C_putc(`'='`);

  out_state ← *normal*;

  break;

case *lt_lt*: *C_putc*(`'<'`);

  C_putc(`'<'`);

  out_state ← *normal*;

  break;

case *gt_eq*: *C_putc*(`'>'`);

  C_putc(`'='`);

  out_state ← *normal*;

  break;

case *lt_eq*: *C_putc*(`'<'`);

  C_putc(`'='`);

  out_state ← *normal*;

  break;

case *not_eq*: *C_putc*(`'!'`);

  C_putc(`'='`);

  out_state ← *normal*;

  break;

case *and_and*: *C_putc*(`'&'`);

  C_putc(`'&'`);

  out_state ← *normal*;

  break;

case *or_or*: *C_putc*(`'|'`);

  C_putc(`'|'`);

  out_state ← *normal*;

  break;

case *dot_dot_dot*: *C_putc*(`'.'`);

  C_putc(`'.'`);

  C_putc(`'.'`);

  out_state ← *normal*;

  break;

case *colon_colon*: *C_putc*(`':'`);

  C_putc(`':'`);

```
    out_state ← normal;
  break;
case period_ast: C_putc('.');
  C_putc('*');
  out_state ← normal;
  break;
case minus_gt_ast: C_putc('-');
  C_putc('>');
  C_putc('*');
  out_state ← normal;
  break;
```

This code is used in section 49.

51.   When an identifier is output to the C file, characters in the range 128–255 must be changed into something else, so the C compiler won't complain. By default, **CTANGLE** converts the character with code $16x + y$ to the three characters 'Xxy', but a different transliteration table can be specified. Thus a German might want *grün* to appear as a still readable **gruen**. This makes debugging a lot less confusing.

#define *translit_length*   10
⟨ Global variables 17 ⟩ +≡
  char *translit*[128][*translit_length*];

52.   ⟨ Set initial values 18 ⟩ +≡
```
  {
    int i;
    for (i ← 0; i < 128; i++) sprintf(translit[i], "X%02X", (unsigned)(128 + i));
  }
```

53.   ⟨ Case of an identifier 53 ⟩ ≡
```
case identifier:
  if (out_state ≡ num_or_id) C_putc(' ');
  j ← (cur_val + name_dir)→byte_start;
  k ← (cur_val + name_dir + 1)→byte_start;
  while (j < k) {
    if ((unsigned char)(*j) < °200) C_putc(*j);
    else C_printf("%s", translit[(unsigned char)(*j) − °200]);
    j++;
  }
  out_state ← num_or_id;
  break;
```

This code is used in section 49.

54. ⟨ Case of a section number 54 ⟩ ≡

```
case section_number:
   if (cur_val > 0) C_printf("/*%d:*/", cur_val);
   else if (cur_val < 0) C_printf("/*:%d*/", −cur_val);
   else if (protect) {
      cur_byte += 4;        /* skip line number and file name */
      cur_char ← '\n';
      goto restart;
   }
   else {
      sixteen_bits a;

      a ← °400 * *cur_byte ++;
      a += *cur_byte ++;        /* gets the line number */
      C_printf("\n#line␣%d␣\"", a);
      cur_val ← *cur_byte ++;
      cur_val ← °400 * (cur_val − °200) + *cur_byte ++;    /* points to the file name */
      for (j ← (cur_val + name_dir)‑byte_start, k ← (cur_val + name_dir + 1)‑byte_start; j < k; j++) {
         if (*j ≡ '\\' ∨ *j ≡ '"') C_putc('\\');
         C_putc(*j);
      }
      C_printf("%s", "\"\n");
   }
   break;
```

This code is used in section 49.

55. Introduction to the input phase.   We have now seen that CTANGLE will be able to output the full C program, if we can only get that program into the byte memory in the proper format. The input process is something like the output process in reverse, since we compress the text as we read it in and we expand it as we write it out.

There are three main input routines. The most interesting is the one that gets the next token of a C text; the other two are used to scan rapidly past TEX text in the CWEB source code. One of the latter routines will jump to the next token that starts with '@', and the other skips to the end of a C comment.

56.   Control codes in CWEB begin with '@', and the next character identifies the code. Some of these are of interest only to CWEAVE, so CTANGLE ignores them; the others are converted by CTANGLE into internal code numbers by the *ccode* table below. The ordering of these internal code numbers has been chosen to simplify the program logic; larger numbers are given to the control codes that denote more significant milestones.

#define *ignore*   0   /∗ control code of no interest to CTANGLE ∗/
#define *ord*   °302   /∗ control code for '@'' ∗/
#define *control_text*   °303   /∗ control code for '@t', '@^', etc. ∗/
#define *translit_code*   °304   /∗ control code for '@l' ∗/
#define *output_defs_code*   °305   /∗ control code for '@h' ∗/
#define *format_code*   °306   /∗ control code for '@f' ∗/
#define *definition*   °307   /∗ control code for '@d' ∗/
#define *begin_C*   °310   /∗ control code for '@c' ∗/
#define *section_name*   °311   /∗ control code for '@<' ∗/
#define *new_section*   °312   /∗ control code for '@␣' and '@∗' ∗/
⟨ Global variables 17 ⟩ +≡
  eight_bits *ccode*[256];   /∗ meaning of a char following @ ∗/

57.   ⟨ Set initial values 18 ⟩ +≡
  {
    int *c*;   /∗ must be **int** so the **for** loop will end ∗/
    for (*c* ← 0; *c* < 256; *c*++) *ccode*[*c*] ← *ignore*;
    ccode['␣'] ← *ccode*['\t'] ← *ccode*['\n'] ← *ccode*['\v'] ← *ccode*['\r'] ← *ccode*['\f'] ← *ccode*['∗'] ←
        new_section;
    ccode['@'] ← '@';
    ccode['='] ← *string*;
    ccode['d'] ← *ccode*['D'] ← *definition*;
    ccode['f'] ← *ccode*['F'] ← *ccode*['s'] ← *ccode*['S'] ← *format_code*;
    ccode['c'] ← *ccode*['C'] ← *ccode*['p'] ← *ccode*['P'] ← *begin_C*;
    ccode['^'] ← *ccode*[':'] ← *ccode*['.'] ← *ccode*['t'] ← *ccode*['T'] ← *ccode*['q'] ← *ccode*['Q'] ←
        control_text;
    ccode['h'] ← *ccode*['H'] ← *output_defs_code*;
    ccode['l'] ← *ccode*['L'] ← *translit_code*;
    ccode['&'] ← *join*;
    ccode['<'] ← *ccode*['('] ← *section_name*;
    ccode['\''] ← *ord*;
  }

58. The *skip_ahead* procedure reads through the input at fairly high speed until finding the next non-ignorable control code, which it returns.

eight_bits *skip_ahead*( )   /∗ skip to next control code ∗/
{
  eight_bits *c*;   /∗ control code found ∗/
  while (1) {
    if (*loc* > *limit* ∧ (*get_line*( ) ≡ 0)) **return** (*new_section*);
    ∗(*limit* + 1) ← '@';
    while (∗*loc* ≠ '@') *loc*++;
    if (*loc* ≤ *limit*) {
      loc++;
      c ← *ccode*[(**eight_bits**) ∗*loc*];
      loc++;
      if (*c* ≠ *ignore* ∨ ∗(*loc* − 1) ≡ '>') **return** (*c*);
    }
  }
}

59. The *skip_comment* procedure reads through the input at somewhat high speed in order to pass over comments, which CTANGLE does not transmit to the output. If the comment is introduced by /∗, *skip_comment* proceeds until finding the end-comment token ∗/ or a newline; in the latter case *skip_comment* will be called again by *get_next*, since the comment is not finished. This is done so that the each newline in the C part of a section is copied to the output; otherwise the #**line** commands inserted into the C file by the output routines become useless. On the other hand, if the comment is introduced by // (i.e., if it is a C++ "short comment"), it always is simply delimited by the next newline. The boolean argument *is_long_comment* distinguishes between the two types of comments.

If *skip_comment* comes to the end of the section, it prints an error message. No comment, long or short, is allowed to contain '@␣' or '@∗'.

⟨ Global variables 17 ⟩ +≡
  boolean *comment_continues* ← 0;   /∗ are we scanning a comment? ∗/

60.   **int** *skip_comment*(*is_long_comment*)   /* skips over comments */
        boolean *is_long_comment*;
    {
      char *c*;   /* current character */
      while (1) {
        if (*loc* > *limit*) {
          if (*is_long_comment*) {
            if (*get_line*( )) **return** (*comment_continues* ← 1);
            else {
              err_print("!␣Input␣ended␣in␣mid-comment");
              return (*comment_continues* ← 0);
            }
          }
          else return (*comment_continues* ← 0);
        }
        c ← *(*loc*++);
        if (*is_long_comment* ∧ *c* ≡ '*' ∧ *loc* ≡ '/') {
          loc++;
          return (*comment_continues* ← 0);
        }
        if (*c* ≡ '@') {
          if (*ccode*[(**eight_bits**) *loc*] ≡ *new_section*) {
            err_print("!␣Section␣name␣ended␣in␣mid-comment");
            loc−−;
            return (*comment_continues* ← 0);
          }
          else *loc*++;
        }
      }
    }

61.   Inputting the next token.

#define *constant* °3

⟨ Global variables 17 ⟩ +≡
   name_pointer *cur_section_name*;   /* name of section just scanned */
   int *no_where*;   /* suppress *print_where*? */

62. ⟨ Include files 6 ⟩ +≡
#include <ctype.h>   /* definition of *isalpha*, *isdigit* and so on */
#include <stdlib.h>   /* definition of *exit* */

63.   As one might expect, *get_next* consists mostly of a big switch that branches to the various special cases that can arise.

#define *isxalpha*(c)   ((c) ≡ '_' ∨ (c) ≡ '$')   /* non-alpha characters allowed in identifier */
#define *ishigh*(c)   ((**unsigned char**)(c) > °177)
   eight_bits *get_next*( )   /* produces the next input token */
   {
     static int *preprocessing* ← 0;
     eight_bits *c*;   /* the current character */
     while (1) {
       if (*loc* > *limit*) {
         if (*preprocessing* ∧ *(*limit* − 1) ≠ '\\') *preprocessing* ← 0;
         if (*get_line*( ) ≡ 0) **return** (*new_section*);
         else if (*print_where* ∧ ¬*no_where*) {
           print_where ← 0;
           ⟨ Insert the line number into *tok_mem* 77 ⟩;
         }
         else return ('\n');
       }
       c ← *loc;
       if (*comment_continues* ∨ (*c* ≡ '/' ∧ (*(*loc* + 1) ≡ '*' ∨ *(*loc* + 1) ≡ '/'))) {
         skip_comment(*comment_continues* ∨ *(*loc* + 1) ≡ '*');
           /* scan to end of comment or newline */
         if (*comment_continues*) **return** ('\n');
         else continue;
       }
       loc++;
       if (*xisdigit*(c) ∨ c ≡ '\\' ∨ c ≡ '.') ⟨ Get a constant 66 ⟩
       else if (c ≡ '\'' ∨ c ≡ '"' ∨ (c ≡ 'L' ∧ (*loc ≡ '\'' ∨ *loc ≡ '"'))) ⟨ Get a string 67 ⟩
       else if (*isalpha*(c) ∨ *isxalpha*(c) ∨ *ishigh*(c)) ⟨ Get an identifier 65 ⟩
       else if (c ≡ '@') ⟨ Get control code and possible section name 68 ⟩
       else if (*xisspace*(c)) {
         if (¬*preprocessing* ∨ *loc* > *limit*) **continue**;
             /* we don't want a blank after a final backslash */
         else return ('␣');   /* ignore spaces and tabs, unless preprocessing */
       }
       else if (c ≡ '#' ∧ *loc* ≡ *buffer* + 1) *preprocessing* ← 1;
     mistake: ⟨ Compress two-symbol operator 64 ⟩
       return (c);
     }
   }

64. The following code assigns values to the combinations `++`, `--`, `->`, `>=`, `<=`, `==`, `<<`, `>>`, `!=`, and `&&`, and to the C++ combinations `...`, `::`, `.*` and `->*`. The compound assignment operators (e.g., `+=`) are treated as separate tokens.

#define $compress(c)$ **if** $(loc\mathbin{++} \le limit)$ **return** (c)

$\langle$ Compress two-symbol operator 64 $\rangle \equiv$
```
  switch (c) {
  case '+':
    if (*loc ≡ '+') compress(plus_plus);
    break;
  case '-':
    if (*loc ≡ '-') {
      compress(minus_minus);
    }
    else if (*loc ≡ '>')
      if (*(loc + 1) ≡ '*') {
        loc++;
        compress(minus_gt_ast);
      }
      else compress(minus_gt);
    break;
  case '.':
    if (*loc ≡ '*') {
      compress(period_ast);
    }
    else if (*loc ≡ '.' ∧ *(loc + 1) ≡ '.') {
      loc++;
      compress(dot_dot_dot);
    }
    break;
  case ':':
    if (*loc ≡ ':') compress(colon_colon);
    break;
  case '=':
    if (*loc ≡ '=') compress(eq_eq);
    break;
  case '>':
    if (*loc ≡ '=') {
      compress(gt_eq);
    }
    else if (*loc ≡ '>') compress(gt_gt);
    break;
  case '<':
    if (*loc ≡ '=') {
      compress(lt_eq);
    }
    else if (*loc ≡ '<') compress(lt_lt);
    break;
  case '&':
    if (*loc ≡ '&') compress(and_and);
    break;
  case '|':
    if (*loc ≡ '|') compress(or_or);
```

```
        break;
      case '!':
        if (*loc ≡ '=') compress(not_eq);
        break;
      }
```

This code is used in section 63.

65. ⟨ Get an identifier 65 ⟩ ≡
```
      {
        id_first ← −−loc;
        while (isalpha(*++loc) ∨ isdigit(*loc) ∨ isxalpha(*loc) ∨ ishigh(*loc)) ;
        id_loc ← loc;
        return (identifier);
      }
```

This code is used in section 63.

66. ⟨ Get a constant 66 ⟩ ≡
```
      {
        id_first ← loc − 1;
        if (*id_first ≡ '.' ∧ ¬xisdigit(*loc)) goto mistake;        /* not a constant */
        if (*id_first ≡ '\\')
          while (xisdigit(*loc)) loc++;       /* octal constant */
        else {
          if (*id_first ≡ '0') {
            if (*loc ≡ 'x' ∨ *loc ≡ 'X') {       /* hex constant */
              loc++;
              while (xisxdigit(*loc)) loc++;
              goto found;
            }
          }
          while (xisdigit(*loc)) loc++;
          if (*loc ≡ '.') {
            loc++;
            while (xisdigit(*loc)) loc++;
          }
          if (*loc ≡ 'e' ∨ *loc ≡ 'E') {       /* float constant */
            if (*++loc ≡ '+' ∨ *loc ≡ '-') loc++;
            while (xisdigit(*loc)) loc++;
          }
        }
      found:
        while (*loc ≡ 'u' ∨ *loc ≡ 'U' ∨ *loc ≡ 'l' ∨ *loc ≡ 'L' ∨ *loc ≡ 'f' ∨ *loc ≡ 'F') loc++;
        id_loc ← loc;
        return (constant);
      }
```

This code is used in section 63.

67. C strings and character constants, delimited by double and single quotes, respectively, can contain newlines or instances of their own delimiters if they are protected by a backslash. We follow this convention, but do not allow the string to be longer than *longest_name*.

⟨ Get a string 67 ⟩ ≡

```
{
  char delim ← c;        /* what started the string */
  id_first ← section_text + 1;
  id_loc ← section_text;
  *++id_loc ← delim;
  if (delim ≡ 'L') {         /* wide character constant */
    delim ← *loc++;
    *++id_loc ← delim;
  }
  while (1) {
    if (loc ≥ limit) {
      if (*(limit − 1) ≠ '\\') {
        err_print("!␣String␣didn't␣end");
        loc ← limit;
        break;
      }
      if (get_line( ) ≡ 0) {
        err_print("!␣Input␣ended␣in␣middle␣of␣string");
        loc ← buffer;
        break;
      }
      else if (++id_loc ≤ section_text_end) *id_loc ← '\n';     /* will print as "\\n" */
    }
    if ((c ← *loc++) ≡ delim) {
      if (++id_loc ≤ section_text_end) *id_loc ← c;
      break;
    }
    if (c ≡ '\\') {
      if (loc ≥ limit) continue;
      if (++id_loc ≤ section_text_end) *id_loc ← '\\';
      c ← *loc++;
    }
    if (++id_loc ≤ section_text_end) *id_loc ← c;
  }
  if (id_loc ≥ section_text_end) {
    printf("\n!␣String␣too␣long:␣");
    term_write(section_text + 1, 25);
    err_print("...");
  }
  id_loc++;
  return (string);
}
```

This code is used in section 63.

68.   After an @ sign has been scanned, the next character tells us whether there is more work to do.

⟨ Get control code and possible section name 68 ⟩ ≡

```
{
    c ← ccode[(eight_bits) *loc ++];
    switch (c) {
    case ignore: continue;
    case output_defs_code: output_defs_seen ← 1;
        return (c);
    case translit_code: err_print("!␣Use␣@l␣in␣limbo␣only");
        continue;
    case control_text:
        while ((c ← skip_ahead( )) ≡ '@') ;        /* only @@ and @> are expected */
        if (*(loc − 1) ≠ '>') err_print("!␣Double␣@␣should␣be␣used␣in␣control␣text");
        continue;
    case section_name: cur_section_name_char ← *(loc − 1);
        ⟨ Scan the section name and make cur_section_name point to it 70 ⟩;
    case string: ⟨ Scan a verbatim string 74 ⟩;
    case ord: ⟨ Scan an ASCII constant 69 ⟩;
    default: return (c);
    }
}
```

This code is cited in section 84.

This code is used in section 63.

69.   After scanning a valid ASCII constant that follows @', this code plows ahead until it finds the next single quote. (Special care is taken if the quote is part of the constant.) Anything after a valid ASCII constant is ignored; thus, @'\nopq' gives the same result as @'\n'.

⟨ Scan an ASCII constant 69 ⟩ ≡

```
    id_first ← loc;
    if (*loc ≡ '\\') {
        if (*++loc ≡ '\'') loc ++;
    }
    while (*loc ≠ '\'') {
        if (*loc ≡ '@') {
            if (*(loc + 1) ≠ '@') err_print("!␣Double␣@␣should␣be␣used␣in␣ASCII␣constant");
            else loc ++;
        }
        loc ++;
        if (loc > limit) {
            err_print("!␣String␣didn't␣end");
            loc ← limit − 1;
            break;
        }
    }
    loc ++;
    return (ord);
```

This code is used in section 68.

70. ⟨ Scan the section name and make *cur_section_name* point to it 70 ⟩ ≡
  {
    char *k;   /∗ pointer into *section_text* ∗/
    ⟨ Put section name into *section_text* 72 ⟩;
    if $(k - section\_text > 3 \wedge strncmp(k - 2, "...", 3) \equiv 0)$
      $cur\_section\_name \leftarrow section\_lookup(section\_text + 1, k - 3, 1);$ /∗ 1 means is a prefix ∗/
    else $cur\_section\_name \leftarrow section\_lookup(section\_text + 1, k, 0);$
    if $(cur\_section\_name\_char \equiv \text{'('})$
      ⟨ If it's not there, add *cur_section_name* to the output file stack, or complain we're out of room 40 ⟩;
    return (*section_name*);
  }
This code is used in section 68.

71. Section names are placed into the *section_text* array with consecutive spaces, tabs, and carriage-returns replaced by single spaces. There will be no spaces at the beginning or the end. (We set $section\_text[0] \leftarrow \text{'␣'}$ to facilitate this, since the *section_lookup* routine uses $section\_text[1]$ as the first character of the name.)
⟨ Set initial values 18 ⟩ +≡
  $section\_text[0] \leftarrow \text{'␣'};$

72. ⟨ Put section name into *section_text* 72 ⟩ ≡
  $k \leftarrow section\_text;$
  while (1) {
    if $(loc > limit \wedge get\_line(\,) \equiv 0)$ {
      $err\_print(\text{"!␣Input␣ended␣in␣section␣name"});$
      $loc \leftarrow buffer + 1;$
      break;
    }
    $c \leftarrow {*}loc;$
    ⟨ If end of name or erroneous nesting, **break** 73 ⟩;
    $loc{+}{+};$
    if $(k < section\_text\_end)$ $k{+}{+};$
    if $(xisspace(c))$ {
      $c \leftarrow \text{'␣'};$
      if $({*}(k - 1) \equiv \text{'␣'})$ $k{-}{-};$
    }
    ${*}k \leftarrow c;$
  }
  if $(k \geq section\_text\_end)$ {
    $printf(\text{"\textbackslash n!␣Section␣name␣too␣long:␣"});$
    $term\_write(section\_text + 1, 25);$
    $printf(\text{"..."});$
    $mark\_harmless;$
  }
  if $({*}k \equiv \text{'␣'} \wedge k > section\_text)$ $k{-}{-};$
This code is used in section 70.

73. ⟨ If end of name or erroneous nesting, **break** 73 ⟩ ≡
  if $(c \equiv \texttt{'@'})$ {
    $c \leftarrow *(loc + 1)$;
    if $(c \equiv \texttt{'>'})$ {
      $loc \mathrel{+}= 2$;
      break;
    }
    if $(ccode\,[(\textbf{eight\_bits})\,c] \equiv new\_section)$ {
      $err\_print(\texttt{"!\_Section\_name\_didn't\_end"})$;
      break;
    }
    if $(ccode\,[(\textbf{eight\_bits})\,c] \equiv section\_name)$ {
      $err\_print(\texttt{"!\_Nesting\_of\_section\_names\_not\_allowed"})$;
      break;
    }
    $*(\mathop{++}k) \leftarrow \texttt{'@'}$;
    $loc\mathop{++}$;   /* now $c \equiv *loc$ again */
  }
This code is used in section 72.

74.   At the present point in the program we have $*(loc - 1) \equiv string$; we set id_first to the beginning of the string itself, and id_loc to its ending-plus-one location in the buffer. We also set loc to the position just after the ending delimiter.
⟨ Scan a verbatim string 74 ⟩ ≡
  {
    $id\_first \leftarrow loc\mathop{++}$;
    $*(limit + 1) \leftarrow \texttt{'@'}$;
    $*(limit + 2) \leftarrow \texttt{'>'}$;
    while $(*loc \neq \texttt{'@'} \vee *(loc + 1) \neq \texttt{'>'})$ $loc\mathop{++}$;
    if $(loc \geq limit)$ $err\_print(\texttt{"!\_Verbatim\_string\_didn't\_end"})$;
    $id\_loc \leftarrow loc$;
    $loc \mathrel{+}= 2$;
    return $(string)$;
  }
This code is used in section 68.

75. Scanning a macro definition.   The rules for generating the replacement texts corresponding to macros and C texts of a section are almost identical; the only differences are that

a) Section names are not allowed in macros; in fact, the appearance of a section name terminates such macros and denotes the name of the current section.

b) The symbols @d and @f and @c are not allowed after section names, while they terminate macro definitions.

c) Spaces are inserted after right parentheses in macros, because the ANSI C preprocessor sometimes requires it.

Therefore there is a single procedure *scan_repl* whose parameter t specifies either *macro* or *section_name*. After *scan_repl* has acted, *cur_text* will point to the replacement text just generated, and *next_control* will contain the control code that terminated the activity.

#define *macro*   0
#define *app_repl*(*c*)
$\qquad$ {
$\qquad\qquad$ **if** (*tok_ptr* $\equiv$ *tok_mem_end*) *overflow*("token");
$\qquad\qquad$ *tok_ptr* ++ $\leftarrow$ *c*;
$\qquad$ }
⟨ Global variables 17 ⟩ +≡
$\quad$ **text_pointer** *cur_text*;$\qquad$ /* replacement text formed by *scan_repl* */
$\quad$ **eight_bits** *next_control*;

76.   **void** *scan_repl*(*t*)$\qquad$ /* creates a replacement text */
$\qquad$ **eight_bits** *t*;
$\quad$ {
$\quad$ **sixteen_bits** *a*;$\qquad$ /* the current token */
$\quad$ **if** (*t* $\equiv$ *section_name*) {
$\qquad$ ⟨ Insert the line number into *tok_mem* 77 ⟩;
$\quad$ }
$\quad$ **while** (1)
$\qquad$ **switch** (*a* $\leftarrow$ *get_next*( )) {
$\qquad\qquad$ ⟨ In cases that *a* is a non-**char** token (*identifier*, *section_name*, etc.), either process it and change
$\qquad\qquad\qquad$ *a* to a byte that should be stored, or **continue** if *a* should be ignored, or **goto** *done* if *a*
$\qquad\qquad\qquad$ signals the end of this replacement text 78 ⟩
$\qquad$ **case** ')': *app_repl*(*a*);
$\qquad\qquad$ **if** (*t* $\equiv$ *macro*) *app_repl*('␣');
$\qquad\qquad$ **break**;
$\qquad$ **default**: *app_repl*(*a*);$\qquad$ /* store *a* in *tok_mem* */
$\qquad$ }
done: *next_control* $\leftarrow$ (**eight_bits**) *a*;
$\quad$ **if** (*text_ptr* > *text_info_end*) *overflow*("text");
$\quad$ *cur_text* $\leftarrow$ *text_ptr*;
$\quad$ (++*text_ptr*)→*tok_start* $\leftarrow$ *tok_ptr*;
$\quad$ }

77.   Here is the code for the line number: first a **sixteen_bits** equal to $°150000$; then the numeric line number; then a pointer to the file name.

⟨ Insert the line number into *tok_mem* 77 ⟩ ≡
   store_two_bytes ($°150000$);
   if (*changing*) *id_first* ← *change_file_name*;
   else *id_first* ← *cur_file_name*;
   id_loc ← *id_first* + *strlen*(*id_first*);
   if (*changing*) *store_two_bytes*((**sixteen_bits**) *change_line*);
   else *store_two_bytes*((**sixteen_bits**) *cur_line*);
   {
     int *a* ← *id_lookup*(*id_first*, *id_loc*, 0) − *name_dir*;
     app_repl(($a/°400$) + $°200$);
     app_repl(a % $°400$);
   }
This code is used in sections 63, 76, and 78.

78.   ⟨ In cases that *a* is a non-**char** token (*identifier*, *section_name*, etc.), either process it and change *a* to a byte that should be stored, or **continue** if *a* should be ignored, or **goto** *done* if *a* signals the end of this replacement text 78 ⟩ ≡
case *identifier*: *a* ← *id_lookup*(*id_first*, *id_loc*, 0) − *name_dir*;
  app_repl(($a/°400$) + $°200$);
  app_repl(a % $°400$);
  break;
case *section_name*:
  if ($t ≠$ *section_name*) **goto** *done*;
  else {
    ⟨ Was an '@' missed here? 79 ⟩;
    a ← *cur_section_name* − *name_dir*;
    app_repl(($a/°400$) + $°250$);
    app_repl(a % $°400$);
    ⟨ Insert the line number into *tok_mem* 77 ⟩;
    break;
  }
case *output_defs_code*: *a* ← *output_defs_flag*;
  app_repl(($a/°400$) + $°200$);
  app_repl(a % $°400$);
  ⟨ Insert the line number into *tok_mem* 77 ⟩;
  break;
case *constant*: **case** *string*: ⟨ Copy a string or verbatim construction or numerical constant 80 ⟩;
case *ord*: ⟨ Copy an ASCII constant 81 ⟩;
case *definition*: **case** *format_code*: **case** *begin_C*:
  if ($t ≠$ *section_name*) **goto** *done*;
  else {
    err_print("!␣@d,␣@f␣and␣@c␣are␣ignored␣in␣C␣text");
    continue;
  }
case *new_section*: **goto** *done*;
This code is used in section 76.

79. ⟨ Was an '@' missed here? 79 ⟩ ≡
  {
      char ∗*try_loc* ← *loc*;
      while (∗*try_loc* ≡ '␣' ∧ *try_loc* < *limit*) *try_loc*++;
      if (∗*try_loc* ≡ '+' ∧ *try_loc* < *limit*) *try_loc*++;
      while (∗*try_loc* ≡ '␣' ∧ *try_loc* < *limit*) *try_loc*++;
      if (∗*try_loc* ≡ '=') *err_print*("!␣Missing␣'@␣'␣before␣a␣named␣section");   /∗ user who isn't
          defining a section should put newline after the name, as explained in the manual ∗/
  }
This code is used in section 78.

80.   ⟨ Copy a string or verbatim construction or numerical constant 80 ⟩ ≡
    app_repl(*a*);   /∗ *string* or *constant* ∗/
    while (*id_first* < *id_loc*) {   /∗ simplify @@ pairs ∗/
      if (∗*id_first* ≡ '@') {
        if (∗(*id_first* + 1) ≡ '@') *id_first*++;
        else *err_print*("!␣Double␣@␣should␣be␣used␣in␣string");
      }
      app_repl(∗*id_first*++);
    }
    app_repl(*a*);
    break;
This code is used in section 78.

81.   This section should be rewritten on machines that don't use ASCII code internally.

$\langle$ Copy an ASCII constant 81 $\rangle \equiv$

```
{
    int c ← (eight_bits) *id_first;
    if (c ≡ '\\') {
        c ← *++id_first;
        if (c ≥ '0' ∧ c ≤ '7') {
            c −= '0';
            if (*(id_first + 1) ≥ '0' ∧ *(id_first + 1) ≤ '7') {
                c ← 8 * c + *(++id_first) − '0';
                if (*(id_first + 1) ≥ '0' ∧ *(id_first + 1) ≤ '7' ∧ c < 32)  c ← 8 * c + *(++id_first) − '0';
            }
        }
        else
            switch (c) {
            case 't': c ← '\t'; break;
            case 'n': c ← '\n'; break;
            case 'b': c ← '\b'; break;
            case 'f': c ← '\f'; break;
            case 'v': c ← '\v'; break;
            case 'r': c ← '\r'; break;
            case 'a': c ← '\7'; break;
            case '?': c ← '?'; break;
            case 'x':
                if (xisdigit(*(id_first + 1)))  c ← *(++id_first) − '0';
                else if (xisxdigit(*(id_first + 1))) {
                    ++id_first;
                    c ← toupper(*id_first) − 'A' + 10;
                }
                if (xisdigit(*(id_first + 1)))  c ← 16 * c + *(++id_first) − '0';
                else if (xisxdigit(*(id_first + 1))) {
                    ++id_first;
                    c ← 16 * c + toupper(*id_first) − 'A' + 10;
                }
                break;
            case '\\': c ← '\\'; break;
            case '\'': c ← '\''; break;
            case '\"': c ← '\"'; break;
            default: err_print("! Unrecognized escape sequence");
            }
    }    /* at this point c should have been converted to its ASCII code number */
    app_repl(constant);
    if (c ≥ 100)  app_repl('0' + c/100);
    if (c ≥ 10)  app_repl('0' + (c/10) % 10);
    app_repl('0' + c % 10);
    app_repl(constant);
}
break;
```

This code is used in section 78.

82. Scanning a section.   The *scan_section* procedure starts when '@␣' or '@*' has been sensed in the input, and it proceeds until the end of that section. It uses *section_count* to keep track of the current section number; with luck, CWEAVE and CTANGLE will both assign the same numbers to sections.

⟨ Global variables 17 ⟩ +≡
  extern sixteen_bits *section_count*;   /* the current section number */

83.   The body of *scan_section* is a loop where we look for control codes that are significant to CTANGLE: those that delimit a definition, the C part of a module, or a new module.

```
void scan_section( )
{
  name_pointer p;      /* section name for the current section */
  text_pointer q;      /* text for the current section */
  sixteen_bits a;      /* token for left-hand side of definition */
  section_count ++;  no_where ← 1;
  if (*(loc − 1) ≡ '*' ∧ show_progress) {      /* starred section */
    printf("*%d", section_count);
    update_terminal;
  }
  next_control ← 0;
  while (1) {
    ⟨ Skip ahead until next_control corresponds to @d, @<, @␣ or the like 84 ⟩;
    if (next_control ≡ definition) {      /* @d */
      ⟨ Scan a definition 85 ⟩
      continue;
    }
    if (next_control ≡ begin_C) {      /* @c or @p */
      p ← name_dir;
      break;
    }
    if (next_control ≡ section_name) {      /* @< or @( */
      p ← cur_section_name;
      ⟨ If section is not being defined, continue 86 ⟩;
      break;
    }
    return;      /* @␣ or @* */
  }
  no_where ← print_where ← 0;
  ⟨ Scan the C part of the current section 87 ⟩;
}
```

84.   At the top of this loop, if *next_control* ≡ *section_name*, the section name has already been scanned (see ⟨ Get control code and possible section name 68 ⟩). Thus, if we encounter *next_control* ≡ *section_name* in the skip-ahead process, we should likewise scan the section name, so later processing will be the same in both cases.

⟨ Skip ahead until *next_control* corresponds to @d, @<, @␣ or the like 84 ⟩ ≡
```
  while (next_control < definition)      /* definition is the lowest of the "significant" codes */
    if ((next_control ← skip_ahead( )) ≡ section_name) {
      loc −= 2;
      next_control ← get_next( );
    }
```
This code is used in section 83.

85. ⟨ Scan a definition 85 ⟩ ≡
```
  {
    while ((next_control ← get_next( )) ≡ '\n') ;        /* allow newline before definition */
    if (next_control ≠ identifier) {
      err_print("!␣Definition␣flushed,␣must␣start␣with␣identifier");
      continue;
    }
    app_repl(((a ← id_lookup(id_first, id_loc, 0) − name_dir)/°400) + °200);        /* append the lhs */
    app_repl(a % °400);
    if (*loc ≠ '(') {        /* identifier must be separated from replacement text */
      app_repl(string);
      app_repl('␣');
      app_repl(string);
    }
    scan_repl(macro);
    cur_text→text_link ← 0;        /* text_link ≡ 0 characterizes a macro */
  }
```
This code is used in section 83.

86. If the section name is not followed by = or +=, no C code is forthcoming: the section is being cited, not being defined. This use is illegal after the definition part of the current section has started, except inside a comment, but CTANGLE does not enforce this rule; it simply ignores the offending section name and everything following it, up to the next significant control code.

⟨ If section is not being defined, **continue** 86 ⟩ ≡
```
    while ((next_control ← get_next( )) ≡ '+') ;        /* allow optional += */
    if (next_control ≠ '=' ∧ next_control ≠ eq_eq) continue;
```
This code is used in section 83.

87. ⟨ Scan the C part of the current section 87 ⟩ ≡
```
    ⟨ Insert the section number into tok_mem 88 ⟩;
    scan_repl(section_name);        /* now cur_text points to the replacement text */
    ⟨ Update the data structure so that the replacement text is accessible 89 ⟩;
```
This code is used in section 83.

88. ⟨ Insert the section number into tok_mem 88 ⟩ ≡
```
    store_two_bytes((sixteen_bits)(°150000 + section_count));        /* °150000 ≡ °320 * °400 */
```
This code is used in section 87.

89. ⟨ Update the data structure so that the replacement text is accessible 89 ⟩ ≡
```
    if (p ≡ name_dir ∨ p ≡ 0) {        /* unnamed section, or bad section name */
      (last_unnamed)→text_link ← cur_text − text_info;
      last_unnamed ← cur_text;
    }
    else if (p→equiv ≡ (char *) text_info) p→equiv ← (char *) cur_text;        /* first section of this name */
    else {
      q ← (text_pointer) p→equiv;
      while (q→text_link < section_flag) q ← q→text_link + text_info;        /* find end of list */
      q→text_link ← cur_text − text_info;
    }
    cur_text→text_link ← section_flag;        /* mark this replacement text as a nonmacro */
```
This code is used in section 87.

90. ⟨ Predeclaration of procedures 2 ⟩ +≡
   void *phase_one* ( );

91.   **void** *phase_one* ( )
   {
      phase ← 1;
      section_count ← 0;
      reset_input ( );
      skip_limbo ( );
      while (¬*input_has_ended*) *scan_section* ( );
      check_complete ( );
      phase ← 2;
   }

92.   Only a small subset of the control codes is legal in limbo, so limbo processing is straightforward.
⟨ Predeclaration of procedures 2 ⟩ +≡
   void *skip_limbo* ( );

93.   **void** *skip_limbo* ( )
   {
      char *c*;
      while (1) {
         if (*loc* > *limit* ∧ *get_line* ( ) ≡ 0) **return**;
         ∗(*limit* + 1) ← '@';
         while (∗*loc* ≠ '@') *loc*++;
         if (*loc*++ ≤ *limit*) {
            c ← ∗*loc*++;
            if (*ccode*[(**eight_bits**) *c*] ≡ *new_section*) **break**;
            switch (*ccode*[(**eight_bits**) *c*]) {
            case *translit_code*: ⟨ Read in transliteration of a character 94 ⟩;
               break;
            case *format_code*: **case** '@': **break**;
            case *control_text*:
               if (*c* ≡ 'q' ∨ *c* ≡ 'Q') {
                  while ((*c* ← *skip_ahead* ( )) ≡ '@') ;
                  if (∗(*loc* − 1) ≠ '>') *err_print* ("!␣Double␣@␣should␣be␣used␣in␣control␣text");
                  break;
               }   /∗ otherwise fall through ∗/
            default: *err_print* ("!␣Double␣@␣should␣be␣used␣in␣limbo");
            }
         }
      }
   }

94.   ⟨ Read in transliteration of a character 94 ⟩ ≡
   while $(xisspace(*loc) \wedge loc < limit)$ $loc{+}{+}$;
   $loc \mathrel{+}= 3$;
   if $(loc > limit \vee \neg xisxdigit(*(loc - 3)) \vee \neg xisxdigit(*(loc - 2))$
       $\vee (*(loc - 3) \geq \text{'0'} \wedge *(loc - 3) \leq \text{'7'}) \vee \neg xisspace(*(loc - 1)))$
    $err\_print(\texttt{"!}\sqcup\texttt{Improper}\sqcup\texttt{hex}\sqcup\texttt{number}\sqcup\texttt{following}\sqcup\texttt{@l"})$;
   else {
     unsigned i;
     char $*beg$;
     $sscanf(loc - 3, \texttt{"\%x"}, \&i)$;
     while $(xisspace(*loc) \wedge loc < limit)$ $loc{+}{+}$;
     $beg \leftarrow loc$;
     while $(loc < limit \wedge (xisalpha(*loc) \vee xisdigit(*loc) \vee *loc \equiv \text{'\_'}))$ $loc{+}{+}$;
     if $(loc - beg \geq translit\_length)$ $err\_print(\texttt{"!}\sqcup\texttt{Replacement}\sqcup\texttt{string}\sqcup\texttt{in}\sqcup\texttt{@l}\sqcup\texttt{too}\sqcup\texttt{long"})$;
     else {
       $strncpy(translit[i - {}^{\circ}200], beg, loc - beg)$;
       $translit[i - {}^{\circ}200][loc - beg] \leftarrow \text{'\textbackslash 0'}$;
     }
   }
This code is used in section 93.

95.   Because on some systems the difference between two pointers is a **long** but not an **int**, we use **%ld** to print these quantities.
   void $print\_stats(\,)$
   {
     $printf(\texttt{"\textbackslash nMemory}\sqcup\texttt{usage}\sqcup\texttt{statistics:\textbackslash n"})$;
     $printf(\texttt{"\%ld}\sqcup\texttt{names}\sqcup\texttt{(out}\sqcup\texttt{of}\sqcup\texttt{\%ld)\textbackslash n"}, (\textbf{long})(name\_ptr - name\_dir), (\textbf{long})\ max\_names)$;
     $printf(\texttt{"\%ld}\sqcup\texttt{replacement}\sqcup\texttt{texts}\sqcup\texttt{(out}\sqcup\texttt{of}\sqcup\texttt{\%ld)\textbackslash n"}, (\textbf{long})(text\_ptr - text\_info), (\textbf{long})\ max\_texts)$;
     $printf(\texttt{"\%ld}\sqcup\texttt{bytes}\sqcup\texttt{(out}\sqcup\texttt{of}\sqcup\texttt{\%ld)\textbackslash n"}, (\textbf{long})(byte\_ptr - byte\_mem), (\textbf{long})\ max\_bytes)$;
     $printf(\texttt{"\%ld}\sqcup\texttt{tokens}\sqcup\texttt{(out}\sqcup\texttt{of}\sqcup\texttt{\%ld)\textbackslash n"}, (\textbf{long})(tok\_ptr - tok\_mem), (\textbf{long})\ max\_toks)$;
   }

96. Index.   Here is a cross-reference table for **CTANGLE**. All sections in which an identifier is used are listed with that identifier, except that reserved words are indexed only when they appear in format definitions, and the appearances of identifiers in section names are not indexed. Underlined entries correspond to where the identifier was declared. Error messages and a few other things like "ASCII code dependencies" are indexed here too.

⟨ Case of a section number 54 ⟩   Used in section 49.

⟨ Case of an identifier 53 ⟩   Used in section 49.

⟨ Cases like != 50 ⟩   Used in section 49.

⟨ Common code for **CWEAVE** and **CTANGLE** 5, 7, 8, 9, 10, 11, 12, 13, 14, 15 ⟩   Used in section 1.

⟨ Compress two-symbol operator 64 ⟩   Used in section 63.

⟨ Copy a string or verbatim construction or numerical constant 80 ⟩   Used in section 78.

⟨ Copy an ASCII constant 81 ⟩   Used in section 78.

⟨ Expand section $a - °24000$, **goto** *restart* 34 ⟩   Used in section 33.

⟨ Get a constant 66 ⟩   Used in section 63.

⟨ Get a string 67 ⟩   Used in section 63.

⟨ Get an identifier 65 ⟩   Used in section 63.

⟨ Get control code and possible section name 68 ⟩   Cited in section 84.   Used in section 63.

⟨ Global variables 17, 23, 28, 32, 36, 38, 45, 51, 56, 59, 61, 75, 82 ⟩   Used in section 1.

⟨ If end of name or erroneous nesting, **break** 73 ⟩   Used in section 72.

⟨ If it's not there, add *cur_section_name* to the output file stack, or complain we're out of room 40 ⟩   Used in section 70.

⟨ If section is not being defined, **continue** 86 ⟩   Used in section 83.

⟨ In cases that a is a non-**char** token (*identifier*, *section_name*, etc.), either process it and change a to a byte that should be stored, or **continue** if a should be ignored, or **goto** *done* if a signals the end of this replacement text 78 ⟩   Used in section 76.

⟨ Include files 6, 62 ⟩   Used in section 1.

⟨ Initialize the output stacks 29 ⟩   Used in section 42.

⟨ Insert the line number into *tok_mem* 77 ⟩   Used in sections 63, 76, and 78.

⟨ Insert the section number into *tok_mem* 88 ⟩   Used in section 87.

⟨ Output macro definitions if appropriate 44 ⟩   Used in section 42.

⟨ Predeclaration of procedures 2, 41, 46, 48, 90, 92 ⟩   Used in section 1.

⟨ Put section name into *section_text* 72 ⟩   Used in section 70.

⟨ Read in transliteration of a character 94 ⟩   Used in section 93.

⟨ Scan a definition 85 ⟩   Used in section 83.

⟨ Scan a verbatim string 74 ⟩   Used in section 68.

⟨ Scan an ASCII constant 69 ⟩   Used in section 68.

⟨ Scan the C part of the current section 87 ⟩   Used in section 83.

⟨ Scan the section name and make *cur_section_name* point to it 70 ⟩   Used in section 68.

⟨ Set initial values 18, 20, 24, 39, 52, 57, 71 ⟩   Used in section 3.

⟨ Skip ahead until *next_control* corresponds to @d, @<, @␣ or the like 84 ⟩   Used in section 83.

⟨ Typedef declarations 16, 27 ⟩   Used in section 1.

⟨ Update the data structure so that the replacement text is accessible 89 ⟩   Used in section 87.

⟨ Was an '@' missed here? 79 ⟩   Used in section 78.

⟨ Write all the named output files 43 ⟩   Used in section 42.

The CWEAVE processor

(Version 3.61)

1. Introduction. This is the CWEAVE program by Silvio Levy and Donald E. Knuth, based on WEAVE by Knuth. We are thankful to Steve Avery, Nelson Beebe, Hans-Hermann Bode (to whom the original C++ adaptation is due), Klaus Guntermann, Norman Ramsey, Tomas Rokicki, Joachim Schnitter, Joachim Schrod, Lee Wittenberg, Saroj Mahapatra, Cesar Augusto Rorato Crusius, and others who have contributed improvements.

The "banner line" defined here should be changed whenever CWEAVE is modified.

#**define** *banner*   "This␣is␣CWEAVE␣(Version␣3.61)\n"

⟨ Include files 6 ⟩
⟨ Preprocessor definitions ⟩
⟨ Common code for CWEAVE and CTANGLE 5 ⟩
⟨ Typedef declarations 18 ⟩
⟨ Global variables 17 ⟩
⟨ Predeclaration of procedures 2 ⟩

2. We predeclare several standard system functions here instead of including their system header files, because the names of the header files are not as standard as the names of the functions. (For example, some C environments have <string.h> where others have <strings.h>.)

⟨ Predeclaration of procedures 2 ⟩ ≡
  extern int *strlen*( );   /* length of string */
  extern int *strcmp*( );   /* compare strings lexicographically */
  extern char *strcpy*( );   /* copy one string to another */
  extern int *strncmp*( );   /* compare up to n string characters */
  extern char *strncpy*( );   /* copy up to n string characters */
See also sections 34, 39, 55, 59, 62, 64, 74, 83, 91, 114, 181, 194, 205, 212, 221, 225, 237, and 246.
This code is used in section 1.

3. CWEAVE has a fairly straightforward outline. It operates in three phases: First it inputs the source file and stores cross-reference data, then it inputs the source once again and produces the TEX output file, finally it sorts and outputs the index.

Please read the documentation for **common**, the set of routines common to CTANGLE and CWEAVE, before proceeding further.

  int *main*(*ac*, *av*)
    int *ac*;   /* argument count */
    char **av*;   /* argument values */
{
  argc ← *ac*;
  argv ← *av*;
  program ← *cweave*;
  make_xrefs ← *force_lines* ← 1;   /* controlled by command-line options */
  common_init( );
  ⟨ Set initial values 20 ⟩;
  if (*show_banner*) *printf*(*banner*);   /* print a "banner line" */
  ⟨ Store all the reserved words 28 ⟩;
  phase_one( );   /* read all the user's text and store the cross-references */
  phase_two( );   /* read all the text again and translate it to TEX form */
  phase_three( );   /* output the cross-reference index */
  return *wrap_up*( );   /* and exit gracefully */
}

4. The following parameters were sufficient in the original WEAVE to handle TₑX, so they should be sufficient for most applications of CWEAVE. If you change *max_bytes*, *max_names*, *hash_size*, or *buf_size* you have to change them also in the file "common.w".

#define *max_bytes* 90000   /* the number of bytes in identifiers, index entries, and section names */
#define *max_names* 4000   /* number of identifiers, strings, section names; must be less than 10240;
           used in "common.w" */
#define *max_sections* 2000   /* greater than the total number of sections */
#define *hash_size* 353   /* should be prime */
#define *buf_size* 100   /* maximum length of input line, plus one */
#define *longest_name* 10000   /* section names and strings shouldn't be longer than this */
#define *long_buf_size* (*buf_size* + *longest_name*)
#define *line_length* 80
          /* lines of TₑX output have at most this many characters; should be less than 256 */
#define *max_refs* 20000   /* number of cross-references; must be less than 65536 */
#define *max_toks* 20000   /* number of symbols in C texts being parsed; must be less than 65536 */
#define *max_texts* 4000   /* number of phrases in C texts being parsed; must be less than 10240 */
#define *max_scraps* 2000   /* number of tokens in C texts being parsed */
#define *stack_size* 400   /* number of simultaneous output levels */

5. The next few sections contain stuff from the file "common.w" that must be included in both "ctangle.w" and "cweave.w". It appears in file "common.h", which needs to be updated when "common.w" changes.

First comes general stuff:

#define *ctangle* 0
#define *cweave* 1

⟨ Common code for CWEAVE and CTANGLE 5 ⟩ ≡
   typedef short boolean;
   typedef char unsigned eight_bits;
   extern boolean *program*;   /* CWEAVE or CTANGLE? */
   extern int *phase*;   /* which phase are we in? */

See also sections 7, 8, 9, 10, 11, 12, 13, 14, and 15.

This code is used in section 1.

6. ⟨ Include files 6 ⟩ ≡
#include <stdio.h>

See also section 38.

This code is used in section 1.

7.   Code related to the character set:

#**define** *and_and* °*4*   /* '&&'; corresponds to MIT's ∧ */
#**define** *lt_lt* °*20*   /* '<<'; corresponds to MIT's ⊂ */
#**define** *gt_gt* °*21*   /* '>>'; corresponds to MIT's ⊃ */
#**define** *plus_plus* °*13*   /* '++'; corresponds to MIT's ↑ */
#**define** *minus_minus* °*1*   /* '--'; corresponds to MIT's ↓ */
#**define** *minus_gt* °*31*   /* '->'; corresponds to MIT's → */
#**define** *not_eq* °*32*   /* '!='; corresponds to MIT's ≠ */
#**define** *lt_eq* °*34*   /* '<='; corresponds to MIT's ≤ */
#**define** *gt_eq* °*35*   /* '>='; corresponds to MIT's ≥ */
#**define** *eq_eq* °*36*   /* '=='; corresponds to MIT's ≡ */
#**define** *or_or* °*37*   /* '||'; corresponds to MIT's ∨ */
#**define** *dot_dot_dot* °*16*   /* '...'; corresponds to MIT's ∞ */
#**define** *colon_colon* °*6*   /* '::'; corresponds to MIT's ∈ */
#**define** *period_ast* °*26*   /* '.*'; corresponds to MIT's ⊛ */
#**define** *minus_gt_ast* °*27*   /* '->*'; corresponds to MIT's ⇆ */

⟨ Common code for CWEAVE and CTANGLE 5 ⟩ +≡
    char *section_text*[*longest_name* + 1];   /* name being sought for */
    char **section_text_end* ← *section_text* + *longest_name*;   /* end of *section_text* */
    char **id_first*;   /* where the current identifier begins in the buffer */
    char **id_loc*;   /* just after the current identifier in the buffer */

8.   Code related to input routines:

#**define** *xisalpha*(*c*)   (*isalpha*(*c*) ∧ ((**eight_bits**) *c* < °*200*))
#**define** *xisdigit*(*c*)   (*isdigit*(*c*) ∧ ((**eight_bits**) *c* < °*200*))
#**define** *xisspace*(*c*)   (*isspace*(*c*) ∧ ((**eight_bits**) *c* < °*200*))
#**define** *xislower*(*c*)   (*islower*(*c*) ∧ ((**eight_bits**) *c* < °*200*))
#**define** *xisupper*(*c*)   (*isupper*(*c*) ∧ ((**eight_bits**) *c* < °*200*))
#**define** *xisxdigit*(*c*)   (*isxdigit*(*c*) ∧ ((**eight_bits**) *c* < °*200*))

⟨ Common code for CWEAVE and CTANGLE 5 ⟩ +≡
    extern char *buffer*[];   /* where each line of input goes */
    extern char **buffer_end*;   /* end of *buffer* */
    extern char **loc*;   /* points to the next character to be read from the buffer */
    extern char **limit*;   /* points to the last character in the buffer */

9.   Code related to identifier and section name storage:

#define $length(c)$ $(c+1)$-*byte_start* $-$ (c)-*byte_start*   /* the length of a name */
#define $print\_id(c)$ $term\_write((c)$-*byte_start*$, length((c)))$ /* print identifier */
#define *llink*   *link*   /* left link in binary search tree for section names */
#define *rlink*   *dummy.Rlink*   /* right link in binary search tree for section names */
#define *root*   *name_dir*-*rlink*   /* the root of the binary search tree for section names */
#define *chunk_marker*   0

⟨ Common code for **CWEAVE** and **CTANGLE** 5 ⟩ +≡
  typedef struct name_info {
    char **byte_start*;   /* beginning of the name in *byte_mem* */
    struct name_info **link*;
    union {
      struct name_info **Rlink*;   /* right link in binary search tree for section names */
      char *Ilk*;   /* used by identifiers in **CWEAVE** only */
    } *dummy*;
    char **equiv_or_xref*;   /* info corresponding to names */
  } **name_info**;   /* contains information about an identifier or section name */
  typedef name_info **name_pointer*;   /* pointer into array of **name_info**s */
  typedef name_pointer **hash_pointer*;
  extern char *byte_mem*[];   /* characters of names */
  extern char **byte_mem_end*;   /* end of *byte_mem* */
  extern name_info *name_dir*[];   /* information about names */
  extern name_pointer *name_dir_end*;   /* end of *name_dir* */
  extern name_pointer *name_ptr*;   /* first unused position in *byte_start* */
  extern char **byte_ptr*;   /* first unused position in *byte_mem* */
  extern name_pointer *hash*[];   /* heads of hash lists */
  extern hash_pointer *hash_end*;   /* end of *hash* */
  extern hash_pointer *h*;   /* index into hash-head array */
  extern name_pointer *id_lookup*( );   /* looks up a string in the identifier table */
  extern name_pointer *section_lookup*( );   /* finds section name */
  extern void *print_section_name*( ), *sprint_section_name*( );

10.   Code related to error handling:

#define *spotless*   0   /* *history* value for normal jobs */
#define *harmless_message*   1   /* *history* value when non-serious info was printed */
#define *error_message*   2   /* *history* value when an error was noted */
#define *fatal_message*   3   /* *history* value when we had to stop prematurely */
#define *mark_harmless*
        {
          if ($history \equiv spotless$) $history \leftarrow harmless\_message$;
        }
#define *mark_error* $history \leftarrow error\_message$
#define $confusion(s)$ $fatal(\texttt{"!\_This\_can't\_happen:\_"}, s)$

⟨ Common code for **CWEAVE** and **CTANGLE** 5 ⟩ +≡
  extern *history*;   /* indicates how bad this run was */
  extern *err_print*( );   /* print error message and context */
  extern *wrap_up*( );   /* indicate *history* and exit */
  extern void *fatal*( );   /* issue error message and die */
  extern void *overflow*( );   /* succumb because a table has overflowed */

11.   Code related to file handling:

    format *line*   *x*   /∗ make *line* an unreserved word ∗/
#define *max_file_name_length* 60
#define *cur_file* *file*[*include_depth*]   /∗ current file ∗/
#define *cur_file_name* *file_name*[*include_depth*]   /∗ current file name ∗/
#define *web_file_name* *file_name*[0]   /∗ main source file name ∗/
#define *cur_line* *line*[*include_depth*]   /∗ number of current line in current file ∗/
⟨ Common code for **CWEAVE** and **CTANGLE** 5 ⟩ +≡
  extern *include_depth*;   /∗ current level of nesting ∗/
  extern FILE ∗*file*[ ];   /∗ stack of non-change files ∗/
  extern FILE ∗*change_file*;   /∗ change file ∗/
  extern char *C_file_name*[ ];   /∗ name of *C_file* ∗/
  extern char *tex_file_name*[ ];   /∗ name of *tex_file* ∗/
  extern char *idx_file_name*[ ];   /∗ name of *idx_file* ∗/
  extern char *scn_file_name*[ ];   /∗ name of *scn_file* ∗/
  extern char *file_name*[ ][*max_file_name_length*];   /∗ stack of non-change file names ∗/
  extern char *change_file_name*[ ];   /∗ name of change file ∗/
  extern *line*[ ];   /∗ number of current line in the stacked files ∗/
  extern *change_line*;   /∗ number of current line in change file ∗/
  extern boolean *input_has_ended*;   /∗ if there is no more input ∗/
  extern boolean *changing*;   /∗ if the current line is from *change_file* ∗/
  extern boolean *web_file_open*;   /∗ if the web file is being read ∗/
  extern *reset_input*( );   /∗ initialize to read the web file and change file ∗/
  extern *get_line*( );   /∗ inputs the next line ∗/
  extern *check_complete*( );   /∗ checks that all changes were picked up ∗/

12.   Code related to section numbers:
⟨ Common code for **CWEAVE** and **CTANGLE** 5 ⟩ +≡
  typedef unsigned short sixteen_bits;
  extern sixteen_bits *section_count*;   /∗ the current section number ∗/
  extern boolean *changed_section*[ ];   /∗ is the section changed? ∗/
  extern boolean *change_pending*;   /∗ is a decision about change still unclear? ∗/
  extern boolean *print_where*;   /∗ tells **CTANGLE** to print line and file info ∗/

13.   Code related to command line arguments:
#define *show_banner* *flags*['b']   /∗ should the banner line be printed? ∗/
#define *show_progress* *flags*['p']   /∗ should progress reports be printed? ∗/
#define *show_happiness* *flags*['h']   /∗ should lack of errors be announced? ∗/
⟨ Common code for **CWEAVE** and **CTANGLE** 5 ⟩ +≡
  extern int *argc*;   /∗ copy of *ac* parameter to *main* ∗/
  extern char ∗∗*argv*;   /∗ copy of *av* parameter to *main* ∗/
  extern boolean *flags*[ ];   /∗ an option for each 7-bit code ∗/

14.   Code relating to output:

#define *update_terminal* *fflush*(*stdout*)   /* empty the terminal output buffer */
#define *new_line* *putchar*('\n')
#define *putxchar* *putchar*
#define *term_write*(*a*, *b*) *fflush*(*stdout*), *fwrite*(*a*, **sizeof**(**char**), *b*, *stdout*)
#define *C_printf*(*c*, *a*) *fprintf*(*C_file*, *c*, *a*)
#define *C_putc*(*c*) *putc*(*c*, *C_file*)
⟨ Common code for **CWEAVE** and **CTANGLE** 5 ⟩ +≡
  extern FILE *∗C_file*;   /* where output of **CTANGLE** goes */
  extern FILE *∗tex_file*;   /* where output of **CWEAVE** goes */
  extern FILE *∗idx_file*;   /* where index from **CWEAVE** goes */
  extern FILE *∗scn_file*;   /* where list of sections from **CWEAVE** goes */
  extern FILE *∗active_file*;   /* currently active file for **CWEAVE** output */

15.   The procedure that gets everything rolling:
⟨ Common code for **CWEAVE** and **CTANGLE** 5 ⟩ +≡
  extern void *common_init*( );

16.   Data structures exclusive to CWEAVE.   As explained in `common.w`, the field of a **name_info** structure that contains the *rlink* of a section name is used for a completely different purpose in the case of identifiers. It is then called the *ilk* of the identifier, and it is used to distinguish between various types of identifiers, as follows:

normal and *func_template* identifiers are part of the C program that will appear in italic type (or in typewriter type if all uppercase).

custom identifiers are part of the C program that will be typeset in special ways.

roman identifiers are index entries that appear after `@^` in the CWEB file.

wildcard identifiers are index entries that appear after `@:` in the CWEB file.

typewriter identifiers are index entries that appear after `@.` in the CWEB file.

alfop, ..., *template_like* identifiers are C or C++ reserved words whose *ilk* explains how they are to be treated when C code is being formatted.

#**define**   *ilk*   *dummy.Ilk*
#**define**   *normal*   0   /* ordinary identifiers have *normal* ilk */
#**define**   *roman*   1   /* normal index entries have *roman* ilk */
#**define**   *wildcard*   2   /* user-formatted index entries have *wildcard* ilk */
#**define**   *typewriter*   3   /* 'typewriter type' entries have *typewriter* ilk */
#**define**   *abnormal*(a)   (a→*ilk* > *typewriter*)   /* tells if a name is special */
#**define**   *func_template*   4   /* identifiers that can be followed by optional template */
#**define**   *custom*   5   /* identifiers with user-given control sequence */
#**define**   *alfop*   22   /* alphabetic operators like **and** or **not_eq** */
#**define**   *else_like*   26   /* **else** */
#**define**   *public_like*   40   /* **public**, **private**, **protected** */
#**define**   *operator_like*   41   /* **operator** */
#**define**   *new_like*   42   /* **new** */
#**define**   *catch_like*   43   /* **catch** */
#**define**   *for_like*   45   /* **for**, **switch**, **while** */
#**define**   *do_like*   46   /* **do** */
#**define**   *if_like*   47   /* **if**, **ifdef**, **endif**, **pragma**, ... */
#**define**   *delete_like*   48   /* **delete** */
#**define**   *raw_ubin*   49   /* '**&**' or '*****' when looking for **const** following */
#**define**   *const_like*   50   /* **const**, **volatile** */
#**define**   *raw_int*   51   /* **int**, **char**, ...; also structure and class names */
#**define**   *int_like*   52   /* same, when not followed by left parenthesis or :: */
#**define**   *case_like*   53   /* **case**, **return**, **goto**, **break**, **continue** */
#**define**   *sizeof_like*   54   /* **sizeof** */
#**define**   *struct_like*   55   /* **struct**, **union**, **enum**, **class** */
#**define**   *typedef_like*   56   /* **typedef** */
#**define**   *define_like*   57   /* **define** */
#**define**   *template_like*   58   /* **template** */

17.   We keep track of the current section number in *section_count*, which is the total number of sections that have started. Sections which have been altered by a change file entry have their *changed_section* flag turned on during the first phase.

⟨ Global variables 17 ⟩ ≡
   boolean *change_exists*;   /* has any section changed? */

See also sections 19, 25, 31, 37, 41, 43, 58, 68, 73, 77, 97, 104, 108, 168, 187, 191, 207, 216, 227, 229, 233, 235, and 244.

This code is used in section 1.

18. The other large memory area in **CWEAVE** keeps the cross-reference data. All uses of the name p are recorded in a linked list beginning at $p\text{-}xref$, which points into the $xmem$ array. The elements of $xmem$ are structures consisting of an integer, num, and a pointer $xlink$ to another element of $xmem$. If $x \leftarrow p\text{-}xref$ is a pointer into $xmem$, the value of $x\text{-}num$ is either a section number where p is used, or $cite\_flag$ plus a section number where p is mentioned, or def_flag plus a section number where p is defined; and $x\text{-}xlink$ points to the next such cross-reference for p, if any. This list of cross-references is in decreasing order by section number. The next unused slot in $xmem$ is $xref\_ptr$. The linked list ends at $\&xmem[0]$.

The global variable $xref\_switch$ is set either to def_flag or to zero, depending on whether the next cross-reference to an identifier is to be underlined or not in the index. This switch is set to def_flag when @! or @d is scanned, and it is cleared to zero when the next identifier or index entry cross-reference has been made. Similarly, the global variable $section\_xref\_switch$ is either def_flag or $cite\_flag$ or zero, depending on whether a section name is being defined, cited or used in C text.

⟨ Typedef declarations 18 ⟩ ≡
  typedef struct xref_info {
    sixteen_bits num;   /∗ section number plus zero or def_flag ∗/
    struct xref_info ∗$xlink$;   /∗ pointer to the previous cross-reference ∗/
  } **xref_info**;
  typedef xref_info ∗**xref_pointer**;

See also sections 24, 103, and 186.

This code is used in section 1.

19. ⟨ Global variables 17 ⟩ +≡
  xref_info $xmem[max\_refs]$;   /∗ contains cross-reference information ∗/
  xref_pointer $xmem\_end \leftarrow xmem + max\_refs - 1$;
  xref_pointer $xref\_ptr$;   /∗ the largest occupied position in $xmem$ ∗/
  sixteen_bits $xref\_switch, section\_xref\_switch$;   /∗ either zero or def_flag ∗/

20. A section that is used for multi-file output (with the @(feature) has a special first cross-reference whose num field is $file\_flag$.

#**define** $file\_flag$ $(3 * cite\_flag)$
#**define** def_flag $(2 * cite\_flag)$
#**define** $cite\_flag$ 10240   /∗ must be strictly larger than $max\_sections$ ∗/
#**define** $xref$ $equiv\_or\_xref$

⟨ Set initial values 20 ⟩ ≡
  $xref\_ptr \leftarrow xmem$;
  $name\_dir\text{-}xref \leftarrow$ (**char** ∗) $xmem$;
  $xref\_switch \leftarrow 0$;
  $section\_xref\_switch \leftarrow 0$;
  $xmem\text{-}num \leftarrow 0$;   /∗ sentinel value ∗/

See also sections 26, 32, 52, 80, 82, 98, 105, 188, 234, and 236.

This code is used in section 3.

21. A new cross-reference for an identifier is formed by calling *new_xref*, which discards duplicate entries and ignores non-underlined references to one-letter identifiers or C's reserved words.

If the user has sent the *no_xref* flag (the **-x** option of the command line), it is unnecessary to keep track of cross-references for identifiers. If one were careful, one could probably make more changes around section 100 to avoid a lot of identifier looking up.

#define *append_xref*(c)
        if (*xref_ptr* ≡ *xmem_end*) *overflow*("cross-reference");
        else (++*xref_ptr*)→*num* ← c;
#define *no_xref* (*flags*['x'] ≡ 0)
#define *make_xrefs* *flags*['x']   /* should cross references be output? */
#define *is_tiny*(p) ((p + 1)→*byte_start* ≡ (p)→*byte_start* + 1)
#define *unindexed*(a) (a < *res_wd_end* ∧ a→*ilk* ≥ *custom*)
        /* tells if uses of a name are to be indexed */

  void *new_xref*(p)
     name_pointer p;
  {
    xref_pointer q;   /* pointer to previous cross-reference */
    sixteen_bits m, n;   /* new and previous cross-reference value */
    if (*no_xref*) **return**;
    if ((*unindexed*(p) ∨ *is_tiny*(p)) ∧ *xref_switch* ≡ 0) **return**;
    m ← *section_count* + *xref_switch*;
    xref_switch ← 0;
    q ← (**xref_pointer**) p→*xref*;
    if (q ≠ *xmem*) {
      n ← q→*num*;
      if (n ≡ m ∨ n ≡ m + *def_flag*) **return**;
      else if (m ≡ n + *def_flag*) {
        q→*num* ← m;
        return;
      }
    }
    append_xref(m);
    xref_ptr→*xlink* ← q;
    p→*xref* ← (**char** *) *xref_ptr*;
  }

22.   The cross-reference lists for section names are slightly different. Suppose that a section name is defined in sections $m_1, \ldots, m_k$, cited in sections $n_1, \ldots, n_l$, and used in sections $p_1, \ldots, p_j$. Then its list will contain $m_1 + def\_flag, \ldots, m_k + def\_flag, n_1 + cite\_flag, \ldots, n_l + cite\_flag, p_1, \ldots, p_j$, in this order.

Although this method of storage takes quadratic time with respect to the length of the list, under foreseeable uses of **CWEAVE** this inefficiency is insignificant.

```
void new_section_xref(p)
    name_pointer p;
{
    xref_pointer q, r;      /* pointers to previous cross-references */
    q ← (xref_pointer) p→xref;
    r ← xmem;
    if (q > xmem)
        while (q→num > section_xref_switch) {
            r ← q;
            q ← q→xlink;
        }
    if (r→num ≡ section_count + section_xref_switch) return;    /* don't duplicate entries */
    append_xref(section_count + section_xref_switch);
    xref_ptr→xlink ← q;
    section_xref_switch ← 0;
    if (r ≡ xmem) p→xref ← (char *) xref_ptr;
    else r→xlink ← xref_ptr;
}
```

23.   The cross-reference list for a section name may also begin with *file_flag*. Here's how that flag gets put in.

```
void set_file_flag(p)
    name_pointer p;
{
    xref_pointer q;
    q ← (xref_pointer) p→xref;
    if (q→num ≡ file_flag) return;
    append_xref(file_flag);
    xref_ptr→xlink ← q;
    p→xref ← (char *) xref_ptr;
}
```

24.   A third large area of memory is used for sixteen-bit 'tokens', which appear in short lists similar to the strings of characters in *byte_mem*. Token lists are used to contain the result of C code translated into TEX form; further details about them will be explained later. A *text_pointer* variable is an index into *tok_start*.

⟨ Typedef declarations 18 ⟩ +≡
```
    typedef sixteen_bits token;
    typedef token *token_pointer;
    typedef token_pointer *text_pointer;
```

25. The first position of *tok_mem* that is unoccupied by replacement text is called *tok_ptr*, and the first unused location of *tok_start* is called *text_ptr*. Thus, we usually have $*text\_ptr \equiv tok\_ptr$.

⟨ Global variables 17 ⟩ +≡
  token *tok_mem*[*max_toks*];   /* tokens */
  token_pointer *tok_mem_end* ← *tok_mem* + *max_toks* − 1;   /* end of *tok_mem* */
  token_pointer *tok_start*[*max_texts*];   /* directory into *tok_mem* */
  token_pointer *tok_ptr*;   /* first unused position in *tok_mem* */
  text_pointer *text_ptr*;   /* first unused position in *tok_start* */
  text_pointer *tok_start_end* ← *tok_start* + *max_texts* − 1;   /* end of *tok_start* */
  token_pointer *max_tok_ptr*;   /* largest value of *tok_ptr* */
  text_pointer *max_text_ptr*;   /* largest value of *text_ptr* */

26. ⟨ Set initial values 20 ⟩ +≡
  tok_ptr ← *tok_mem* + 1;
  text_ptr ← *tok_start* + 1;
  tok_start[0] ← *tok_mem* + 1;
  tok_start[1] ← *tok_mem* + 1;
  max_tok_ptr ← *tok_mem* + 1;
  max_text_ptr ← *tok_start* + 1;

27. Here are the three procedures needed to complete *id_lookup*:

```
int names_match(p, first, l, t)
    name_pointer p;       /* points to the proposed match */
    char *first;       /* position of first character of string */
    int l;       /* length of identifier */
    eight_bits t;       /* desired ilk */
{
  if (length(p) ≠ l) return 0;
  if (p⃗ilk ≠ t ∧ ¬(t ≡ normal ∧ abnormal(p))) return 0;
  return ¬strncmp(first, p⃗byte_start, l);
}
void init_p(p, t)
    name_pointer p;
    eight_bits t;
{
  p⃗ilk ← t;
  p⃗xref ← (char *) xmem;
}
void init_node(p)
    name_pointer p;
{
  p⃗xref ← (char *) xmem;
}
```

28. We have to get C's reserved words into the hash table, and the simplest way to do this is to insert them every time CWEAVE is run. Fortunately there are relatively few reserved words. (Some of these are not strictly "reserved," but are defined in header files of the ISO Standard C Library.)

⟨ Store all the reserved words 28 ⟩ ≡
  id_lookup("and", Λ, *alfop*);
  id_lookup("and_eq", Λ, *alfop*);
  id_lookup("asm", Λ, *sizeof_like*);
  id_lookup("auto", Λ, *int_like*);
  id_lookup("bitand", Λ, *alfop*);
  id_lookup("bitor", Λ, *alfop*);
  id_lookup("bool", Λ, *raw_int*);
  id_lookup("break", Λ, *case_like*);
  id_lookup("case", Λ, *case_like*);
  id_lookup("catch", Λ, *catch_like*);
  id_lookup("char", Λ, *raw_int*);
  id_lookup("class", Λ, *struct_like*);
  id_lookup("clock_t", Λ, *raw_int*);
  id_lookup("compl", Λ, *alfop*);
  id_lookup("const", Λ, *const_like*);
  id_lookup("const_cast", Λ, *raw_int*);
  id_lookup("continue", Λ, *case_like*);
  id_lookup("default", Λ, *case_like*);
  id_lookup("define", Λ, *define_like*);
  id_lookup("defined", Λ, *sizeof_like*);
  id_lookup("delete", Λ, *delete_like*);
  id_lookup("div_t", Λ, *raw_int*);
  id_lookup("do", Λ, *do_like*);
  id_lookup("double", Λ, *raw_int*);
  id_lookup("dynamic_cast", Λ, *raw_int*);
  id_lookup("elif", Λ, *if_like*);
  id_lookup("else", Λ, *else_like*);
  id_lookup("endif", Λ, *if_like*);
  id_lookup("enum", Λ, *struct_like*);
  id_lookup("error", Λ, *if_like*);
  id_lookup("explicit", Λ, *int_like*);
  id_lookup("export", Λ, *int_like*);
  id_lookup("extern", Λ, *int_like*);
  id_lookup("FILE", Λ, *raw_int*);
  id_lookup("float", Λ, *raw_int*);
  id_lookup("for", Λ, *for_like*);
  id_lookup("fpos_t", Λ, *raw_int*);
  id_lookup("friend", Λ, *int_like*);
  id_lookup("goto", Λ, *case_like*);
  id_lookup("if", Λ, *if_like*);
  id_lookup("ifdef", Λ, *if_like*);
  id_lookup("ifndef", Λ, *if_like*);
  id_lookup("include", Λ, *if_like*);
  id_lookup("inline", Λ, *int_like*);
  id_lookup("int", Λ, *raw_int*);
  id_lookup("jmp_buf", Λ, *raw_int*);
  id_lookup("ldiv_t", Λ, *raw_int*);
  id_lookup("line", Λ, *if_like*);

id_lookup("long", Λ, *raw_int*);
id_lookup("mutable", Λ, *int_like*);
id_lookup("namespace", Λ, *struct_like*);
id_lookup("new", Λ, *new_like*);
id_lookup("not", Λ, *alfop*);
id_lookup("not_eq", Λ, *alfop*);
id_lookup("NULL", Λ, *custom*);
id_lookup("offsetof", Λ, *raw_int*);
id_lookup("operator", Λ, *operator_like*);
id_lookup("or", Λ, *alfop*);
id_lookup("or_eq", Λ, *alfop*);
id_lookup("pragma", Λ, *if_like*);
id_lookup("private", Λ, *public_like*);
id_lookup("protected", Λ, *public_like*);
id_lookup("ptrdiff_t", Λ, *raw_int*);
id_lookup("public", Λ, *public_like*);
id_lookup("register", Λ, *int_like*);
id_lookup("reinterpret_cast", Λ, *raw_int*);
id_lookup("return", Λ, *case_like*);
id_lookup("short", Λ, *raw_int*);
id_lookup("sig_atomic_t", Λ, *raw_int*);
id_lookup("signed", Λ, *raw_int*);
id_lookup("size_t", Λ, *raw_int*);
id_lookup("sizeof", Λ, *sizeof_like*);
id_lookup("static", Λ, *int_like*);
id_lookup("static_cast", Λ, *raw_int*);
id_lookup("struct", Λ, *struct_like*);
id_lookup("switch", Λ, *for_like*);
id_lookup("template", Λ, *template_like*);
id_lookup("this", Λ, *custom*);
id_lookup("throw", Λ, *case_like*);
id_lookup("time_t", Λ, *raw_int*);
id_lookup("try", Λ, *else_like*);
id_lookup("typedef", Λ, *typedef_like*);
id_lookup("typeid", Λ, *raw_int*);
id_lookup("typename", Λ, *struct_like*);
id_lookup("undef", Λ, *if_like*);
id_lookup("union", Λ, *struct_like*);
id_lookup("unsigned", Λ, *raw_int*);
id_lookup("using", Λ, *int_like*);
id_lookup("va_dcl", Λ, *decl*);   /* Berkeley's variable-arg-list convention */
id_lookup("va_list", Λ, *raw_int*);   /* ditto */
id_lookup("virtual", Λ, *int_like*);
id_lookup("void", Λ, *raw_int*);
id_lookup("volatile", Λ, *const_like*);
id_lookup("wchar_t", Λ, *raw_int*);
id_lookup("while", Λ, *for_like*);
id_lookup("xor", Λ, *alfop*);
id_lookup("xor_eq", Λ, *alfop*);
res_wd_end ← *name_ptr*;
id_lookup("TeX", Λ, *custom*);
id_lookup("make_pair", Λ, *func_template*);

This code is used in section 3.

29.   Lexical scanning.   Let us now consider the subroutines that read the CWEB source file and break it into meaningful units. There are four such procedures: One simply skips to the next '@␣' or '@*' that begins a section; another passes over the TEX text at the beginning of a section; the third passes over the TEX text in a C comment; and the last, which is the most interesting, gets the next token of a C text. They all use the pointers *limit* and *loc* into the line of input currently being studied.

30.   Control codes in CWEB, which begin with '@', are converted into a numeric code designed to simplify CWEAVE's logic; for example, larger numbers are given to the control codes that denote more significant milestones, and the code of *new_section* should be the largest of all. Some of these numeric control codes take the place of **char** control codes that will not otherwise appear in the output of the scanning routines.

#define *ignore* °0   /∗ control code of no interest to CWEAVE ∗/
#define *verbatim* °2   /∗ takes the place of extended ASCII *α* ∗/
#define *begin_short_comment* °3   /∗ C++ short comment ∗/
#define *begin_comment* '\t'   /∗ tab marks will not appear ∗/
#define *underline* '\n'   /∗ this code will be intercepted without confusion ∗/
#define *noop* °177   /∗ takes the place of ASCII delete ∗/
#define *xref_roman* °203   /∗ control code for '@^' ∗/
#define *xref_wildcard* °204   /∗ control code for '@:' ∗/
#define *xref_typewriter* °205   /∗ control code for '@.' ∗/
#define *TEX_string* °206   /∗ control code for '@t' ∗/
    format *TeX_string* *TeX*
#define *ord* °207   /∗ control code for '@'' ∗/
#define *join* °210   /∗ control code for '@&' ∗/
#define *thin_space* °211   /∗ control code for '@,' ∗/
#define *math_break* °212   /∗ control code for '@|' ∗/
#define *line_break* °213   /∗ control code for '@/' ∗/
#define *big_line_break* °214   /∗ control code for '@#' ∗/
#define *no_line_break* °215   /∗ control code for '@+' ∗/
#define *pseudo_semi* °216   /∗ control code for '@;' ∗/
#define *macro_arg_open* °220   /∗ control code for '@[' ∗/
#define *macro_arg_close* °221   /∗ control code for '@]' ∗/
#define *trace* °222   /∗ control code for '@0', '@1' and '@2' ∗/
#define *translit_code* °223   /∗ control code for '@l' ∗/
#define *output_defs_code* °224   /∗ control code for '@h' ∗/
#define *format_code* °225   /∗ control code for '@f' and '@s' ∗/
#define *definition* °226   /∗ control code for '@d' ∗/
#define *begin_C* °227   /∗ control code for '@c' ∗/
#define *section_name* °230   /∗ control code for '@<' ∗/
#define *new_section* °231   /∗ control code for '@␣' and '@*' ∗/

31.   Control codes are converted to CWEAVE's internal representation by means of the table *ccode*.
⟨ Global variables 17 ⟩ +≡
    eight_bits *ccode*[256];   /∗ meaning of a char following @ ∗/

32.   ⟨ Set initial values 20 ⟩ +≡
```
{
  int c;
  for (c ← 0; c < 256; c++) ccode[c] ← 0;
}
```
$ccode['\textvisiblespace'] \leftarrow ccode['\backslash t'] \leftarrow ccode['\backslash n'] \leftarrow ccode['\backslash v'] \leftarrow ccode['\backslash r'] \leftarrow ccode['\backslash f'] \leftarrow ccode['*'] \leftarrow$
  new_section;
$ccode['@'] \leftarrow '@';$ /* 'quoted' at sign */
$ccode['='] \leftarrow$ *verbatim*;
$ccode['d'] \leftarrow ccode['D'] \leftarrow$ *definition*;
$ccode['f'] \leftarrow ccode['F'] \leftarrow ccode['s'] \leftarrow ccode['S'] \leftarrow$ *format_code*;
$ccode['c'] \leftarrow ccode['C'] \leftarrow ccode['p'] \leftarrow ccode['P'] \leftarrow$ *begin_C*;
$ccode['t'] \leftarrow ccode['T'] \leftarrow$ *TEX_string*;
$ccode['l'] \leftarrow ccode['L'] \leftarrow$ *translit_code*;
$ccode['q'] \leftarrow ccode['Q'] \leftarrow$ *noop*;
$ccode['h'] \leftarrow ccode['H'] \leftarrow$ *output_defs_code*;
$ccode['\&'] \leftarrow$ *join*;
$ccode['<'] \leftarrow ccode['('] \leftarrow$ *section_name*;
$ccode['!'] \leftarrow$ *underline*;
$ccode['\^{}'] \leftarrow$ *xref_roman*;
$ccode[':'] \leftarrow$ *xref_wildcard*;
$ccode['.'] \leftarrow$ *xref_typewriter*;
$ccode[','] \leftarrow$ *thin_space*;
$ccode['|'] \leftarrow$ *math_break*;
$ccode['/'] \leftarrow$ *line_break*;
$ccode['\#'] \leftarrow$ *big_line_break*;
$ccode['+'] \leftarrow$ *no_line_break*;
$ccode[';'] \leftarrow$ *pseudo_semi*;
$ccode['['] \leftarrow$ *macro_arg_open*;
$ccode[']'] \leftarrow$ *macro_arg_close*;
$ccode['\backslash''] \leftarrow$ *ord*;
⟨ Special control codes for debugging 33 ⟩

33.   Users can write @2, @1, and @0 to turn tracing fully on, partly on, and off, respectively.

⟨ Special control codes for debugging 33 ⟩ ≡
  $ccode['0'] \leftarrow ccode['1'] \leftarrow ccode['2'] \leftarrow$ *trace*;
This code is used in section 32.

34.   The *skip_limbo* routine is used on the first pass to skip through portions of the input that are not in any sections, i.e., that precede the first section. After this procedure has been called, the value of *input_has_ended* will tell whether or not a section has actually been found.

   There's a complication that we will postpone until later: If the @s operation appears in limbo, we want to use it to adjust the default interpretation of identifiers.

⟨ Predeclaration of procedures 2 ⟩ +≡
  void *skip_limbo*( );

35.   **void** *skip_limbo*( )
```
{
  while (1) {
    if (loc > limit ∧ get_line( ) ≡ 0) return;
    *(limit + 1) ← '@';
    while (*loc ≠ '@') loc ++;      /* look for '@', then skip two chars */
    if (loc ++ ≤ limit) {
      int c ← ccode[(eight_bits) *loc ++];
      if (c ≡ new_section) return;
      if (c ≡ noop) skip_restricted( );
      else if (c ≡ format_code) ⟨Process simple format in limbo 71⟩;
    }
  }
}
```

36.   The *skip_TEX* routine is used on the first pass to skip through the TEX code at the beginning of a section. It returns the next control code or '|' found in the input. A *new_section* is assumed to exist at the very end of the file.

format   *skip_TeX*   *TeX*

unsigned *skip_TEX*( )   /* skip past pure TEX code */
```
{
  while (1) {
    if (loc > limit ∧ get_line( ) ≡ 0) return (new_section);
    *(limit + 1) ← '@';
    while (*loc ≠ '@' ∧ *loc ≠ '|') loc ++;
    if (*loc ++ ≡ '|') return ('|');
    if (loc ≤ limit) return (ccode[(eight_bits) *(loc ++)]);
  }
}
```

37. Inputting the next token.   As stated above, CWEAVE's most interesting lexical scanning routine is the *get_next* function that inputs the next token of C input. However, *get_next* is not especially complicated.

The result of *get_next* is either a **char** code for some special character, or it is a special code representing a pair of characters (e.g., '!='), or it is the numeric value computed by the *ccode* table, or it is one of the following special codes:

identifier: In this case the global variables *id_first* and *id_loc* will have been set to the beginning and ending-plus-one locations in the buffer, as required by the *id_lookup* routine.

string: The string will have been copied into the array *section_text*; *id_first* and *id_loc* are set as above (now they are pointers into *section_text*).

constant: The constant is copied into *section_text*, with slight modifications; *id_first* and *id_loc* are set.

Furthermore, some of the control codes cause *get_next* to take additional actions:

xref_roman, *xref_wildcard*, *xref_typewriter*, *TEX_string*, *verbatim*: The values of *id_first* and *id_loc* will have been set to the beginning and ending-plus-one locations in the buffer.

section_name: In this case the global variable *cur_section* will point to the *byte_start* entry for the section name that has just been scanned. The value of *cur_section_char* will be '(' if the section name was preceded by @(instead of @<.

If *get_next* sees '@!' it sets *xref_switch* to *def_flag* and goes on to the next token.

```
#define  constant   °200      /* C constant */
#define  string      °201      /* C string */
#define  identifier  °202      /* C identifier or reserved word */
```

⟨ Global variables 17 ⟩ +≡
  name_pointer *cur_section*;   /* name of section just scanned */
  char *cur_section_char*;   /* the character just before that name */

38.   ⟨ Include files 6 ⟩ +≡
```
#include <ctype.h>     /* definition of isalpha, isdigit and so on */
#include <stdlib.h>      /* definition of exit */
```

39.   As one might expect, *get_next* consists mostly of a big switch that branches to the various special cases that can arise. C allows underscores to appear in identifiers, and some C compilers even allow the dollar sign.

```
#define  isxalpha(c)  ((c) ≡ '_' ∨ (c) ≡ '$')     /* non-alpha characters allowed in identifier */
#define  ishigh(c)    ((eight_bits)(c) > °177)
```

⟨ Predeclaration of procedures 2 ⟩ +≡
  eight_bits *get_next*( );

40.   **eight_bits** $get\_next()$ /* produces the next input token */
  { **eight_bits** c;   /* the current character */
    while (1) {
      ⟨ Check if we're at the end of a preprocessor command 45 ⟩;
      if $(loc > limit \wedge get\_line() \equiv 0)$ **return** $(new\_section)$;
      $c \leftarrow *(loc \mathbin{++})$;
      if $(xisdigit(c) \vee c \equiv \text{'\textbackslash\textbackslash'} \vee c \equiv \text{'.'})$ ⟨ Get a constant 48 ⟩
      else if $(c \equiv \text{'\textbackslash''} \vee c \equiv \text{'"'} \vee (c \equiv \text{'L'} \wedge (*loc \equiv \text{'\textbackslash''} \vee *loc \equiv \text{'"'}))$
            $\vee \ (c \equiv \text{'<'} \wedge sharp\_include\_line \equiv 1))$ ⟨ Get a string 49 ⟩
      else if $(xisalpha(c) \vee isxalpha(c) \vee ishigh(c))$ ⟨ Get an identifier 47 ⟩
      else if $(c \equiv \text{'@'})$ ⟨ Get control code and possible section name 50 ⟩
      else if $(xisspace(c))$ **continue**;   /* ignore spaces and tabs */
      if $(c \equiv \text{'\#'} \wedge loc \equiv buffer + 1)$ ⟨ Raise preprocessor flag 42 ⟩;
    $mistake$: ⟨ Compress two-symbol operator 46 ⟩
      return (c);
    }
  }

41.   Because preprocessor commands do not fit in with the rest of the syntax of C, we have to deal with them separately. One solution is to enclose such commands between special markers. Thus, when a # is seen as the first character of a line, get_next returns a special code $left\_preproc$ and raises a flag $preprocessing$.

  We can use the same internal code number for $left\_preproc$ as we do for ord, since get_next changes ord into a string.

#define $left\_preproc$ ord /* begins a preprocessor command */
#define $right\_preproc$ $°217$ /* ends a preprocessor command */
⟨ Global variables 17 ⟩ +≡
  boolean $preprocessing \leftarrow 0$;   /* are we scanning a preprocessor command? */

42.   ⟨ Raise preprocessor flag 42 ⟩ ≡
  {
    $preprocessing \leftarrow 1$;
    ⟨ Check if next token is **include** 44 ⟩;
    return $(left\_preproc)$;
  }
This code is used in section 40.

43.   An additional complication is the freakish use of < and > to delimit a file name in lines that start with #include. We must treat this file name as a string.
⟨ Global variables 17 ⟩ +≡
  boolean $sharp\_include\_line \leftarrow 0$;   /* are we scanning a # **include** line? */

44.   ⟨ Check if next token is **include** 44 ⟩ ≡
  while $(loc \leq buffer\_end - 7 \wedge xisspace(*loc))$ $loc \mathbin{++}$;
  if $(loc \leq buffer\_end - 6 \wedge strncmp(loc, \text{"include"}, 7) \equiv 0)$ $sharp\_include\_line \leftarrow 1$;
This code is used in section 42.

45.   When we get to the end of a preprocessor line, we lower the flag and send a code *right_preproc*, unless the last character was a \.

⟨ Check if we're at the end of a preprocessor command 45 ⟩ ≡
 while (*loc* ≡ *limit* − 1 ∧ *preprocessing* ∧ *loc ≡ ' \\ ')
  if (*get_line*( ) ≡ 0) **return** (*new_section*); /* still in preprocessor mode */
 if (*loc* ≥ *limit* ∧ *preprocessing*) {
  preprocessing ← *sharp_include_line* ← 0;
  return (*right_preproc*);
 }

This code is used in section 40.

46.   The following code assigns values to the combinations ++, --, ->, >=, <=, ==, <<, >>, !=, ||, and
&&, and to the C++ combinations ..., ::, .* and ->*. The compound assignment operators (e.g., +=) are
treated as separate tokens.

#define *compress*(*c*) **if** (*loc* ++ ≤ *limit*) **return** (*c*)
⟨ Compress two-symbol operator 46 ⟩ ≡
  switch (*c*) {
  case '/':
    if (∗*loc* ≡ '∗') {
      compress(*begin_comment*);
    }
    else if (∗*loc* ≡ '/') *compress*(*begin_short_comment*);
    break;
  case '+':
    if (∗*loc* ≡ '+') *compress*(*plus_plus*);
    break;
  case '-':
    if (∗*loc* ≡ '-') {
      compress(*minus_minus*);
    }
    else if (∗*loc* ≡ '>')
      if (∗(*loc* + 1) ≡ '∗') {
        loc ++;
        compress(*minus_gt_ast*);
      }
      else *compress*(*minus_gt*);
    break;
  case '.':
    if (∗*loc* ≡ '∗') {
      compress(*period_ast*);
    }
    else if (∗*loc* ≡ '.' ∧ ∗(*loc* + 1) ≡ '.') {
      loc ++;
      compress(*dot_dot_dot*);
    }
    break;
  case ':':
    if (∗*loc* ≡ ':') *compress*(*colon_colon*);
    break;
  case '=':
    if (∗*loc* ≡ '=') *compress*(*eq_eq*);
    break;
  case '>':
    if (∗*loc* ≡ '=') {
      compress(*gt_eq*);
    }
    else if (∗*loc* ≡ '>') *compress*(*gt_gt*);
    break;
  case '<':
    if (∗*loc* ≡ '=') {
      compress(*lt_eq*);
    }
    else if (∗*loc* ≡ '<') *compress*(*lt_lt*);

```
    break;
case '&':
    if (*loc ≡ '&') compress(and_and);
    break;
case '|':
    if (*loc ≡ '|') compress(or_or);
    break;
case '!':
    if (*loc ≡ '=') compress(not_eq);
    break;
}
```

This code is used in section 40.

47. ⟨ Get an identifier 47 ⟩ ≡

```
{
    id_first ← −−loc;
    while (isalpha(*++loc) ∨ isdigit(*loc) ∨ isxalpha(*loc) ∨ ishigh(*loc)) ;
    id_loc ← loc;
    return (identifier);
}
```

This code is used in section 40.

48.   Different conventions are followed by TEX and C to express octal and hexadecimal numbers; it is reasonable to stick to each convention within its realm. Thus the C part of a **CWEB** file has octals introduced by 0 and hexadecimals by 0x, but **CWEAVE** will print with TEX/ macros that the user can redefine to fit the context. In order to simplify such macros, we replace some of the characters.

Notice that in this section and the next, id_first and id_loc are pointers into the array $section\_text$, not into $buffer$.

⟨ Get a constant 48 ⟩ ≡
```
  {
    id_first ← id_loc ← section_text + 1;
    if (*(loc − 1) ≡ '\\') {
      *id_loc ++ ← '~';
      while (xisdigit(*loc)) *id_loc ++ ← *loc ++;
    }     /* octal constant */
    else if (*(loc − 1) ≡ '0') {
      if (*loc ≡ 'x' ∨ *loc ≡ 'X') {
        *id_loc ++ ← '^';
        loc ++;
        while (xisxdigit(*loc)) *id_loc ++ ← *loc ++;
      }     /* hex constant */
      else if (xisdigit(*loc)) {
        *id_loc ++ ← '~';
        while (xisdigit(*loc)) *id_loc ++ ← *loc ++;
      }     /* octal constant */
      else goto dec;      /* decimal constant */
    }
    else {      /* decimal constant */
      if (*(loc − 1) ≡ '.' ∧ ¬xisdigit(*loc)) goto mistake;      /* not a constant */
  dec: *id_loc ++ ← *(loc − 1);
      while (xisdigit(*loc) ∨ *loc ≡ '.') *id_loc ++ ← *loc ++;
      if (*loc ≡ 'e' ∨ *loc ≡ 'E') {      /* float constant */
        *id_loc ++ ← '_';
        loc ++;
        if (*loc ≡ '+' ∨ *loc ≡ '-') *id_loc ++ ← *loc ++;
        while (xisdigit(*loc)) *id_loc ++ ← *loc ++;
      }
    }
    while (*loc ≡ 'u' ∨ *loc ≡ 'U' ∨ *loc ≡ 'l' ∨ *loc ≡ 'L' ∨ *loc ≡ 'f' ∨ *loc ≡ 'F') {
      *id_loc ++ ← '$';
      *id_loc ++ ← toupper(*loc);
      loc ++;
    }
    return (constant);
  }
```
This code is used in section 40.

49. C strings and character constants, delimited by double and single quotes, respectively, can contain newlines or instances of their own delimiters if they are protected by a backslash. We follow this convention, but do not allow the string to be longer than *longest_name*.

⟨ Get a string 49 ⟩ ≡
```
  {
    char delim ← c;        /* what started the string */
    id_first ← section_text + 1;
    id_loc ← section_text;
    if (delim ≡ '\'' ∧ *(loc − 2) ≡ '@') {
      *++id_loc ← '@';
      *++id_loc ← '@';
    }
    *++id_loc ← delim;
    if (delim ≡ 'L') {        /* wide character constant */
      delim ← *loc ++;
      *++id_loc ← delim;
    }
    if (delim ≡ '<') delim ← '>';        /* for file names in # include lines */
    while (1) {
      if (loc ≥ limit) {
        if (*(limit − 1) ≠ '\\') {
          err_print("!␣String␣didn't␣end");
          loc ← limit;
          break;
        }
        if (get_line( ) ≡ 0) {
          err_print("!␣Input␣ended␣in␣middle␣of␣string");
          loc ← buffer;
          break;
        }
      }
      if ((c ← *loc ++) ≡ delim) {
        if (++id_loc ≤ section_text_end) *id_loc ← c;
        break;
      }
      if (c ≡ '\\')
        if (loc ≥ limit) continue;
        else if (++id_loc ≤ section_text_end) {
          *id_loc ← '\\';
          c ← *loc ++;
        }
      if (++id_loc ≤ section_text_end) *id_loc ← c;
    }
    if (id_loc ≥ section_text_end) {
      printf("\n!␣String␣too␣long:␣");
      term_write(section_text + 1, 25);
      printf("...");
      mark_error;
    }
    id_loc ++;
    return (string);
  }
```

This code is used in sections 40 and 50.

50. After an @ sign has been scanned, the next character tells us whether there is more work to do.

⟨ Get control code and possible section name 50 ⟩ ≡
```
  {
    c ← *loc++;
    switch (ccode[(eight_bits) c]) {
    case translit_code: err_print("!␣Use␣@l␣in␣limbo␣only");
      continue;
    case underline: xref_switch ← def_flag;
      continue;
    case trace: tracing ← c − '0';
      continue;
    case xref_roman: case xref_wildcard: case xref_typewriter: case noop: case TEX_string:
      c ← ccode[c];
      skip_restricted();
      return(c);
    case section_name: ⟨ Scan the section name and make cur_section point to it 51 ⟩;
    case verbatim: ⟨ Scan a verbatim string 57 ⟩;
    case ord: ⟨ Get a string 49 ⟩;
    default: return(ccode[(eight_bits) c]);
    }
  }
```

This code is used in section 40.

51. The occurrence of a section name sets *xref_switch* to zero, because the section name might (for example) follow **int**.

⟨ Scan the section name and make cur_section point to it 51 ⟩ ≡
```
  {
    char *k;      /* pointer into section_text */
    cur_section_char ← *(loc − 1);
    ⟨ Put section name into section_text 53 ⟩;
    if (k − section_text > 3 ∧ strncmp(k − 2, "...", 3) ≡ 0)
      cur_section ← section_lookup(section_text + 1, k − 3, 1);      /* 1 indicates a prefix */
    else cur_section ← section_lookup(section_text + 1, k, 0);
    xref_switch ← 0;
    return(section_name);
  }
```

This code is used in section 50.

52. Section names are placed into the *section_text* array with consecutive spaces, tabs, and carriage-returns replaced by single spaces. There will be no spaces at the beginning or the end. (We set *section_text*[0] ← '␣' to facilitate this, since the *section_lookup* routine uses *section_text*[1] as the first character of the name.)

⟨ Set initial values 20 ⟩ +≡
```
  section_text[0] ← '␣';
```

53.   ⟨ Put section name into *section_text* 53 ⟩ ≡

$k \leftarrow section\_text$;

while (1) {

  if $(loc > limit \wedge get\_line\,( ) \equiv 0)$ {

    $err\_print\,(\texttt{"!}\sqcup\texttt{Input}\sqcup\texttt{ended}\sqcup\texttt{in}\sqcup\texttt{section}\sqcup\texttt{name"})$;

    $loc \leftarrow buffer + 1$;

    break;

  }

  $c \leftarrow *loc$;

  ⟨ If end of name or erroneous control code, **break** 54 ⟩;

  $loc\,{+}{+}$;

  if $(k < section\_text\_end)\ k{+}{+}$;

  if $(xisspace\,(c))$ {

    $c \leftarrow \text{'}\sqcup\text{'}$;

    if $(*(k-1) \equiv \text{'}\sqcup\text{'})\ k{-}{-}$;

  }

  $*k \leftarrow c$;

}

if $(k \geq section\_text\_end)$ {

  $printf\,(\texttt{"\textbackslash n!}\sqcup\texttt{Section}\sqcup\texttt{name}\sqcup\texttt{too}\sqcup\texttt{long:}\sqcup\texttt{"})$;

  $term\_write\,(section\_text + 1, 25)$;

  $printf\,(\texttt{"...}\texttt{"})$;

  $mark\_harmless$;

}

if $(*k \equiv \text{'}\sqcup\text{'} \wedge k > section\_text)\ k{-}{-}$;

This code is used in section 51.

54.   ⟨ If end of name or erroneous control code, **break** 54 ⟩ ≡

if $(c \equiv \text{'@'})$ {

  $c \leftarrow *(loc + 1)$;

  if $(c \equiv \text{'>'})$ {

    $loc \mathrel{+}= 2$;

    break;

  }

  if $(ccode\,[(\textbf{eight\_bits})\ c] \equiv new\_section)$ {

    $err\_print\,(\texttt{"!}\sqcup\texttt{Section}\sqcup\texttt{name}\sqcup\texttt{didn't}\sqcup\texttt{end"})$;

    break;

  }

  if $(c \neq \text{'@'})$ {

    $err\_print\,(\texttt{"!}\sqcup\texttt{Control}\sqcup\texttt{codes}\sqcup\texttt{are}\sqcup\texttt{forbidden}\sqcup\texttt{in}\sqcup\texttt{section}\sqcup\texttt{name"})$;

    break;

  }

  $*({+}{+}k) \leftarrow \text{'@'}$;

  $loc\,{+}{+}$;   /* now $c \equiv *loc$ again */

}

This code is used in section 53.

55.   This function skips over a restricted context at relatively high speed.

⟨ Predeclaration of procedures 2 ⟩ +≡

  void $skip\_restricted\,( )$;

56.   **void** *skip_restricted*( )
{
    id_first ← *loc*;
    *(*limit* + 1) ← '@';
false_alarm:
    while (*∗loc* ≠ '@') *loc*++;
    id_loc ← *loc*;
    if (*loc*++ > *limit*) {
      err_print("!␣Control␣text␣didn't␣end");
      loc ← *limit*;
    }
    else {
      if (*∗loc* ≡ '@' ∧ *loc* ≤ *limit*) {
        loc++;
        goto *false_alarm*;
      }
      if (*∗loc*++ ≠ '>') *err_print*("!␣Control␣codes␣are␣forbidden␣in␣control␣text");
    }
}

57.   At the present point in the program we have *∗(loc − 1)* ≡ *verbatim*; we set *id_first* to the beginning of the string itself, and *id_loc* to its ending-plus-one location in the buffer. We also set *loc* to the position just after the ending delimiter.

⟨ Scan a verbatim string 57 ⟩ ≡
{
    id_first ← *loc*++;
    *(*limit* + 1) ← '@';
    *(*limit* + 2) ← '>';
    while (*∗loc* ≠ '@' ∨ *∗(loc* + 1) ≠ '>') *loc*++;
    if (*loc* ≥ *limit*) *err_print*("!␣Verbatim␣string␣didn't␣end");
    id_loc ← *loc*;
    loc += 2;
    return (*verbatim*);
}
This code is used in section 50.

58.   Phase one processing.   We now have accumulated enough subroutines to make it possible to carry out CWEAVE's first pass over the source file. If everything works right, both phase one and phase two of CWEAVE will assign the same numbers to sections, and these numbers will agree with what CTANGLE does.

The global variable *next_control* often contains the most recent output of *get_next*; in interesting cases, this will be the control code that ended a section or part of a section.

⟨ Global variables 17 ⟩ +≡
  eight_bits *next_control*;   /∗ control code waiting to be acting upon ∗/

59.   The overall processing strategy in phase one has the following straightforward outline.

⟨ Predeclaration of procedures 2 ⟩ +≡
  void *phase_one*( );

60.   **void** *phase_one*( )
  {
    phase ← 1;
    reset_input( );
    section_count ← 0;
    skip_limbo( );
    change_exists ← 0;
    while (¬*input_has_ended*) ⟨ Store cross-reference data for the current section 61 ⟩;
    changed_section[*section_count*] ← *change_exists*;   /∗ the index changes if anything does ∗/
    phase ← 2;   /∗ prepare for second phase ∗/
    ⟨ Print error messages about unused or undefined section names 76 ⟩;
  }

61.   ⟨ Store cross-reference data for the current section 61 ⟩ ≡
  {
    if (++*section_count* ≡ *max_sections*) *overflow*("section␣number");
    changed_section[*section_count*] ← *changing*;   /∗ it will become 1 if any line changes ∗/
    if (∗(*loc* − 1) ≡ '∗' ∧ *show_progress*) {
      printf("∗%d", *section_count*);
      update_terminal;   /∗ print a progress report ∗/
    }
    ⟨ Store cross-references in the TEX part of a section 66 ⟩;
    ⟨ Store cross-references in the definition part of a section 69 ⟩;
    ⟨ Store cross-references in the C part of a section 72 ⟩;
    if (*changed_section*[*section_count*]) *change_exists* ← 1;
  }
This code is used in section 60.

62. The *C_xref* subroutine stores references to identifiers in C text material beginning with the current value of *next_control* and continuing until *next_control* is '{' or '|', or until the next "milestone" is passed (i.e., *next_control* $\geq$ *format_code*). If *next_control* $\geq$ *format_code* when *C_xref* is called, nothing will happen; but if *next_control* $\equiv$ '|' upon entry, the procedure assumes that this is the '|' preceding C text that is to be processed.

The parameter *spec_ctrl* is used to change this behavior. In most cases *C_xref* is called with *spec_ctrl* $\equiv$ *ignore*, which triggers the default processing described above. If *spec_ctrl* $\equiv$ *section_name*, section names will be gobbled. This is used when C text in the TEX part or inside comments is parsed: It allows for section names to appear in | ... |, but these strings will not be entered into the cross reference lists since they are not definitions of section names.

The program uses the fact that our internal code numbers satisfy the relations *xref_roman* $\equiv$ *identifier* + *roman* and *xref_wildcard* $\equiv$ *identifier* + *wildcard* and *xref_typewriter* $\equiv$ *identifier* + *typewriter*, as well as *normal* $\equiv$ 0.

⟨ Predeclaration of procedures 2 ⟩ +≡
  void *C_xref* ( );

63.   **void** *C_xref* (*spec_ctrl*)   /∗ makes cross-references for C identifiers ∗/
        eight_bits *spec_ctrl*;
  {
    name_pointer *p*;   /∗ a referenced name ∗/
    while (*next_control* < *format_code* ∨ *next_control* $\equiv$ *spec_ctrl*) {
      if (*next_control* $\geq$ *identifier* ∧ *next_control* $\leq$ *xref_typewriter*) {
        if (*next_control* > *identifier*) ⟨ Replace "@@" by "@" 67 ⟩
        p ← *id_lookup* (*id_first*, *id_loc*, *next_control* − *identifier*);
        new_xref (*p*);
      }
      if (*next_control* $\equiv$ *section_name*) {
        section_xref_switch ← *cite_flag*;
        new_section_xref (*cur_section*);
      }
      next_control ← *get_next* ( );
      if (*next_control* $\equiv$ '|' ∨ *next_control* $\equiv$ *begin_comment* ∨ *next_control* $\equiv$ *begin_short_comment*)
        return;
    }
  }

64.   The *outer_xref* subroutine is like *C_xref* except that it begins with *next_control* $\neq$ '|' and ends with *next_control* $\geq$ *format_code*. Thus, it handles C text with embedded comments.

⟨ Predeclaration of procedures 2 ⟩ +≡
  void *outer_xref* ( );

65.   **void** *outer_xref* ( )   /∗ extension of *C_xref* ∗/
  {
    int *bal*;   /∗ brace level in comment ∗/
    while (*next_control* < *format_code*)
      if (*next_control* ≠ *begin_comment* ∧ *next_control* ≠ *begin_short_comment*) *C_xref* (*ignore*);
      else {
        boolean *is_long_comment* ← (*next_control* ≡ *begin_comment*);
        bal ← *copy_comment* (*is_long_comment*, 1);
        next_control ← ' | ';
        while (*bal* > 0) {
          C_xref (*section_name*);   /∗ do not reference section names in comments ∗/
          if (*next_control* ≡ ' | ') *bal* ← *copy_comment* (*is_long_comment*, *bal*);
          else *bal* ← 0;   /∗ an error message will occur in phase two ∗/
        }
      }
  }

66.   In the TEX part of a section, cross-reference entries are made only for the identifiers in C texts enclosed in | . . . |, or for control texts enclosed in @^ . . . @> or @. . . . @> or @: . . . @>.

⟨ Store cross-references in the TEX part of a section 66 ⟩ ≡
  while (1) {
    switch (*next_control* ← *skip_TEX* ( )) {
    case *translit_code*: *err_print* ("!␣Use␣@l␣in␣limbo␣only");
      continue;
    case *underline*: *xref_switch* ← *def_flag*;
      continue;
    case *trace*: *tracing* ← ∗(*loc* − 1) − '0';
      continue;
    case ' | ': *C_xref* (*section_name*);
      break;
    case *xref_roman*: **case** *xref_wildcard*: **case** *xref_typewriter*: **case** *noop*: **case** *section_name*: *loc* −= 2;
      next_control ← *get_next* ( );   /∗ scan to @> ∗/
      if (*next_control* ≥ *xref_roman* ∧ *next_control* ≤ *xref_typewriter*) {
        ⟨ Replace "@@" by "@" 67 ⟩
        new_xref (*id_lookup* (*id_first*, *id_loc*, *next_control* − *identifier*));
      }
      break;
    }
    if (*next_control* ≥ *format_code*) **break**;
  }
This code is used in section 61.

67.   ⟨ Replace "`@@`" by "`@`" 67 ⟩ ≡
  {
    char $*src \leftarrow id\_first$, $*dst \leftarrow id\_first$;
    while $(src < id\_loc)$ {
      if $(*src \equiv$ '`@`') $src\mathbin{+}\mathbin{+}$;
      $*dst\mathbin{+}\mathbin{+} \leftarrow *src\mathbin{+}\mathbin{+}$;
    }
    $id\_loc \leftarrow dst$;
    while $(dst < src)$ $*dst\mathbin{+}\mathbin{+} \leftarrow$ '␣';   /* clean up in case of error message display */
  }

This code is used in sections 63 and 66.

68.   During the definition and C parts of a section, cross-references are made for all identifiers except reserved words. However, the right identifier in a format definition is not referenced, and the left identifier is referenced only if it has been explicitly underlined (preceded by `@!`). The TEX code in comments is, of course, ignored, except for C portions enclosed in | ... |; the text of a section name is skipped entirely, even if it contains | ... | constructions.

The variables *lhs* and *rhs* point to the respective identifiers involved in a format definition.

⟨ Global variables 17 ⟩ +≡
  name_pointer lhs, rhs;   /* pointers to *byte_start* for format identifiers */
  name_pointer res_wd_end;   /* pointer to the first nonreserved identifier */

69.   When we get to the following code we have $next\_control \geq format\_code$.

⟨ Store cross-references in the definition part of a section 69 ⟩ ≡
  while $(next\_control \leq definition)$ {   /* *format_code* or *definition* */
    if $(next\_control \equiv definition)$ {
      $xref\_switch \leftarrow def\_flag$;   /* implied `@!` */
      $next\_control \leftarrow get\_next(\,)$;
    }
    else ⟨ Process a format definition 70 ⟩;
    $outer\_xref(\,)$;
  }

This code is used in section 61.

70. Error messages for improper format definitions will be issued in phase two. Our job in phase one is to define the *ilk* of a properly formatted identifier, and to remove cross-references to identifiers that we now discover should be unindexed.

⟨ Process a format definition 70 ⟩ ≡
```
    {
        next_control ← get_next( );
        if (next_control ≡ identifier) {
            lhs ← id_lookup(id_first, id_loc, normal);
            lhs⃗ilk ← normal;
            if (xref_switch)  new_xref(lhs);
            next_control ← get_next( );
            if (next_control ≡ identifier) {
                rhs ← id_lookup(id_first, id_loc, normal);
                lhs⃗ilk ← rhs⃗ilk;
                if (unindexed(lhs)) {        /* retain only underlined entries */
                    xref_pointer q, r ← Λ;
                    for (q ← (xref_pointer) lhs⃗xref; q > xmem; q ← q⃗xlink)
                        if (q⃗num < def_flag)
                            if (r)  r⃗xlink ← q⃗xlink;
                            else lhs⃗xref ← (char ∗) q⃗xlink;
                        else r ← q;
                }
                next_control ← get_next( );
            }
        }
    }
```
This code is used in section 69.

71. A much simpler processing of format definitions occurs when the definition is found in limbo.

⟨ Process simple format in limbo 71 ⟩ ≡
```
    {
        if (get_next( ) ≠ identifier)  err_print("!␣Missing␣left␣identifier␣of␣@s");
        else {
            lhs ← id_lookup(id_first, id_loc, normal);
            if (get_next( ) ≠ identifier)  err_print("!␣Missing␣right␣identifier␣of␣@s");
            else {
                rhs ← id_lookup(id_first, id_loc, normal);
                lhs⃗ilk ← rhs⃗ilk;
            }
        }
    }
```
This code is used in section 35.

72.   Finally, when the TEX and definition parts have been treated, we have $next\_control \geq begin\_C$.

$\langle$ Store cross-references in the C part of a section 72 $\rangle \equiv$

```
if (next_control ≤ section_name) {       /* begin_C or section_name */
  if (next_control ≡ begin_C) section_xref_switch ← 0;
  else {
    section_xref_switch ← def_flag;
    if (cur_section_char ≡ '(' ∧ cur_section ≠ name_dir) set_file_flag(cur_section);
  }
  do {
    if (next_control ≡ section_name ∧ cur_section ≠ name_dir) new_section_xref(cur_section);
    next_control ← get_next();
    outer_xref();
  } while (next_control ≤ section_name);
}
```

This code is used in section 61.

73.   After phase one has looked at everything, we want to check that each section name was both defined and used. The variable cur_xref will point to cross-references for the current section name of interest.

$\langle$ Global variables 17 $\rangle \mathrel{+}\equiv$

```
xref_pointer cur_xref;       /* temporary cross-reference pointer */
boolean an_output;           /* did file_flag precede cur_xref? */
```

74.   The following recursive procedure walks through the tree of section names and prints out anomalies.

$\langle$ Predeclaration of procedures 2 $\rangle \mathrel{+}\equiv$

```
void section_check();
```

75.   **void** *section_check*(*p*)
      name_pointer *p*;   /* print anomalies in subtree *p* */
  {
    if (*p*) {
      section_check(*p*-*llink*);
      cur_xref ← (**xref_pointer**) *p*-*xref*;
      if (*cur_xref*→*num* ≡ *file_flag*) {
        an_output ← 1;
        cur_xref ← *cur_xref*→*xlink*;
      }
      else *an_output* ← 0;
      if (*cur_xref*→*num* < *def_flag*) {
        printf("\n!␣Never␣defined:␣<");
        print_section_name(*p*);
        putchar('>');
        mark_harmless;
      }
      while (*cur_xref*→*num* ≥ *cite_flag*) *cur_xref* ← *cur_xref*→*xlink*;
      if (*cur_xref* ≡ *xmem* ∧ ¬*an_output*) {
        printf("\n!␣Never␣used:␣<");
        print_section_name(*p*);
        putchar('>');
        mark_harmless;
      }
      section_check(*p*-*rlink*);
    }
  }

76.   ⟨ Print error messages about unused or undefined section names 76 ⟩ ≡
  section_check(*root*)

This code is used in section 60.

77. Low-level output routines. The TEX output is supposed to appear in lines at most *line_length* characters long, so we place it into an output buffer. During the output process, *out_line* will hold the current line number of the line about to be output.

⟨ Global variables 17 ⟩ +≡
    char *out_buf* [*line_length* + 1];　　/∗ assembled characters ∗/
    char ∗*out_ptr*;　　/∗ just after last character in *out_buf* ∗/
    char ∗*out_buf_end* ← *out_buf* + *line_length*;　　/∗ end of *out_buf* ∗/
    int *out_line*;　　/∗ number of next line to be output ∗/

78. The *flush_buffer* routine empties the buffer up to a given breakpoint, and moves any remaining characters to the beginning of the next line. If the *per_cent* parameter is 1 a '%' is appended to the line that is being output; in this case the breakpoint *b* should be strictly less than *out_buf_end*. If the *per_cent* parameter is 0, trailing blanks are suppressed. The characters emptied from the buffer form a new line of output; if the *carryover* parameter is true, a "%" in that line will be carried over to the next line (so that TEX will ignore the completion of commented-out text).

#define *c_line_write* (*c*)　*fflush* (*active_file*), *fwrite* (*out_buf* + 1, **sizeof** (**char**), *c*, *active_file*)
#define *tex_putc* (*c*)　*putc* (*c*, *active_file*)
#define *tex_new_line*　*putc* ('\n', *active_file*)
#define *tex_printf* (*c*)　*fprintf* (*active_file*, *c*)

    void *flush_buffer* (*b*, *per_cent*, *carryover*)
        char ∗*b*;　　/∗ outputs from *out_buf* + 1 to *b*, where *b* ≤ *out_ptr* ∗/
        boolean *per_cent*, *carryover*;
  {
    char ∗*j*;

    j ← *b*;　　/∗ pointer into *out_buf* ∗/
    if (¬*per_cent*)　　/∗ remove trailing blanks ∗/
      while (*j* > *out_buf* ∧ ∗*j* ≡ '␣') *j*−−;
    c_line_write (*j* − *out_buf*);
    if (*per_cent*) *tex_putc* ('%');
    tex_new_line;
    out_line ++;
    if (*carryover*)
      while (*j* > *out_buf*)
        if (∗*j*−− ≡ '%' ∧ (*j* ≡ *out_buf* ∨ ∗*j* ≠ '\\')) {
          ∗*b*−− ← '%';
          break;
        }
    if (*b* < *out_ptr*) *strncpy* (*out_buf* + 1, *b* + 1, *out_ptr* − *b*);
    out_ptr −= *b* − *out_buf*;
  }

79.   When we are copying TEX source material, we retain line breaks that occur in the input, except that an empty line is not output when the TEX source line was nonempty. For example, a line of the TEX file that contains only an index cross-reference entry will not be copied. The *finish_line* routine is called just before *get_line* inputs a new line, and just after a line break token has been emitted during the output of translated C text.

```
void finish_line( )      /* do this at the end of a line */
{
  char *k;       /* pointer into buffer */
  if (out_ptr > out_buf ) flush_buffer(out_ptr, 0, 0);
  else {
    for (k ← buffer; k ≤ limit; k++)
      if (¬(xisspace(*k))) return;
    flush_buffer(out_buf, 0, 0);
  }
}
```

80.   In particular, the *finish_line* procedure is called near the very beginning of phase two. We initialize the output variables in a slightly tricky way so that the first line of the output file will be '\input cwebmac'.

⟨ Set initial values 20 ⟩ +≡
  $out\_ptr ← out\_buf + 1;$
  $out\_line ← 1;$
  $active\_file ← tex\_file;$
  $*out\_ptr ← \texttt{'c'};$
  $tex\_printf(\texttt{"\\\\input\_cwebma"});$

81.   When we wish to append one character c to the output buffer, we write '$out(c)$'; this will cause the buffer to be emptied if it was already full. If we want to append more than one character at once, we say $out\_str(s)$, where s is a string containing the characters.

   A line break will occur at a space or after a single-nonletter TEX control sequence.

```
#define  out(c)
          {
             if (out_ptr ≥ out_buf_end ) break_out( );
             *(++ out_ptr) ← c;
          }
  void out_str(s)     /* output characters from s to end of string */
     char *s;
{
  while (*s) out(*s++);
}
```

82.   The *break_out* routine is called just before the output buffer is about to overflow. To make this routine a little faster, we initialize position 0 of the output buffer to '\'; this character isn't really output.

⟨ Set initial values 20 ⟩ +≡
  $out\_buf[0] ← \texttt{'\\\\'};$

83.   A long line is broken at a blank space or just before a backslash that isn't preceded by another backslash. In the latter case, a '%' is output at the break.

⟨ Predeclaration of procedures 2 ⟩ +≡
  void break_out( );

84.   **void** *break_out*( )   /* finds a way to break the output line */
{
   char *$*k \leftarrow out\_ptr$;   /* pointer into *out_buf* */
   while (1) {
     if ($k \equiv out\_buf$) ⟨Print warning message, break the line, **return** 85⟩;
     if ($*k \equiv$ '␣') {
       flush_buffer$(k, 0, 1)$;
       return;
     }
     if ($*(k\!-\!-) \equiv$ '\\' $\wedge *k \neq$ '\\') {   /* we've decreased k */
       flush_buffer$(k, 1, 1)$;
       return;
     }
   }
}

85.   We get to this section only in the unusual case that the entire output line consists of a string of backslashes followed by a string of nonblank non-backslashes. In such cases it is almost always safe to break the line by putting a '%' just before the last character.

⟨Print warning message, break the line, **return** 85⟩ ≡
{
   printf("\n!␣Line␣had␣to␣be␣broken␣(output␣1.␣%d):\n", *out_line*);
   term_write($out\_buf + 1, out\_ptr - out\_buf - 1$);
   new_line;
   mark_harmless;
   flush_buffer$(out\_ptr - 1, 1, 1)$;
   return;
}
This code is used in section 84.

86.   Here is a macro that outputs a section number in decimal notation. The number to be converted by *out_section* is known to be less than *def_flag*, so it cannot have more than five decimal digits. If the section is changed, we output '*' just after the number.

   void *out_section*(n)
      sixteen_bits n;
{
   char $s[6]$;
   sprintf(s, "%d", n);
   out_str(s);
   if (*changed_section*$[n]$) *out_str*("*");
}

87.   The *out_name* procedure is used to output an identifier or index entry, enclosing it in braces.

```
void out_name(p, quote_xalpha)
    name_pointer p;
    boolean quote_xalpha;
{
    char *k, *k_end ← (p + 1)→byte_start;      /* pointers into byte_mem */
    out('{');
    for (k ← p→byte_start; k < k_end; k++) {
        if (isxalpha(*k) ∧ quote_xalpha) out('\\');
        out(*k);
    }
    out('}');
}
```

88. Routines that copy TEX material.   During phase two, we use subroutines *copy_limbo*, *copy_TEX*, and *copy_comment* in place of the analogous *skip_limbo*, *skip_TEX*, and *skip_comment* that were used in phase one. (Well, *copy_comment* was actually written in such a way that it functions as *skip_comment* in phase one.)

The *copy_limbo* routine, for example, takes TEX material that is not part of any section and transcribes it almost verbatim to the output file. The use of '@' signs is severely restricted in such material: '@@' pairs are replaced by singletons; '@l' and '@q' and '@s' are interpreted.

```
void copy_limbo( )
{
  char c;
  while (1) {
    if (loc > limit ∧ (finish_line( ), get_line( ) ≡ 0))  return;
    *(limit + 1) ← '@';
    while (*loc ≠ '@')  out(*(loc ++));
    if (loc ++ ≤ limit)  {
      c ← *loc ++;
      if (ccode [(eight_bits) c] ≡ new_section)  break;
      switch (ccode [(eight_bits) c])  {
      case translit_code: out_str("\\ATL");
        break;
      case '@': out('@');
        break;
      case noop: skip_restricted( );
        break;
      case format_code:
        if (get_next( ) ≡ identifier)  get_next( );
        if (loc ≥ limit)  get_line( );     /* avoid blank lines in output */
        break;     /* the operands of @s are ignored on this pass */
      default: err_print("! Double @ should be used in limbo");
        out('@');
      }
    }
  }
}
```

89.   The *copy_TEX* routine processes the TEX code at the beginning of a section; for example, the words you are now reading were copied in this way. It returns the next control code or '|' found in the input. We don't copy spaces or tab marks into the beginning of a line. This makes the test for empty lines in *finish_line* work.

90.   **format** *copy_TeX*   *TeX*

  eight_bits *copy_TEX*( )

  {

    char c;   /* current character being copied */

    while (1) {

      if ($loc > limit \wedge (finish\_line(\,), get\_line(\,) \equiv 0)$) **return** (*new_section*);

      $*(limit + 1) \leftarrow$ '@';

      while (($c \leftarrow *(loc\!+\!+)) \neq$ '|' $\wedge c \neq$ '@') {

        out(c);

        if ($out\_ptr \equiv out\_buf + 1 \wedge (xisspace(c))$) $out\_ptr\!-\!-$;

      }

      if ($c \equiv$ '|') **return** ('|');

      if ($loc \leq limit$) **return** (*ccode*[(**eight_bits**) $*(loc\!+\!+)$]);

    }

  }

91.   The *copy_comment* function issues a warning if more braces are opened than closed, and in the case of a more serious error it supplies enough braces to keep TEX from complaining about unbalanced braces. Instead of copying the TEX material into the output buffer, this function copies it into the token memory (in phase two only). The abbreviation *app_tok*(t) is used to append token t to the current token list, and it also makes sure that it is possible to append at least one further token without overflow.

#define *app_tok*(c)

        {

          if ($tok\_ptr + 2 > tok\_mem\_end$) *overflow*("token");

          $*(tok\_ptr\!+\!+) \leftarrow c$;

        }

⟨ Predeclaration of procedures 2 ⟩ +≡

  int *copy_comment*( );

92.   **int** *copy_comment* (*is_long_comment*, *bal*)   /∗ copies TEX code in comments ∗/
    boolean *is_long_comment*;   /∗ is this a traditional C comment? ∗/
    int *bal*;   /∗ brace balance ∗/
{
  char *c*;   /∗ current character being copied ∗/
  while (1) {
    if (*loc* > *limit*) {
      if (*is_long_comment*) {
        if (*get_line*( ) ≡ 0) {
          err_print("!␣Input␣ended␣in␣mid-comment");
          loc ← *buffer* + 1;
          goto *done*;
        }
      }
      else {
        if (*bal* > 1) *err_print*("!␣Missing␣}␣in␣comment");
        goto *done*;
      }
    }
    c ← ∗(*loc*++);
    if (*c* ≡ '|') **return** (*bal*);
    if (*is_long_comment*) ⟨Check for end of comment 93⟩;
    if (*phase* ≡ 2) {
      if (*ishigh*(*c*)) *app_tok*(*quoted_char*);
      app_tok(*c*);
    }
    ⟨Copy special things when *c* ≡ '@', '\\' 94⟩;
    if (*c* ≡ '{') *bal*++;
    else if (*c* ≡ '}') {
      if (*bal* > 1) *bal*−−;
      else {
        err_print("!␣Extra␣}␣in␣comment");
        if (*phase* ≡ 2) *tok_ptr*−−;
      }
    }
  }
done: ⟨Clear *bal* and **return** 95⟩;
}

93.   ⟨Check for end of comment 93⟩ ≡
  if (*c* ≡ '∗' ∧ ∗*loc* ≡ '/') {
    loc++;
    if (*bal* > 1) *err_print*("!␣Missing␣}␣in␣comment");
    goto *done*;
  }

This code is used in section 92.

94.   ⟨Copy special things when $c \equiv$ '$@$', '$\backslash\backslash$' 94⟩ ≡

  if $(c \equiv$ '$@$') $\{$

    if $(*(loc\text{++}) \neq$ '$@$') $\{$

      $err\_print($"$!_\sqcup$Illegal$_\sqcup$use$_\sqcup$of$_\sqcup$@$_\sqcup$in$_\sqcup$comment"$);$

      $loc\ \text{--}= 2;$

      if $(phase \equiv 2)\ *(tok\_ptr - 1) \leftarrow$ '$_\sqcup$';

      goto $done;$

    $\}$

  $\}$

  else if $(c \equiv$ '$\backslash\backslash$' $\wedge *loc \neq$ '$@$') **if** $(phase \equiv 2)\ app\_tok(*(loc\text{++}))$

  else $loc\text{++};$

This code is used in section 92.

95.   We output enough right braces to keep TEX happy.

⟨Clear bal and **return** 95⟩ ≡

  if $(phase \equiv 2)$

    while $(bal\text{--} > 0)\ app\_tok($'$\}$'$);$

  return $(0);$

This code is used in section 92.

96. Parsing.   The most intricate part of CWEAVE is its mechanism for converting C-like code into TEX code, and we might as well plunge into this aspect of the program now. A "bottom up" approach is used to parse the C-like material, since CWEAVE must deal with fragmentary constructions whose overall "part of speech" is not known.

At the lowest level, the input is represented as a sequence of entities that we shall call *scraps*, where each scrap of information consists of two parts, its *category* and its *translation*. The category is essentially a syntactic class, and the translation is a token list that represents TEX code. Rules of syntax and semantics tell us how to combine adjacent scraps into larger ones, and if we are lucky an entire C text that starts out as hundreds of small scraps will join together into one gigantic scrap whose translation is the desired TEX code. If we are unlucky, we will be left with several scraps that don't combine; their translations will simply be output, one by one.

The combination rules are given as context-sensitive productions that are applied from left to right. Suppose that we are currently working on the sequence of scraps $s_1 s_2 \ldots s_n$. We try first to find the longest production that applies to an initial substring $s_1 s_2 \ldots$; but if no such productions exist, we try to find the longest production applicable to the next substring $s_2 s_3 \ldots$; and if that fails, we try to match $s_3 s_4 \ldots$, etc.

A production applies if the category codes have a given pattern. For example, one of the productions (see rule 3) is

$$exp \; \left\{ \begin{array}{c} binop \\ ubinop \end{array} \right\} \; exp \; \rightarrow \; exp$$

and it means that three consecutive scraps whose respective categories are *exp*, *binop* (or *ubinop*), and *exp* are converted to one scrap whose category is *exp*. The translations of the original scraps are simply concatenated. The case of

$$exp \; comma \; exp \; \rightarrow \; exp \qquad E_1 C \; opt9 \, E_2$$

(rule 4) is only slightly more complicated: Here the resulting *exp* translation consists not only of the three original translations, but also of the tokens *opt* and 9 between the translations of the *comma* and the following *exp*. In the TEX file, this will specify an optional line break after the comma, with penalty 90.

At each opportunity the longest possible production is applied. For example, if the current sequence of scraps is *int_like cast lbrace*, rule 31 is applied; but if the sequence is *int_like cast* followed by anything other than *lbrace*, rule 32 takes effect.

Translation rules such as '$E_1 C \; opt9 \, E_2$' above use subscripts to distinguish between translations of scraps whose categories have the same initial letter; these subscripts are assigned from left to right.

97.   Here is a list of the category codes that scraps can have. (A few others, like *int_like*, have already been defined; the *cat_name* array contains a complete list.)

#define	*exp*	1	/* denotes an expression, including perhaps a single identifier */
#define	*unop*	2	/* denotes a unary operator */
#define	*binop*	3	/* denotes a binary operator */
#define	*ubinop*	4	/* denotes an operator that can be unary or binary, depending on context */
#define	*cast*	5	/* denotes a cast */
#define	*question*	6	/* denotes a question mark and possibly the expressions flanking it */
#define	*lbrace*	7	/* denotes a left brace */
#define	*rbrace*	8	/* denotes a right brace */
#define	*decl_head*	9	/* denotes an incomplete declaration */
#define	*comma*	10	/* denotes a comma */
#define	*lpar*	11	/* denotes a left parenthesis or left bracket */
#define	*rpar*	12	/* denotes a right parenthesis or right bracket */
#define	*prelangle*	13	/* denotes '<' before we know what it is */
#define	*prerangle*	14	/* denotes '>' before we know what it is */
#define	*langle*	15	/* denotes '<' when it's used as angle bracket in a template */
#define	*colcol*	18	/* denotes '::' */
#define	*base*	19	/* denotes a colon that introduces a base specifier */
#define	*decl*	20	/* denotes a complete declaration */
#define	*struct_head*	21	/* denotes the beginning of a structure specifier */
#define	*stmt*	23	/* denotes a complete statement */
#define	*function*	24	/* denotes a complete function */
#define	*fn_decl*	25	/* denotes a function declarator */
#define	*semi*	27	/* denotes a semicolon */
#define	*colon*	28	/* denotes a colon */
#define	*tag*	29	/* denotes a statement label */
#define	*if_head*	30	/* denotes the beginning of a compound conditional */
#define	*else_head*	31	/* denotes a prefix for a compound statement */
#define	*if_clause*	32	/* pending **if** together with a condition */
#define	*lproc*	35	/* begins a preprocessor command */
#define	*rproc*	36	/* ends a preprocessor command */
#define	*insert*	37	/* a scrap that gets combined with its neighbor */
#define	*section_scrap*	38	/* section name */
#define	*dead*	39	/* scrap that won't combine */
#define	*ftemplate*	59	/* *make_pair* */
#define	*new_exp*	60	/* **new** and a following type identifier */
#define	*begin_arg*	61	/* @[*/
#define	*end_arg*	62	/* @] */

⟨ Global variables 17 ⟩ +≡
  char *cat_name*[256][12];
  eight_bits *cat_index*;

98.   ⟨ Set initial values 20 ⟩ +≡
    for ($cat\_index \leftarrow 0$; $cat\_index < 255$; cat_index ++) $strcpy(cat\_name[cat\_index], \texttt{"UNKNOWN"})$;
  $strcpy(cat\_name[exp], \texttt{"exp"})$;
  $strcpy(cat\_name[unop], \texttt{"unop"})$;
  $strcpy(cat\_name[binop], \texttt{"binop"})$;
  $strcpy(cat\_name[ubinop], \texttt{"ubinop"})$;
  $strcpy(cat\_name[cast], \texttt{"cast"})$;
  $strcpy(cat\_name[question], \texttt{"?"})$;
  $strcpy(cat\_name[lbrace], \texttt{"\{"})$;
  $strcpy(cat\_name[rbrace], \texttt{"\}"})$;
  $strcpy(cat\_name[decl\_head], \texttt{"decl\_head"})$;
  $strcpy(cat\_name[comma], \texttt{","})$;
  $strcpy(cat\_name[lpar], \texttt{"("})$;
  $strcpy(cat\_name[rpar], \texttt{")"})$;
  $strcpy(cat\_name[prelangle], \texttt{"<"})$;
  $strcpy(cat\_name[prerangle], \texttt{">"})$;
  $strcpy(cat\_name[langle], \texttt{"\\\\<"})$;
  $strcpy(cat\_name[colcol], \texttt{"::"})$;
  $strcpy(cat\_name[base], \texttt{"\\\\:"})$;
  $strcpy(cat\_name[decl], \texttt{"decl"})$;
  $strcpy(cat\_name[struct\_head], \texttt{"struct\_head"})$;
  $strcpy(cat\_name[alfop], \texttt{"alfop"})$;
  $strcpy(cat\_name[stmt], \texttt{"stmt"})$;
  $strcpy(cat\_name[function], \texttt{"function"})$;
  $strcpy(cat\_name[fn\_decl], \texttt{"fn\_decl"})$;
  $strcpy(cat\_name[else\_like], \texttt{"else\_like"})$;
  $strcpy(cat\_name[semi], \texttt{";"})$;
  $strcpy(cat\_name[colon], \texttt{":"})$;
  $strcpy(cat\_name[tag], \texttt{"tag"})$;
  $strcpy(cat\_name[if\_head], \texttt{"if\_head"})$;
  $strcpy(cat\_name[else\_head], \texttt{"else\_head"})$;
  $strcpy(cat\_name[if\_clause], \texttt{"if()"})$;
  $strcpy(cat\_name[lproc], \texttt{"\#\{"})$;
  $strcpy(cat\_name[rproc], \texttt{"\#\}"})$;
  $strcpy(cat\_name[insert], \texttt{"insert"})$;
  $strcpy(cat\_name[section\_scrap], \texttt{"section"})$;
  $strcpy(cat\_name[dead], \texttt{"@d"})$;
  $strcpy(cat\_name[public\_like], \texttt{"public"})$;
  $strcpy(cat\_name[operator\_like], \texttt{"operator"})$;
  $strcpy(cat\_name[new\_like], \texttt{"new"})$;
  $strcpy(cat\_name[catch\_like], \texttt{"catch"})$;
  $strcpy(cat\_name[for\_like], \texttt{"for"})$;
  $strcpy(cat\_name[do\_like], \texttt{"do"})$;
  $strcpy(cat\_name[if\_like], \texttt{"if"})$;
  $strcpy(cat\_name[delete\_like], \texttt{"delete"})$;
  $strcpy(cat\_name[raw\_ubin], \texttt{"ubinop?"})$;
  $strcpy(cat\_name[const\_like], \texttt{"const"})$;
  $strcpy(cat\_name[raw\_int], \texttt{"raw"})$;
  $strcpy(cat\_name[int\_like], \texttt{"int"})$;
  $strcpy(cat\_name[case\_like], \texttt{"case"})$;
  $strcpy(cat\_name[sizeof\_like], \texttt{"sizeof"})$;
  $strcpy(cat\_name[struct\_like], \texttt{"struct"})$;

```
strcpy(cat_name[typedef_like], "typedef");
strcpy(cat_name[define_like], "define");
strcpy(cat_name[template_like], "template");
strcpy(cat_name[ftemplate], "ftemplate");
strcpy(cat_name[new_exp], "new_exp");
strcpy(cat_name[begin_arg], "@[");
strcpy(cat_name[end_arg], "@]");
strcpy(cat_name[0], "zero");
```

99. This code allows CWEAVE to display its parsing steps.

```
void print_cat(c)        /* symbolic printout of a category */
    eight_bits c;
{
  printf(cat_name[c]);
}
```

100.   The token lists for translated TEX output contain some special control symbols as well as ordinary characters. These control symbols are interpreted by **CWEAVE** before they are written to the output file.

break_space denotes an optional line break or an en space;

force denotes a line break;

big_force denotes a line break with additional vertical space;

preproc_line denotes that the line will be printed flush left;

opt denotes an optional line break (with the continuation line indented two ems with respect to the normal starting position)—this code is followed by an integer n, and the break will occur with penalty $10n$;

backup denotes a backspace of one em;

cancel obliterates any *break_space*, *opt*, *force*, or *big_force* tokens that immediately precede or follow it and also cancels any *backup* tokens that follow it;

indent causes future lines to be indented one more em;

outdent causes future lines to be indented one less em.

All of these tokens are removed from the TEX output that comes from C text between | ... | signs; *break_space* and *force* and *big_force* become single spaces in this mode. The translation of other C texts results in TEX control sequences \1, \2, \3, \4, \5, \6, \7, \8 corresponding respectively to *indent*, *outdent*, *opt*, *backup*, *break_space*, *force*, *big_force* and *preproc_line*. However, a sequence of consecutive '␣', *break_space*, *force*, and/or *big_force* tokens is first replaced by a single token (the maximum of the given ones).

The token *math_rel* will be translated into \MRL{, and it will get a matching } later. Other control sequences in the TEX output will be '\\{ ... }' surrounding identifiers, '\&{ ... }' surrounding reserved words, '\.{ ... }' surrounding strings, '\C{ ... } *force*' surrounding comments, and '\X$n$: ... \X' surrounding section names, where n is the section number.

```
#define  math_rel       °206
#define  big_cancel      °210        /* like cancel, also overrides spaces */
#define  cancel          °211        /* overrides backup, break_space, force, big_force */
#define  indent          °212        /* one more tab (\1) */
#define  outdent         °213        /* one less tab (\2) */
#define  opt             °214      /* optional break in mid-statement (\3) */
#define  backup          °215        /* stick out one unit to the left (\4) */
#define  break_space     °216       /* optional break between statements (\5) */
#define  force           °217      /* forced break between statements (\6) */
#define  big_force       °220        /* forced break with additional space (\7) */
#define  preproc_line    °221        /* begin line without indentation (\8) */
#define  quoted_char     °222        /* introduces a character token in the range °200–°377 */
#define  end_translation °223        /* special sentinel token at end of list */
#define  inserted        °224        /* sentinel to mark translations of inserts */
#define  qualifier       °225        /* introduces an explicit namespace qualifier */
```

101.   The raw input is converted into scraps according to the following table, which gives category codes followed by the translations. The symbol '**' stands for '\&{identifier}', i.e., the identifier itself treated as a reserved word. The right-hand column is the so-called *mathness*, which is explained further below.

An identifier c of length 1 is translated as \|c instead of as \\{c}. An identifier CAPS in all caps is translated as \.{CAPS} instead of as \\{CAPS}. An identifier that has become a reserved word via **typedef** is translated with \& replacing \\ and *raw_int* replacing *exp*.

A string of length greater than 20 is broken into pieces of size at most 20 with discretionary breaks in between.

!=	*binop:* \I	yes
<=	*binop:* \Z	yes
>=	*binop:* \G	yes
==	*binop:* \E	yes
&&	*binop:* \W	yes
||	*binop:* \V	yes
++	*unop:* \PP	yes
--	*unop:* \MM	yes
->	*binop:* \MG	yes
>>	*binop:* \GG	yes
<<	*binop:* \LL	yes
::	*colcol:* \DC	maybe
.*	*binop:* \PA	yes
->*	*binop:* \MGA	yes
...	*raw_int:* \,\ldots\,	yes
"string"	*exp:* \.{string with special characters quoted}	maybe
@=string@>	*exp:* \vb{string with special characters quoted}	maybe
@'7'	*exp:* \.{@'7'}	maybe
077 or \77	*exp:* \T{\~77}	maybe
0x7f	*exp:* \T{\^7f}	maybe
77	*exp:* \T{77}	maybe
77L	*exp:* \T{77\$L}	maybe
0.1E5	*exp:* \T{0.1_5}	maybe
+	*ubinop:* +	yes
−	*ubinop:* −	yes
*	*raw_ubin:* *	yes
/	*binop:* /	yes
<	*prelangle:* \langle	yes
=	*binop:* \K	yes
>	*prerangle:* \rangle	yes
.	*binop:* .	yes
|	*binop:* \OR	yes
^	*binop:* \XOR	yes
%	*binop:* \MOD	yes
?	*question:* \?	yes
!	*unop:* \R	yes
~	*unop:* \CM	yes
&	*raw_ubin:* \AND	maybe
(	*lpar:* (	maybe
[	*lpar:* [	maybe
)	*rpar:*)	maybe
]	*rpar:*]	maybe
{	*lbrace:* {	yes
}	*lbrace:* }	yes

,	*comma*: ,	yes
;	*semi*: ;	maybe
:	*colon*: :	no
# (within line)	*ubinop*: \#	yes
# (at beginning)	*lproc*: *force preproc_line* \#	no
end of # line	*rproc*: *force*	no
identifier	*exp*: \\{identifier with underlines and dollar signs quoted}	maybe
and	*alfop*: **	yes
and_eq	*alfop*: **	yes
asm	*sizeof_like*: **	maybe
auto	*int_like*: **	maybe
bitand	*alfop*: **	yes
bitor	*alfop*: **	yes
bool	*raw_int*: **	maybe
break	*case_like*: **	maybe
case	*case_like*: **	maybe
catch	*catch_like*: **	maybe
char	*raw_int*: **	maybe
class	*struct_like*: **	maybe
clock_t	*raw_int*: **	maybe
compl	*alfop*: **	yes
const	*const_like*: **	maybe
const_cast	*raw_int*: **	maybe
continue	*case_like*: **	maybe
default	*case_like*: **	maybe
define	*define_like*: **	maybe
defined	*sizeof_like*: **	maybe
delete	*delete_like*: **	maybe
div_t	*raw_int*: **	maybe
do	*do_like*: **	maybe
double	*raw_int*: **	maybe
dynamic_cast	*raw_int*: **	maybe
elif	*if_like*: **	maybe
else	*else_like*: **	maybe
endif	*if_like*: **	maybe
enum	*struct_like*: **	maybe
error	*if_like*: **	maybe
explicit	*int_like*: **	maybe
export	*int_like*: **	maybe
extern	*int_like*: **	maybe
FILE	*raw_int*: **	maybe
float	*raw_int*: **	maybe
for	*for_like*: **	maybe
fpos_t	*raw_int*: **	maybe
friend	*int_like*: **	maybe
goto	*case_like*: **	maybe
if	*if_like*: **	maybe
ifdef	*if_like*: **	maybe
ifndef	*if_like*: **	maybe
include	*if_like*: **	maybe
inline	*int_like*: **	maybe
int	*raw_int*: **	maybe

jmp_buf	*raw_int*: **	maybe
ldiv_t	*raw_int*: **	maybe
line	*if_like*: **	maybe
long	*raw_int*: **	maybe
make_pair	*ftemplate*: \\{make_pair}	maybe
mutable	*int_like*: **	maybe
namespace	*struct_like*: **	maybe
new	*new_like*: **	maybe
not	*alfop*: **	yes
not_eq	*alfop*: **	yes
NULL	*exp*: \NULL	yes
offsetof	*raw_int*: **	maybe
operator	*operator_like*: **	maybe
or	*alfop*: **	yes
or_eq	*alfop*: **	yes
pragma	*if_like*: **	maybe
private	*public_like*: **	maybe
protected	*public_like*: **	maybe
ptrdiff_t	*raw_int*: **	maybe
public	*public_like*: **	maybe
register	*int_like*: **	maybe
reinterpret_cast	*raw_int*: **	maybe
return	*case_like*: **	maybe
short	*raw_int*: **	maybe
sig_atomic_t	*raw_int*: **	maybe
signed	*raw_int*: **	maybe
size_t	*raw_int*: **	maybe
sizeof	*sizeof_like*: **	maybe
static	*int_like*: **	maybe
static_cast	*raw_int*: **	maybe
struct	*struct_like*: **	maybe
switch	*for_like*: **	maybe
template	*template_like*: **	maybe
TeX	*exp*: \TeX	yes
this	*exp*: \this	yes
throw	*case_like*: **	maybe
time_t	*raw_int*: **	maybe
try	*else_like*: **	maybe
typedef	*typedef_like*: **	maybe
typeid	*raw_int*: **	maybe
typename	*struct_like*: **	maybe
undef	*if_like*: **	maybe
union	*struct_like*: **	maybe
unsigned	*raw_int*: **	maybe
using	*int_like*: **	maybe
va_dcl	*decl*: **	maybe
va_list	*raw_int*: **	maybe
virtual	*int_like*: **	maybe
void	*raw_int*: **	maybe
volatile	*const_like*: **	maybe
wchar_t	*raw_int*: **	maybe
while	*for_like*: **	maybe

`xor`	*alfop*: **	
`xor_eq`	*alfop*: **	yes
`@,`	*insert*: \,	yes
`@|`	*insert*: *opt* 0	maybe
`@/`	*insert*: *force*	maybe
`@#`	*insert*: *big_force*	no
`@+`	*insert*: *big_cancel* {} *break_space* {} *big_cancel*	no
`@;`	*semi*:	no
`@[`	*begin_arg*:	maybe
`@]`	*end_arg*:	maybe
`@&`	*insert*: \J	maybe
`@h`	*insert*: *force* \ATH *force*	maybe
`@< section name @>`	*section_scrap*: \X*n*: translated section name\X	no
`@( section name @>`	*section_scrap*: \X*n*:\.{section name with special characters quoted␣}\X	maybe
`/*comment*/`	*insert*: *cancel* \C{translated comment} *force*	maybe
`//comment`	*insert*: *cancel* \SHC{translated comment} *force*	no
		no

The construction `@t` stuff `@>` contributes \hbox{ stuff } to the following scrap.

102. Here is a table of all the productions. Each production that combines two or more consecutive scraps implicitly inserts a $ where necessary, that is, between scraps whose abutting boundaries have different *mathness*. In this way we never get double $$.

A translation is provided when the resulting scrap is not merely a juxtaposition of the scraps it comes from. An asterisk* next to a scrap means that its first identifier gets an underlined entry in the index, via the function *make_underlined*. Two asterisks** means that both *make_underlined* and *make_reserved* are called; that is, the identifier's ilk becomes *raw_int*. A dagger † before the production number refers to the notes at the end of this section, which deal with various exceptional cases.

We use *in*, *out*, *back* and *bsp* as shorthands for *indent*, *outdent*, *backup* and *break_space*, respectively.

	LHS	$\to$ RHS	Translation	Example
0	$\left\{\begin{array}{l} any \\ any\ any \\ any\ any\ any \end{array}\right\}$ *insert*	$\to \left\{\begin{array}{l} any \\ any\ any \\ any\ any\ any \end{array}\right\}$		stmt; /* comment */
1	$exp \left\{\begin{array}{l} lbrace \\ int\_like \\ decl \end{array}\right\}$	$\to fn\_decl \left\{\begin{array}{l} lbrace \\ int\_like \\ decl \end{array}\right\}$	$F = E^*\ in\ in$	$main()\{$ $main(ac, av)$ **int** $ac;$
2	$exp\ unop$	$\to exp$		$x{+}{+}$
3	$exp \left\{\begin{array}{l} binop \\ ubinop \end{array}\right\} exp$	$\to exp$		x/y $x + y$
4	$exp\ comma\ exp$	$\to exp$	$EC\ opt9\ E$	$f(x, y)$
5	$exp \left\{\begin{array}{l} lpar\ rpar \\ cast \end{array}\right\} colon$	$\to exp \left\{\begin{array}{l} lpar\ rpar \\ cast \end{array}\right\} base$		$\mathbf{C}():$ $\mathbf{C}\text{int}\ i\ ):$
6	$exp\ semi$	$\to stmt$		$x \leftarrow 0;$
7	$exp\ colon$	$\to tag$	E^*C	$found:$
8	$exp\ rbrace$	$\to stmt\ rbrace$		end of **enum** list
9	$exp \left\{\begin{array}{l} lpar\ rpar \\ cast \end{array}\right\} \left\{\begin{array}{l} const\_like \\ case\_like \end{array}\right\}$	$\to exp \left\{\begin{array}{l} lpar\ rpar \\ cast \end{array}\right\}$	$\left\{\begin{array}{l} R = R_\sqcup C \\ C_1 = C_{1\sqcup} C_2 \end{array}\right\}$	$f()$ **const** $f(\mathbf{int})$ **throw**
10	$exp \left\{\begin{array}{l} exp \\ cast \end{array}\right\}$	$\to exp$		$time()$
11	$lpar \left\{\begin{array}{l} exp \\ ubinop \end{array}\right\} rpar$	$\to exp$		(x) $(*)$
12	$lpar\ rpar$	$\to exp$	$L\backslash, R$	functions, declarations
13	$lpar \left\{\begin{array}{l} decl\_head \\ int\_like \\ cast \end{array}\right\} rpar$	$\to cast$		(**char** $*$)
14	$lpar \left\{\begin{array}{l} decl\_head \\ int\_like \\ exp \end{array}\right\} comma$	$\to lpar$	$L\left\{\begin{array}{l} D \\ I \\ E \end{array}\right\} C\ opt9$	(**int**,
15	$lpar \left\{\begin{array}{l} stmt \\ decl \end{array}\right\}$	$\to lpar$	$\left\{\begin{array}{l} LS_\sqcup \\ LD_\sqcup \end{array}\right\}$	($k \leftarrow 5;$ (**int** $k \leftarrow 5;$
16	$unop \left\{\begin{array}{l} exp \\ int\_like \end{array}\right\}$	$\to exp$		$\neg x$ $\sim\mathbf{C}$
17	$ubinop\ cast\ rpar$	$\to cast\ rpar$	$C = \{U\}C$	$*\mathbf{CPtr})$
18	$ubinop \left\{\begin{array}{l} exp \\ int\_like \end{array}\right\}$	$\to \left\{\begin{array}{l} exp \\ int\_like \end{array}\right\}$	$\{U\}\left\{\begin{array}{l} E \\ I \end{array}\right\}$	$*x$ $*\mathbf{CPtr}$
19	$ubinop\ binop$	$\to binop$	$math\_rel\ U\{B\}\}$	$*{=}$
20	$binop\ binop$	$\to binop$	$math\_rel\ \{B_1\}\{B_2\}\}$	$\gg{=}$

#				
21	$cast \left\{ {lpar \atop exp} \right\}$	$\rightarrow \left\{ {lpar \atop exp} \right\}$	$\left\{ {CL \atop C_\sqcup E} \right\}$	$(\textbf{double})(x+2)\,x$ $(\textbf{double})$
22	$cast\ semi$	$\rightarrow exp\ semi$		$(\textbf{int});$
23	$sizeof\_like\ cast$	$\rightarrow exp$		$\textbf{sizeof}(\textbf{double})$
24	$sizeof\_like\ exp$	$\rightarrow exp$	$S_\sqcup E$	$\textbf{sizeof}\ x$
25	$int\_like \left\{ {int\_like \atop struct\_like} \right\}$	$\rightarrow \left\{ {int\_like \atop struct\_like} \right\}$	$I_\sqcup \left\{ {I \atop S} \right\}$	$\textbf{extern char}$
26	$int\_like\ exp \left\{ {raw\_int \atop struct\_like} \right\}$	$\rightarrow int\_like \left\{ {raw\_int \atop struct\_like} \right\}$		$\textbf{extern"Ada" int}$
27	$int\_like \left\{ {exp \atop ubinop \atop colon} \right\}$	$\rightarrow decl\_head \left\{ {exp \atop ubinop \atop colon} \right\}$	$D = I_\sqcup$	$\textbf{int}$ x $*x$ $\textbf{unsigned}$: $\textbf{int}$
28	$int\_like \left\{ {semi \atop binop} \right\}$	$\rightarrow decl\_head \left\{ {semi \atop binop} \right\}$		$\textbf{int}$ $x;$ $\textbf{int}\ f(\textbf{int} = 4)$
29	$public\_like\ colon$	$\rightarrow tag$		$\textbf{private}:$
30	$public\_like$	$\rightarrow int\_like$		$\textbf{private}$
31	$colcol \left\{ {exp \atop int\_like} \right\}$	$\rightarrow \left\{ {exp \atop int\_like} \right\}$	$qualifier\ C \left\{ {E \atop I} \right\}$	$\textbf{C}::x$
32	$colcol\ colcol$	$\rightarrow colcol$		$\textbf{C}::\textbf{B}::$
33	$decl\_head\ comma$	$\rightarrow decl\_head$	$DC_\sqcup$	$\textbf{int}\ x,$
34	$decl\_head\ ubinop$	$\rightarrow decl\_head$	$D\{U\}$	$\textbf{int}\ *$
†35	$decl\_head\ exp$	$\rightarrow decl\_head$	DE^*	$\textbf{int}\ x$
36	$decl\_head \left\{ {binop \atop colon} \right\} exp \left\{ {comma \atop semi \atop rpar} \right\}$	$\rightarrow decl\_head \left\{ {comma \atop semi \atop rpar} \right\}$	$D = D \left\{ {B \atop C} \right\} E$	$\textbf{int}\ f(\textbf{int}\ x = 2)\ b : 1$ $\textbf{int}$
37	$decl\_head\ cast$	$\rightarrow decl\_head$		$\textbf{int}\ f(\textbf{int})$
38	$decl\_head \left\{ {int\_like \atop lbrace \atop decl} \right\}$	$\rightarrow fn\_decl \left\{ {int\_like \atop lbrace \atop decl} \right\}$	$F = D\ in\ in$	$\textbf{long}\ time(\ )\ \{$
39	$decl\_head\ semi$	$\rightarrow decl$		$\textbf{int}\ n;$
40	$decl\ decl$	$\rightarrow decl$	$D_1\ force\ D_2$	$\textbf{int}\ n;\ \textbf{double}\ x;$
41	$decl \left\{ {stmt \atop function} \right\}$	$\rightarrow \left\{ {stmt \atop function} \right\}$	$D\ big\_force \left\{ {S \atop F} \right\}$	$\textbf{extern}\ n;\ main\ (\,)\{\ \}$
42	$base \left\{ {int\_like \atop exp} \right\} comma$	$\rightarrow base$	$B_\sqcup \left\{ {I \atop E} \right\} C\ opt9$	$: \textbf{public A},$ $: i(5),$
43	$base \left\{ {int\_like \atop exp} \right\} lbrace$	$\rightarrow lbrace$	$B_\sqcup \left\{ {I \atop E} \right\}_\sqcup L$	$\textbf{D} : \textbf{public A}\ \{$
44	$struct\_like\ lbrace$	$\rightarrow struct\_head$	$S_\sqcup L$	$\textbf{struct}\ \{$
45	$struct\_like \left\{ {exp \atop int\_like} \right\} semi$	$\rightarrow decl\_head\ semi$	$S_\sqcup \left\{ {E^{**} \atop I^{**}} \right\}$	$\textbf{struct forward};$
46	$struct\_like \left\{ {exp \atop int\_like} \right\} lbrace$	$\rightarrow struct\_head$	$S_\sqcup \left\{ {E^{**} \atop I^{**}} \right\}_\sqcup L$	$\textbf{struct name\_info}\ \{$
47	$struct\_like \left\{ {exp \atop int\_like} \right\} colon$	$\rightarrow struct\_like \left\{ {exp \atop int\_like} \right\} base$		$\textbf{class C} :$
†48	$struct\_like \left\{ {exp \atop int\_like} \right\}$	$\rightarrow int\_like$	$S_\sqcup \left\{ {E \atop I} \right\}$	$\textbf{struct name\_info}\ z;$

49 $struct\_head$ $\left\{\begin{array}{l} decl \\ stmt \\ function \end{array}\right\}$ $rbrace$ $\rightarrow int\_like$ S in $force$ $\left\{\begin{array}{l} D \\ S \\ F \end{array}\right\}$ out $force$ R **struct** { declaration }

50 $struct\_head$ $rbrace$ $\rightarrow int\_like$ $S\backslash, R$ **class C** { }

51 fn_decl $decl$ $\rightarrow fn\_decl$ F $force$ D $f(z)$ **double** z;

52 fn_decl $stmt$ $\rightarrow function$ F out out $force$ S $main()\ldots$

53 $function$ $\left\{\begin{array}{l} stmt \\ decl \\ function \end{array}\right\}$ $\rightarrow \left\{\begin{array}{l} stmt \\ decl \\ function \end{array}\right\}$ F big_force $\left\{\begin{array}{l} S \\ D \\ F \end{array}\right\}$ outer block

54 $lbrace$ $rbrace$ $\rightarrow stmt$ $L\backslash, R$ empty statement

55 $lbrace$ $\left\{\begin{array}{l} stmt \\ decl \\ function \end{array}\right\}$ $rbrace \rightarrow stmt$ $force$ L in $force$ S $force$ $back$ R out $force$ compound statement

56 $lbrace$ exp $[comma]$ $rbrace$ $\rightarrow exp$ initializer

57 if_like exp $\rightarrow if\_clause$ $I_{\sqcup}E$ **if** (z)

58 $else\_like$ $colon$ $\rightarrow else\_like$ $base$ **try** :

59 $else\_like$ $lbrace$ $\rightarrow else\_head$ $lbrace$ **else** {

60 $else\_like$ $stmt$ $\rightarrow stmt$ $force$ E in bsp S out $force$ **else** $x \leftarrow 0$;

61 $else\_head$ $\left\{\begin{array}{l} stmt \\ exp \end{array}\right\}$ $\rightarrow stmt$ $force$ E bsp $noop$ $cancel$ S bsp **else** { $x \leftarrow 0$; }

62 if_clause $lbrace$ $\rightarrow if\_head$ $lbrace$ **if** (x) {

63 if_clause $stmt$ $else\_like$ if_like $\rightarrow if\_like$ $force$ I in bsp S out $force$ $E_{\sqcup}I$ **if** (x) y; **else if**

64 if_clause $stmt$ $else\_like$ $\rightarrow else\_like$ $force$ I in bsp S out $force$ E **if** (x) y; **else**

65 if_clause $stmt$ $\rightarrow else\_like$ $stmt$ **if** (x)

66 if_head $\left\{\begin{array}{l} stmt \\ exp \end{array}\right\}$ $else\_like$ $if\_like \rightarrow if\_like$ $force$ I bsp $noop$ $cancel$ S $force$ $E_{\sqcup}I$ **if** (x) { y; } **else if**

67 if_head $\left\{\begin{array}{l} stmt \\ exp \end{array}\right\}$ $else\_like$ $\rightarrow else\_like$ $force$ I bsp $noop$ $cancel$ S $force$ E **if** (x) { y; } **else**

68 if_head $\left\{\begin{array}{l} stmt \\ exp \end{array}\right\}$ $\rightarrow else\_head$ $\left\{\begin{array}{l} stmt \\ exp \end{array}\right\}$ **if** (x) { y; }

69 do_like $stmt$ $else\_like$ $semi \rightarrow stmt$ D bsp $noop$ $cancel$ S $cancel$ $noop$ bsp ES **do** $f(x)$; **while** $(g(x))$;

70 $case\_like$ $semi$ $\rightarrow stmt$ **return**;

71 $case\_like$ $colon$ $\rightarrow tag$ **default**:

72 $case\_like$ exp $\rightarrow exp$ $C_{\sqcup}E$ **return** 0

73 $catch\_like$ $\left\{\begin{array}{l} cast \\ exp \end{array}\right\}$ $\rightarrow fn\_decl$ $C\left\{\begin{array}{l} C \\ E \end{array}\right\}$ in in **catch**$(\ldots)$

74 tag tag $\rightarrow tag$ T_1 bsp T_2 **case** 0: **case** 1:

75 tag $\left\{\begin{array}{l} stmt \\ decl \\ function \end{array}\right\}$ $\rightarrow \left\{\begin{array}{l} stmt \\ decl \\ function \end{array}\right\}$ $force$ $back$ T bsp S **case** 0: $z \leftarrow 0$;

†76 $stmt$ $\left\{\begin{array}{l} stmt \\ decl \\ function \end{array}\right\}$ $\rightarrow \left\{\begin{array}{l} stmt \\ decl \\ function \end{array}\right\}$ $S\left\{\begin{array}{l} force\ S \\ big\_force\ D \\ big\_force\ F \end{array}\right\}$ $x \leftarrow 1$; $y \leftarrow 2$;

77 $semi$ $\rightarrow stmt$ $_{\sqcup}S$ empty statement

†78 $lproc$ $\left\{\begin{array}{l} if\_like \\ else\_like \\ define\_like \end{array}\right\}$ $\rightarrow lproc$ **#include**
#else
#define

79 $lproc$ $rproc$ $\rightarrow insert$ **#endif**

80	$lproc \left\{ \begin{array}{c} exp\ [exp] \\ function \end{array} \right\} rproc$	$\rightarrow insert$	$I_{\sqcup} \left\{ \begin{array}{c} E[_{\sqcup}\backslash 5\,E] \\ F \end{array} \right\}$	**#define** a 1 **#define** a { b; }
81	$section\_scrap\ semi$	$\rightarrow stmt$	$MS\ force$	⟨section name⟩;
82	$section\_scrap$	$\rightarrow exp$		⟨section name⟩
83	$insert\ any$	$\rightarrow any$		|#include|
84	$prelangle$	$\rightarrow binop$	<	< not in template
85	$prerangle$	$\rightarrow binop$	>	> not in template
86	$langle\ prerangle$	$\rightarrow cast$	$L\backslash , P$	⟨⟩
87	$langle \left\{ \begin{array}{c} decl\_head \\ int\_like \\ exp \end{array} \right\} prerangle$	$\rightarrow cast$		⟨**class C**⟩
88	$langle \left\{ \begin{array}{c} decl\_head \\ int\_like \\ exp \end{array} \right\} comma$	$\rightarrow langle$	$L \left\{ \begin{array}{c} D \\ I \\ E \end{array} \right\} C\ opt9$	⟨**class C**,
89	$template\_like\ exp\ prelangle$	$\rightarrow template\_like\ exp\ langle$		**template** a⟨100⟩
90	$template\_like \left\{ \begin{array}{c} exp \\ raw\_int \end{array} \right\}$	$\rightarrow \left\{ \begin{array}{c} exp \\ raw\_int \end{array} \right\}$	$T_{\sqcup} \left\{ \begin{array}{c} E \\ R \end{array} \right\}$	**C**::**template** a( )
91	$template\_like$	$\rightarrow raw\_int$		**template**⟨**class T**⟩
92	$new\_like\ lpar\ exp\ rpar$	$\rightarrow new\_like$		**new**($nothrow$)
93	$new\_like\ cast$	$\rightarrow exp$	$N_{\sqcup}C$	**new** (**int** $*$)
†94	new_like	$\rightarrow new\_exp$		**new C**( )
95	$new\_exp \left\{ \begin{array}{c} int\_like \\ const\_like \end{array} \right\}$	$\rightarrow new\_exp$	$N_{\sqcup} \left\{ \begin{array}{c} I \\ C \end{array} \right\}$	**new const int**
96	$new\_exp\ struct\_like \left\{ \begin{array}{c} exp \\ int\_like \end{array} \right\}$	$\rightarrow new\_exp$	$N_{\sqcup}S_{\sqcup} \left\{ \begin{array}{c} E \\ I \end{array} \right\}$	**new struct S**
97	$new\_exp\ raw\_ubin$	$\rightarrow new\_exp$	$N\{R\}$	**new int**$*$[2]
98	$new\_exp \left\{ \begin{array}{c} lpar \\ exp \end{array} \right\}$	$\rightarrow exp \left\{ \begin{array}{c} lpar \\ exp \end{array} \right\}$	$E = N \left\{ \begin{array}{c} \\ _{\sqcup} \end{array} \right\}$	**operator**[ ](**int**) **new int**(2)
†99	new_exp	$\rightarrow exp$		**new int**;
100	$ftemplate\ prelangle$	$\rightarrow ftemplate\ langle$		$make\_pair$⟨**int**, **int**⟩
101	$ftemplate$	$\rightarrow exp$		$make\_pair$(1, 2)
102	$for\_like\ exp$	$\rightarrow else\_like$	$F_{\sqcup}E$	**while** (1)
103	$raw\_ubin\ const\_like$	$\rightarrow raw\_ubin$	$RC\backslash_{\sqcup}$	$*$**const** x
104	raw_ubin	$\rightarrow ubinop$		$*\ x$
105	$const\_like$	$\rightarrow int\_like$		**const** x
106	$raw\_int\ prelangle$	$\rightarrow raw\_int\ langle$		**C**⟨
107	$raw\_int\ colcol$	$\rightarrow colcol$		**C**::
108	$raw\_int\ cast$	$\rightarrow raw\_int$		**C**⟨**class T**⟩
109	$raw\_int\ lpar$	$\rightarrow exp\ lpar$		**complex**(x, y)
†110	raw_int	$\rightarrow int\_like$		**complex** z
†111	$operator\_like \left\{ \begin{array}{c} binop \\ unop \\ ubinop \end{array} \right\}$	$\rightarrow exp$	$O\{ \left\{ \begin{array}{c} B \\ U \\ U \end{array} \right\} \}$	**operator**+
112	$operator\_like \left\{ \begin{array}{c} new\_like \\ delete\_like \end{array} \right\}$	$\rightarrow exp$	$O_{\sqcup} \left\{ \begin{array}{c} N \\ S \end{array} \right\}$	**operator delete**
113	$operator\_like\ comma$	$\rightarrow exp$		**operator**,
†114	$operator\_like$	$\rightarrow new\_exp$		**operator char**$*$
115	$typedef\_like \left\{ \begin{array}{c} int\_like \\ cast \end{array} \right\} \left\{ \begin{array}{c} comma \\ semi \end{array} \right\}$	$\rightarrow typedef\_like\ exp \left\{ \begin{array}{c} comma \\ semi \end{array} \right\}$		**typedef int I**,

116	*typedef_like int_like*	$\rightarrow$ *typedef_like*	$T_{\sqcup}I$	**typedef char**
†117	*typedef_like exp*	$\rightarrow$ *typedef_like*	$T_{\sqcup}E^{**}$	**typedef I @[@] (∗P)**
118	*typedef_like comma*	$\rightarrow$ *typedef_like*	$TC_{\sqcup}$	**typedef int x,**
119	*typedef_like semi*	$\rightarrow$ *decl*		**typedef int x,y;**
120	*typedef_like ubinop* $\left\{ \begin{array}{c} cast \\ ubinop \end{array} \right\}$	$\rightarrow$ *typedef_like* $\left\{ \begin{array}{c} cast \\ ubinop \end{array} \right\}$	$\left\{ \begin{array}{c} C = \{U\}C \\ U_2 = \{U_1\}U_2 \end{array} \right\}$	**typedef ∗∗(CPtr)**
121	*delete_like lpar rpar*	$\rightarrow$ *delete_like*	$DL\backslash\,,R$	**delete[]**
122	*delete_like exp*	$\rightarrow$ *exp*	$D_{\sqcup}E$	**delete p**
†123	*question exp* $\left\{ \begin{array}{c} colon \\ base \end{array} \right\}$	$\rightarrow$ *binop*		**? x :** **? f( ) :**
124	*begin_arg end_arg*	$\rightarrow$ *exp*		**@[char∗@]**
125	*any_other end_arg*	$\rightarrow$ *end_arg*		**char∗@]**

†Notes

Rule 35: The *exp* must not be immediately followed by *lpar*, *exp*, or *cast*.

Rule 48: The *exp* or *int_like* must not be immediately followed by *base*.

Rule 76: The *force* in the *stmt* line becomes *bsp* if CWEAVE has been invoked with the -f option.

Rule 78: The *define_like* case calls *make_underlined* on the following scrap.

Rule 94: The *new_like* must not be immediately followed by *lpar*.

Rule 99: The *new_exp* must not be immediately followed by *raw_int*, *struct_like*, or *colcol*.

Rule 110: The *raw_int* must not be immediately followed by *langle*.

Rule 111: The operator after *operator_like* must not be immediately followed by a *binop*.

Rule 114: The *operator_like* must not be immediately followed by *raw_ubin*.

Rule 117: The *exp* must not be immediately followed by *lpar*, *exp*, or *cast*.

Rule 123: The mathness of the *colon* or *base* changes to 'yes'.

103.   Implementing the productions.   More specifically, a scrap is a structure consisting of a category *cat* and a **text_pointer** *trans*, which points to the translation in *tok_start*. When C text is to be processed with the grammar above, we form an array *scrap_info* containing the initial scraps. Our production rules have the nice property that the right-hand side is never longer than the left-hand side. Therefore it is convenient to use sequential allocation for the current sequence of scraps. Five pointers are used to manage the parsing:

> *pp* is a pointer into *scrap_info*. We will try to match the category codes $pp\text{-}cat$, $(pp+1)\text{-}cat$, ... to the left-hand sides of productions.

> *scrap_base*, *lo_ptr*, *hi_ptr*, and *scrap_ptr* are such that the current sequence of scraps appears in positions *scrap_base* through *lo_ptr* and *hi_ptr* through *scrap_ptr*, inclusive, in the *cat* and *trans* arrays. Scraps located between *scrap_base* and *lo_ptr* have been examined, while those in positions $\geq$ *hi_ptr* have not yet been looked at by the parsing process.

Initially *scrap_ptr* is set to the position of the final scrap to be parsed, and it doesn't change its value. The parsing process makes sure that *lo_ptr* $\geq$ *pp* + 3, since productions have as many as four terms, by moving scraps from *hi_ptr* to *lo_ptr*. If there are fewer than *pp* + 3 scraps left, the positions up to *pp* + 3 are filled with blanks that will not match in any productions. Parsing stops when *pp* $\equiv$ *lo_ptr* + 1 and *hi_ptr* $\equiv$ *scrap_ptr* + 1.

Since the *scrap* structure will later be used for other purposes, we declare its second element as a union.

⟨ Typedef declarations 18 ⟩ +≡
    typedef struct {
      eight_bits *cat*;
      eight_bits *mathness*;
      union {
        text_pointer *Trans*;
        ⟨ Rest of *trans_plus* union 232 ⟩
      } *trans_plus*;
    } **scrap**;
    typedef scrap *∗scrap_pointer*;

104.   #define *trans   trans_plus.Trans*   /∗ translation texts of scraps ∗/
⟨ Global variables 17 ⟩ +≡
    scrap *scrap_info*[*max_scraps*];   /∗ memory array for scraps ∗/
    scrap_pointer *scrap_info_end* ← *scrap_info* + *max_scraps* − 1;   /∗ end of *scrap_info* ∗/
    scrap_pointer *pp*;   /∗ current position for reducing productions ∗/
    scrap_pointer *scrap_base*;   /∗ beginning of the current scrap sequence ∗/
    scrap_pointer *scrap_ptr*;   /∗ ending of the current scrap sequence ∗/
    scrap_pointer *lo_ptr*;   /∗ last scrap that has been examined ∗/
    scrap_pointer *hi_ptr*;   /∗ first scrap that has not been examined ∗/
    scrap_pointer *max_scr_ptr*;   /∗ largest value assumed by *scrap_ptr* ∗/

105.   ⟨ Set initial values 20 ⟩ +≡
    scrap_base ← *scrap_info* + 1;
    max_scr_ptr ← *scrap_ptr* ← *scrap_info*;

106.   Token lists in *tok_mem* are composed of the following kinds of items for TEX output.

- Character codes and special codes like *force* and *math_rel* represent themselves;
- *id_flag* + *p* represents \\{identifier *p*};
- *res_flag* + *p* represents \&{identifier *p*};
- *section_flag* + *p* represents section name *p*;
- *tok_flag* + *p* represents token list number *p*;
- *inner_tok_flag* + *p* represents token list number *p*, to be translated without line-break controls.

#define *id_flag* 10240   /* signifies an identifier */
#define *res_flag* 2 * *id_flag*   /* signifies a reserved word */
#define *section_flag* 3 * *id_flag*   /* signifies a section name */
#define *tok_flag* 4 * *id_flag*   /* signifies a token list */
#define *inner_tok_flag* 5 * *id_flag*   /* signifies a token list in '| ... |' */

  void *print_text*(*p*)   /* prints a token list for debugging; not used in *main* */
    text_pointer *p*;
{
  token_pointer *j*;   /* index into *tok_mem* */
  sixteen_bits *r*;   /* remainder of token after the flag has been stripped off */
  if (*p* ≥ *text_ptr*) *printf*("BAD");
  else
    for (*j* ← *p*; *j* < *(*p*+1); *j*++) {
    r ← *j* % *id_flag*;
    switch (*j*/*id_flag*) {
    case 1: *printf*("\\\\{");
      print_id((*name_dir* + *r*));
      printf("}");
      break;   /* *id_flag* */
    case 2: *printf*("\\&{");
      print_id((*name_dir* + *r*));
      printf("}");
      break;   /* *res_flag* */
    case 3: *printf*("<");
      print_section_name((*name_dir* + *r*));
      printf(">");
      break;   /* *section_flag* */
    case 4: *printf*("[[%d]]",*r*);
      break;   /* *tok_flag* */
    case 5: *printf*("|[[%d]]|",*r*);
      break;   /* *inner_tok_flag* */
    default: ⟨Print token *r* in symbolic form 107⟩;
    }
    }
  fflush(*stdout*);
}

107.   ⟨ Print token r in symbolic form 107 ⟩ ≡

```
switch (r) {
case math_rel: printf ("\\mathrel{");
  break;
case big_cancel: printf ("[ccancel]");
  break;
case cancel: printf ("[cancel]");
  break;
case indent: printf ("[indent]");
  break;
case outdent: printf ("[outdent]");
  break;
case backup: printf ("[backup]");
  break;
case opt: printf ("[opt]");
  break;
case break_space: printf ("[break]");
  break;
case force: printf ("[force]");
  break;
case big_force: printf ("[fforce]");
  break;
case preproc_line: printf ("[preproc]");
  break;
case quoted_char: j++;
  printf ("[%o]", (unsigned) *j);
  break;
case end_translation: printf ("[quit]");
  break;
case inserted: printf ("[inserted]");
  break;
default: putxchar (r);
}
```

This code is used in section 106.

108.   The production rules listed above are embedded directly into **CWEAVE**, since it is easier to do this than to write an interpretive system that would handle production systems in general. Several macros are defined here so that the program for each production is fairly short.

All of our productions conform to the general notion that some k consecutive scraps starting at some position j are to be replaced by a single scrap of some category c whose translation is composed from the translations of the disappearing scraps. After this production has been applied, the production pointer pp should change by an amount d. Such a production can be represented by the quadruple (j, k, c, d). For example, the production '$exp\ comma\ exp \to exp$' would be represented by '$(pp, 3, exp, -2)$'; in this case the pointer pp should decrease by 2 after the production has been applied, because some productions with exp in their second or third positions might now match, but no productions have exp in the fourth position of their left-hand sides. Note that the value of d is determined by the whole collection of productions, not by an individual one. The determination of d has been done by hand in each case, based on the full set of productions but not on the grammar of C or on the rules for constructing the initial scraps.

We also attach a serial number to each production, so that additional information is available when debugging. For example, the program below contains the statement '$reduce(pp, 3, exp, -2, 4)$' when it implements the production just mentioned.

Before calling $reduce$, the program should have appended the tokens of the new translation to the tok_mem array. We commonly want to append copies of several existing translations, and macros are defined to simplify these common cases. For example, $app2(pp)$ will append the translations of two consecutive scraps, $pp\text{-}trans$ and $(pp + 1)\text{-}trans$, to the current token list. If the entire new translation is formed in this way, we write '$squash(j, k, c, d, n)$' instead of '$reduce(j, k, c, d, n)$'. For example, '$squash(pp, 3, exp, -2, 3)$' is an abbreviation for '$app3(pp); reduce(pp, 3, exp, -2, 3)$'.

A couple more words of explanation: Both big_app and app append a token (while big_app1 to big_app4 append the specified number of scrap translations) to the current token list. The difference between big_app and app is simply that big_app checks whether there can be a conflict between math and non-math tokens, and intercalates a '$\$$' token if necessary. When in doubt what to use, use big_app.

The $mathness$ is an attribute of scraps that says whether they are to be printed in a math mode context or not. It is separate from the "part of speech" (the cat) because to make each cat have a fixed $mathness$ (as in the original **WEAVE**) would multiply the number of necessary production rules.

The low two bits (i.e. $mathness \% 4$) control the left boundary. (We need two bits because we allow cases yes_math, no_math and $maybe\_math$, which can go either way.) The next two bits (i.e. $mathness / 4$) control the right boundary. If we combine two scraps and the right boundary of the first has a different mathness from the left boundary of the second, we insert a $\$$ in between. Similarly, if at printing time some irreducible scrap has a yes_math boundary the scrap gets preceded or followed by a $\$$. The left boundary is $maybe\_math$ if and only if the right boundary is.

The code below is an exact translation of the production rules into C, using such macros, and the reader should have no difficulty understanding the format by comparing the code with the symbolic productions as they were listed earlier.

```
#define  no_math    2     /* should be in horizontal mode */
#define  yes_math   1     /* should be in math mode */
#define  maybe_math 0      /* works in either horizontal or math mode */
#define  big_app2(a)  big_app1(a); big_app1(a + 1)
#define  big_app3(a)  big_app2(a); big_app1(a + 2)
#define  big_app4(a)  big_app3(a); big_app1(a + 3)
#define  app(a)  *(tok_ptr ++) ← a
#define  app1(a)  *(tok_ptr ++) ← tok_flag + (int)((a)-trans − tok_start)
```

⟨ Global variables 17 ⟩ +≡
   int $cur\_mathness$, $init\_mathness$;

109.   **void** $app\_str(s)$
    char $*s;$
{
  while $(*s)$ $app\_tok(*(s++));$
}
void $big\_app(a)$
    token $a;$
{
  if $(a \equiv \text{'}\sqcup\text{'} \lor (a \geq big\_cancel \land a \leq big\_force))$ /* non-math token */
  {
    if $(cur\_mathness \equiv maybe\_math)$ $init\_mathness \leftarrow no\_math;$
    else if $(cur\_mathness \equiv yes\_math)$ $app\_str(\texttt{"\{\}\$"});$
    $cur\_mathness \leftarrow no\_math;$
  }
  else {
    if $(cur\_mathness \equiv maybe\_math)$ $init\_mathness \leftarrow yes\_math;$
    else if $(cur\_mathness \equiv no\_math)$ $app\_str(\texttt{"\$\{\}"});$
    $cur\_mathness \leftarrow yes\_math;$
  }
  $app(a);$
}
void $big\_app1(a)$
    scrap_pointer $a;$
{
  switch $(a\text{-}mathness \% 4)$ {   /* left boundary */
  case $(no\_math):$
    if $(cur\_mathness \equiv maybe\_math)$ $init\_mathness \leftarrow no\_math;$
    else if $(cur\_mathness \equiv yes\_math)$ $app\_str(\texttt{"\{\}\$"});$
    $cur\_mathness \leftarrow a\text{-}mathness/4;$ /* right boundary */
    break;
  case $(yes\_math):$
    if $(cur\_mathness \equiv maybe\_math)$ $init\_mathness \leftarrow yes\_math;$
    else if $(cur\_mathness \equiv no\_math)$ $app\_str(\texttt{"\$\{\}"});$
    $cur\_mathness \leftarrow a\text{-}mathness/4;$ /* right boundary */
    break;
  case $(maybe\_math):$ /* no changes */
    break;
  }
  $app(tok\_flag + (\textbf{int})((a)\text{-}trans - tok\_start));$
}

110.   Let us consider the big switch for productions now, before looking at its context. We want to design the program so that this switch works, so we might as well not keep ourselves in suspense about exactly what code needs to be provided with a proper environment.

#define $cat1$ $(pp + 1){\rightarrow}cat$
#define $cat2$ $(pp + 2){\rightarrow}cat$
#define $cat3$ $(pp + 3){\rightarrow}cat$
#define lhs_not_simple

$\quad\quad\quad (pp{\rightarrow}cat \neq public\_like \wedge pp{\rightarrow}cat \neq semi \wedge pp{\rightarrow}cat \neq prelangle \wedge pp{\rightarrow}cat \neq prerangle \wedge pp{\rightarrow}cat \neq$
$\quad\quad\quad\quad template\_like \wedge pp{\rightarrow}cat \neq new\_like \wedge pp{\rightarrow}cat \neq new\_exp \wedge pp{\rightarrow}cat \neq ftemplate \wedge pp{\rightarrow}cat \neq$
$\quad\quad\quad\quad raw\_ubin \wedge pp{\rightarrow}cat \neq const\_like \wedge pp{\rightarrow}cat \neq raw\_int \wedge pp{\rightarrow}cat \neq operator\_like)$
$\quad\quad\quad$ /* not a production with left side length 1 */

⟨ Match a production at pp, or increase pp if there is no match 110 ⟩ ≡
$\quad$ {
$\quad\quad$ **if** ($cat1 \equiv end\_arg \wedge lhs\_not\_simple$)
$\quad\quad\quad$ **if** ($pp{\rightarrow}cat \equiv begin\_arg$) $squash(pp, 2, exp, -2, 124)$;
$\quad\quad\quad$ **else** $squash(pp, 2, end\_arg, -1, 125)$;
$\quad\quad$ **else if** ($cat1 \equiv insert$) $squash(pp, 2, pp{\rightarrow}cat, -2, 0)$;
$\quad\quad$ **else if** ($cat2 \equiv insert$) $squash(pp + 1, 2, (pp + 1){\rightarrow}cat, -1, 0)$;
$\quad\quad$ **else if** ($cat3 \equiv insert$) $squash(pp + 2, 2, (pp + 2){\rightarrow}cat, 0, 0)$;
$\quad\quad$ **else**
$\quad\quad\quad$ **switch** ($pp{\rightarrow}cat$) {
$\quad\quad\quad$ **case** exp: ⟨ Cases for exp 117 ⟩; **break**;
$\quad\quad\quad$ **case** $lpar$: ⟨ Cases for $lpar$ 118 ⟩; **break**;
$\quad\quad\quad$ **case** $unop$: ⟨ Cases for $unop$ 119 ⟩; **break**;
$\quad\quad\quad$ **case** $ubinop$: ⟨ Cases for $ubinop$ 120 ⟩; **break**;
$\quad\quad\quad$ **case** $binop$: ⟨ Cases for $binop$ 121 ⟩; **break**;
$\quad\quad\quad$ **case** $cast$: ⟨ Cases for $cast$ 122 ⟩; **break**;
$\quad\quad\quad$ **case** $sizeof\_like$: ⟨ Cases for $sizeof\_like$ 123 ⟩; **break**;
$\quad\quad\quad$ **case** int_like: ⟨ Cases for int_like 124 ⟩; **break**;
$\quad\quad\quad$ **case** $public\_like$: ⟨ Cases for $public\_like$ 125 ⟩; **break**;
$\quad\quad\quad$ **case** $colcol$: ⟨ Cases for $colcol$ 126 ⟩; **break**;
$\quad\quad\quad$ **case** $decl\_head$: ⟨ Cases for $decl\_head$ 127 ⟩; **break**;
$\quad\quad\quad$ **case** $decl$: ⟨ Cases for $decl$ 128 ⟩; **break**;
$\quad\quad\quad$ **case** $base$: ⟨ Cases for $base$ 129 ⟩; **break**;
$\quad\quad\quad$ **case** $struct\_like$: ⟨ Cases for $struct\_like$ 130 ⟩; **break**;
$\quad\quad\quad$ **case** $struct\_head$: ⟨ Cases for $struct\_head$ 131 ⟩; **break**;
$\quad\quad\quad$ **case** fn_decl: ⟨ Cases for fn_decl 132 ⟩; **break**;
$\quad\quad\quad$ **case** $function$: ⟨ Cases for $function$ 133 ⟩; **break**;
$\quad\quad\quad$ **case** $lbrace$: ⟨ Cases for $lbrace$ 134 ⟩; **break**;
$\quad\quad\quad$ **case** if_like: ⟨ Cases for if_like 135 ⟩; **break**;
$\quad\quad\quad$ **case** $else\_like$: ⟨ Cases for $else\_like$ 136 ⟩; **break**;
$\quad\quad\quad$ **case** $else\_head$: ⟨ Cases for $else\_head$ 137 ⟩; **break**;
$\quad\quad\quad$ **case** if_clause: ⟨ Cases for if_clause 138 ⟩; **break**;
$\quad\quad\quad$ **case** if_head: ⟨ Cases for if_head 139 ⟩; **break**;
$\quad\quad\quad$ **case** do_like: ⟨ Cases for do_like 140 ⟩; **break**;
$\quad\quad\quad$ **case** $case\_like$: ⟨ Cases for $case\_like$ 141 ⟩; **break**;
$\quad\quad\quad$ **case** $catch\_like$: ⟨ Cases for $catch\_like$ 142 ⟩; **break**;
$\quad\quad\quad$ **case** tag: ⟨ Cases for tag 143 ⟩; **break**;
$\quad\quad\quad$ **case** $stmt$: ⟨ Cases for $stmt$ 144 ⟩; **break**;
$\quad\quad\quad$ **case** $semi$: ⟨ Cases for $semi$ 145 ⟩; **break**;
$\quad\quad\quad$ **case** $lproc$: ⟨ Cases for $lproc$ 146 ⟩; **break**;
$\quad\quad\quad$ **case** $section\_scrap$: ⟨ Cases for $section\_scrap$ 147 ⟩; **break**;

```
      case insert: ⟨Cases for insert 148⟩; break;
      case prelangle: ⟨Cases for prelangle 149⟩; break;
      case prerangle: ⟨Cases for prerangle 150⟩; break;
      case langle: ⟨Cases for langle 151⟩; break;
      case template_like: ⟨Cases for template_like 152⟩; break;
      case new_like: ⟨Cases for new_like 153⟩; break;
      case new_exp: ⟨Cases for new_exp 154⟩; break;
      case ftemplate: ⟨Cases for ftemplate 155⟩; break;
      case for_like: ⟨Cases for for_like 156⟩; break;
      case raw_ubin: ⟨Cases for raw_ubin 157⟩; break;
      case const_like: ⟨Cases for const_like 158⟩; break;
      case raw_int: ⟨Cases for raw_int 159⟩; break;
      case operator_like: ⟨Cases for operator_like 160⟩; break;
      case typedef_like: ⟨Cases for typedef_like 161⟩; break;
      case delete_like: ⟨Cases for delete_like 162⟩; break;
      case question: ⟨Cases for question 163⟩; break;
      }
   pp ++;     /* if no match was found, we move to the right */
}
```

This code is used in section 166.

111.   In C, new specifier names can be defined via **typedef**, and we want to make the parser recognize
future occurrences of the identifier thus defined as specifiers. This is done by the procedure *make_reserved*,
which changes the *ilk* of the relevant identifier.

We first need a procedure to recursively seek the first identifier in a token list, because the identifier might
be enclosed in parentheses, as when one defines a function returning a pointer.

If the first identifier found is a keyword like '**case**', we return the special value *case_found*; this prevents
underlining of identifiers in case labels.

If the first identifier is the keyword '**operator**', we give up; users who want to index definitions of over-
loaded C++ operators should say, for example, '`@!@^\&{operator} $+{=}$@>`' (or, more properly alphabetized, '`@!@:operator+=}{\&{operator} $+{=}$@>`').

#define *no_ident_found*   (**token_pointer**) 0   /∗ distinct from any identifier token ∗/
#define *case_found*   (**token_pointer**) 1   /∗ likewise ∗/
#define *operator_found*   (**token_pointer**) 2   /∗ likewise ∗/

  token_pointer *find_first_ident*(p)
    text_pointer *p*;
  {
    token_pointer *q*;   /∗ token to be returned ∗/
    token_pointer *j*;   /∗ token being looked at ∗/
    sixteen_bits *r*;   /∗ remainder of token after the flag has been stripped off ∗/
    if $(p \geq text\_ptr)$ *confusion*(`"find_first_ident"`);
    for $(j \leftarrow *p; \; j < *(p+1); \; j\text{++})$ {
    $r \leftarrow *j \% id\_flag$;
    switch $(*j/id\_flag)$ {
    case 2:   /∗ *res_flag* ∗/
      if $(name\_dir[r].ilk \equiv case\_like)$ **return** *case_found*;
      if $(name\_dir[r].ilk \equiv operator\_like)$ **return** *operator_found*;
      if $(name\_dir[r].ilk \neq raw\_int)$ **break**;
    case 1: **return** *j*;
    case 4: **case** 5:   /∗ *tok_flag* or *inner_tok_flag* ∗/
      if $((q \leftarrow find\_first\_ident(tok\_start + r)) \neq no\_ident\_found)$ **return** *q*;
    default: ;   /∗ char, *section_flag*, fall thru: move on to next token ∗/
      if $(*j \equiv inserted)$ **return** *no_ident_found*;   /∗ ignore inserts ∗/
      else if $(*j \equiv qualifier)$ *j*++;   /∗ bypass namespace qualifier ∗/
    }
    }
    return *no_ident_found*;
  }

112.   The scraps currently being parsed must be inspected for any occurrence of the identifier that we're making reserved; hence the **for** loop below.

> **void** *make_reserved*(*p*)   /* make the first identifier in *p-trans* like **int** */
>   **scrap_pointer** *p*;
> {
>   **sixteen_bits** *tok_value*;   /* the name of this identifier, plus its flag */
>   **token_pointer** *tok_loc*;   /* pointer to *tok_value* */
>   **if** ((*tok_loc* ← *find_first_ident*(*p-trans*)) ≤ *operator_found*) **return**;   /* this should not happen */
>   *tok_value* ← *tok_loc;
>   **for** (; *p* ≤ *scrap_ptr*; *p* ≡ *lo_ptr* ? *p* ← *hi_ptr* : *p*++) {
>   **if** (*p-cat* ≡ *exp*) {
>   **if** (**(*p-trans*) ≡ *tok_value*) {
>   *p-cat* ← *raw_int*;
>   **(*p-trans*) ← *tok_value* % *id_flag* + *res_flag*;
>   }
>   }
>   }
>   (*name_dir* + (**sixteen_bits**)(*tok_value* % *id_flag*))-*ilk* ← *raw_int*;
>   *tok_loc ← *tok_value* % *id_flag* + *res_flag*;
> }

113.   In the following situations we want to mark the occurrence of an identifier as a definition: when *make_reserved* is just about to be used; after a specifier, as in **char** **argv; before a colon, as in *found*:; and in the declaration of a function, as in *main*(){. . . ; }. This is accomplished by the invocation of *make_underlined* at appropriate times. Notice that, in the declaration of a function, we find out that the identifier is being defined only after it has been swallowed up by an *exp*.

> **void** *make_underlined*(*p*)   /* underline the entry for the first identifier in *p-trans* */
>   **scrap_pointer** *p*;
> {
>   **token_pointer** *tok_loc*;   /* where the first identifier appears */
>   **if** ((*tok_loc* ← *find_first_ident*(*p-trans*)) ≤ *operator_found*) **return**;
>   /* this happens, for example, in **case** *found*: */
>   *xref_switch* ← *def_flag*;
>   *underline_xref*(*tok_loc % *id_flag* + *name_dir*);
> }

114.   We cannot use *new_xref* to underline a cross-reference at this point because this would just make a new cross-reference at the end of the list. We actually have to search through the list for the existing cross-reference.

⟨Predeclaration of procedures 2⟩ +≡
   void *underline_xref*( );

115.   **void** *underline_xref* (*p*)
       name_pointer *p*;
   {
       xref_pointer $q \leftarrow$ (**xref_pointer**) *p→xref* ;   /∗ pointer to cross-reference being examined ∗/
       xref_pointer *r*;   /∗ temporary pointer for permuting cross-references ∗/
       sixteen_bits *m*;   /∗ cross-reference value to be installed ∗/
       sixteen_bits *n*;   /∗ cross-reference value being examined ∗/
       if (*no_xref*) **return**;
       $m \leftarrow section\_count + xref\_switch$;
       while ($q \neq xmem$) {
         $n \leftarrow q{\rightarrow}num$;
         if ($n \equiv m$) **return**;
         else if ($m \equiv n + def\_flag$) {
           $q{\rightarrow}num \leftarrow m$;
           return;
         }
         else if ($n \geq def\_flag \wedge n < m$) **break**;
         $q \leftarrow q{\rightarrow}xlink$;
       }
       ⟨ Insert new cross-reference at *q*, not at beginning of list 116 ⟩;
   }

116.   We get to this section only when the identifier is one letter long, so it didn't get a non-underlined entry during phase one. But it may have got some explicitly underlined entries in later sections, so in order to preserve the numerical order of the entries in the index, we have to insert the new cross-reference not at the beginning of the list (namely, at *p→xref*), but rather right before *q*.

⟨ Insert new cross-reference at *q*, not at beginning of list 116 ⟩ ≡
   append_xref (0);   /∗ this number doesn't matter ∗/
   xref_ptr→xlink $\leftarrow$ (**xref_pointer**) *p→xref* ;
   $r \leftarrow xref\_ptr$;
   p→xref $\leftarrow$ (**char** ∗) *xref_ptr*;
   while ($r{\rightarrow}xlink \neq q$) {
     $r{\rightarrow}num \leftarrow r{\rightarrow}xlink{\rightarrow}num$;
     $r \leftarrow r{\rightarrow}xlink$;
   }
   $r{\rightarrow}num \leftarrow m$;   /∗ everything from *q* on is left undisturbed ∗/
This code is used in section 115.

117. Now comes the code that tries to match each production starting with a particular type of scrap. Whenever a match is discovered, the *squash* or *reduce* macro will cause the appropriate action to be performed, followed by **goto** *found*.

⟨ Cases for *exp* 117 ⟩ ≡

 if (*cat1* ≡ *lbrace* ∨ *cat1* ≡ *int_like* ∨ *cat1* ≡ *decl*) {
  make_underlined(*pp*);
  big_app1(*pp*);
  big_app(*indent*);
  app(*indent*);
  reduce(*pp*, 1, *fn_decl*, 0, 1);
 }
 else if (*cat1* ≡ *unop*) *squash*(*pp*, 2, *exp*, −2, 2);
 else if ((*cat1* ≡ *binop* ∨ *cat1* ≡ *ubinop*) ∧ *cat2* ≡ *exp*) *squash*(*pp*, 3, *exp*, −2, 3);
 else if (*cat1* ≡ *comma* ∧ *cat2* ≡ *exp*) {
  big_app2(*pp*);
  app(*opt*);
  app('9');
  big_app1(*pp* + 2);
  reduce(*pp*, 3, *exp*, −2, 4);
 }
 else if (*cat1* ≡ *lpar* ∧ *cat2* ≡ *rpar* ∧ *cat3* ≡ *colon*) *squash*(*pp* + 3, 1, *base*, 0, 5);
 else if (*cat1* ≡ *cast* ∧ *cat2* ≡ *colon*) *squash*(*pp* + 2, 1, *base*, 0, 5);
 else if (*cat1* ≡ *semi*) *squash*(*pp*, 2, *stmt*, −1, 6);
 else if (*cat1* ≡ *colon*) {
  make_underlined(*pp*);
  squash(*pp*, 2, *tag*, −1, 7);
 }
 else if (*cat1* ≡ *rbrace*) *squash*(*pp*, 1, *stmt*, −1, 8);
 else if (*cat1* ≡ *lpar* ∧ *cat2* ≡ *rpar* ∧ (*cat3* ≡ *const_like* ∨ *cat3* ≡ *case_like*)) {
  big_app1(*pp* + 2);
  big_app('␣');
  big_app1(*pp* + 3);
  reduce(*pp* + 2, 2, *rpar*, 0, 9);
 }
 else if (*cat1* ≡ *cast* ∧ (*cat2* ≡ *const_like* ∨ *cat2* ≡ *case_like*)) {
  big_app1(*pp* + 1);
  big_app('␣');
  big_app1(*pp* + 2);
  reduce(*pp* + 1, 2, *cast*, 0, 9);
 }
 else if (*cat1* ≡ *exp* ∨ *cat1* ≡ *cast*) *squash*(*pp*, 2, *exp*, −2, 10);

This code is used in section 110.

118.   ⟨ Cases for *lpar* 118 ⟩ ≡
  if (($cat1 \equiv exp \vee cat1 \equiv ubinop$) $\wedge cat2 \equiv rpar$) $squash(pp, 3, exp, -2, 11)$;
  else if ($cat1 \equiv rpar$) {
    $big\_app1(pp)$;
    $app(\text{'}\backslash\backslash\text{'})$;
    $app(\text{'},\text{'})$;
    $big\_app1(pp + 1)$;
    $reduce(pp, 2, exp, -2, 12)$;
  }
  else if (($cat1 \equiv decl\_head \vee cat1 \equiv int\_like \vee cat1 \equiv cast$) $\wedge cat2 \equiv rpar$) $squash(pp, 3, cast, -2, 13)$;
  else if (($cat1 \equiv decl\_head \vee cat1 \equiv int\_like \vee cat1 \equiv exp$) $\wedge cat2 \equiv comma$) {
    $big\_app3(pp)$;
    $app(opt)$;
    $app(\text{'9'})$;
    $reduce(pp, 3, lpar, -1, 14)$;
  }
  else if ($cat1 \equiv stmt \vee cat1 \equiv decl$) {
    $big\_app2(pp)$;
    $big\_app(\text{'}\sqcup\text{'})$;
    $reduce(pp, 2, lpar, -1, 15)$;
  }
This code is used in section 110.

119.   ⟨ Cases for *unop* 119 ⟩ ≡
  if ($cat1 \equiv exp \vee cat1 \equiv int\_like$) $squash(pp, 2, exp, -2, 16)$;
This code is used in section 110.

120.   ⟨ Cases for *ubinop* 120 ⟩ ≡
  if ($cat1 \equiv cast \wedge cat2 \equiv rpar$) {
    $big\_app(\text{'\{'})$;
    $big\_app1(pp)$;
    $big\_app(\text{'\}'})$;
    $big\_app1(pp + 1)$;
    $reduce(pp, 2, cast, -2, 17)$;
  }
  else if ($cat1 \equiv exp \vee cat1 \equiv int\_like$) {
    $big\_app(\text{'\{'})$;
    $big\_app1(pp)$;
    $big\_app(\text{'\}'})$;
    $big\_app1(pp + 1)$;
    $reduce(pp, 2, cat1, -2, 18)$;
  }
  else if ($cat1 \equiv binop$) {
    $big\_app(math\_rel)$;
    $big\_app1(pp)$;
    $big\_app(\text{'\{'})$;
    $big\_app1(pp + 1)$;
    $big\_app(\text{'\}'})$;
    $big\_app(\text{'\}'})$;
    $reduce(pp, 2, binop, -1, 19)$;
  }
This code is used in section 110.

121.   ⟨Cases for *binop* 121⟩ ≡
  if (*cat1* ≡ *binop*) {
    big_app(*math_rel*);
    big_app('{');
    big_app1(*pp*);
    big_app('}');
    big_app('{');
    big_app1(*pp* + 1);
    big_app('}');
    big_app('}');
    reduce(*pp*, 2, *binop*, −1, 20);
  }
This code is used in section 110.

122.   ⟨Cases for *cast* 122⟩ ≡
  if (*cat1* ≡ *lpar*) *squash*(*pp*, 2, *lpar*, −1, 21);
  else if (*cat1* ≡ *exp*) {
    big_app1(*pp*);
    big_app('␣');
    big_app1(*pp* + 1);
    reduce(*pp*, 2, *exp*, −2, 21);
  }
  else if (*cat1* ≡ *semi*) *squash*(*pp*, 1, *exp*, −2, 22);
This code is used in section 110.

123.   ⟨Cases for *sizeof_like* 123⟩ ≡
  if (*cat1* ≡ *cast*) *squash*(*pp*, 2, *exp*, −2, 23);
  else if (*cat1* ≡ *exp*) {
    big_app1(*pp*);
    big_app('␣');
    big_app1(*pp* + 1);
    reduce(*pp*, 2, *exp*, −2, 24);
  }
This code is used in section 110.

124.   ⟨Cases for *int_like* 124⟩ ≡
  if (*cat1* ≡ *int_like* ∨ *cat1* ≡ *struct_like*) {
    big_app1(*pp*);
    big_app('␣');
    big_app1(*pp* + 1);
    reduce(*pp*, 2, *cat1*, −2, 25);
  }
  else if (*cat1* ≡ *exp* ∧ (*cat2* ≡ *raw_int* ∨ *cat2* ≡ *struct_like*)) *squash*(*pp*, 2, *int_like*, −2, 26);
  else if (*cat1* ≡ *exp* ∨ *cat1* ≡ *ubinop* ∨ *cat1* ≡ *colon*) {
    big_app1(*pp*);
    big_app('␣');
    reduce(*pp*, 1, *decl_head*, −1, 27);
  }
  else if (*cat1* ≡ *semi* ∨ *cat1* ≡ *binop*) *squash*(*pp*, 1, *decl_head*, 0, 28);
This code is used in section 110.

125. $\langle$ Cases for *public_like* 125 $\rangle$ $\equiv$
 if ($cat1 \equiv colon$) $squash(pp, 2, tag, -1, 29)$;
 else $squash(pp, 1, int\_like, -2, 30)$;
This code is used in section 110.

126. $\langle$ Cases for *colcol* 126 $\rangle$ $\equiv$
 if ($cat1 \equiv exp \lor cat1 \equiv int\_like$) {
  $app(qualifier)$;
  $squash(pp, 2, cat1, -2, 31)$;
 } **else if** ($cat1 \equiv colcol$) $squash(pp, 2, colcol, -1, 32)$;
This code is used in section 110.

127. $\langle$ Cases for *decl_head* 127 $\rangle$ $\equiv$
 if ($cat1 \equiv comma$) {
  $big\_app2(pp)$;
  $big\_app(\text{'}\sqcup\text{'})$;
  $reduce(pp, 2, decl\_head, -1, 33)$;
 }
 else if ($cat1 \equiv ubinop$) {
  $big\_app1(pp)$;
  $big\_app(\text{'}\{\text{'})$;
  $big\_app1(pp + 1)$;
  $big\_app(\text{'}\}\text{'})$;
  $reduce(pp, 2, decl\_head, -1, 34)$;
 }
 else if ($cat1 \equiv exp \land cat2 \neq lpar \land cat2 \neq exp \land cat2 \neq cast$) {
  $make\_underlined(pp + 1)$;
  $squash(pp, 2, decl\_head, -1, 35)$;
 }
 else if (($cat1 \equiv binop \lor cat1 \equiv colon$) $\land cat2 \equiv exp \land (cat3 \equiv comma \lor cat3 \equiv semi \lor cat3 \equiv rpar$))
  $squash(pp, 3, decl\_head, -1, 36)$;
 else if ($cat1 \equiv cast$) $squash(pp, 2, decl\_head, -1, 37)$;
 else if ($cat1 \equiv lbrace \lor cat1 \equiv int\_like \lor cat1 \equiv decl$) {
  $big\_app1(pp)$;
  $big\_app(indent)$;
  $app(indent)$;
  $reduce(pp, 1, fn\_decl, 0, 38)$;
 }
 else if ($cat1 \equiv semi$) $squash(pp, 2, decl, -1, 39)$;
This code is used in section 110.

128.   ⟨ Cases for *decl* 128 ⟩ ≡
  if (*cat1* ≡ *decl*) {
    big_app1(*pp*);
    big_app(*force*);
    big_app1(*pp* + 1);
    reduce(*pp*, 2, *decl*, −1, 40);
  }
  else if (*cat1* ≡ *stmt* ∨ *cat1* ≡ *function*) {
    big_app1(*pp*);
    big_app(*big_force*);
    big_app1(*pp* + 1);
    reduce(*pp*, 2, *cat1*, −1, 41);
  }
This code is used in section 110.

129.   ⟨ Cases for *base* 129 ⟩ ≡
  if (*cat1* ≡ *int_like* ∨ *cat1* ≡ *exp*) {
    if (*cat2* ≡ *comma*) {
      big_app1(*pp*);
      big_app('␣');
      big_app2(*pp* + 1);
      app(*opt*);
      app('9');
      reduce(*pp*, 3, *base*, 0, 42);
    }
    else if (*cat2* ≡ *lbrace*) {
      big_app1(*pp*);
      big_app('␣');
      big_app1(*pp* + 1);
      big_app('␣');
      big_app1(*pp* + 2);
      reduce(*pp*, 3, *lbrace*, −2, 43);
    }
  }
This code is used in section 110.

130.   ⟨ Cases for *struct_like* 130 ⟩ ≡
   if (*cat1* ≡ *lbrace*) {
     big_app1(*pp*);
     big_app(' ⊔ ');
     big_app1(*pp* + 1);
     reduce(*pp*, 2, *struct_head*, 0, 44);
   }
   else if (*cat1* ≡ *exp* ∨ *cat1* ≡ *int_like*) {
     if (*cat2* ≡ *lbrace* ∨ *cat2* ≡ *semi*) {
       make_underlined(*pp* + 1);
       make_reserved(*pp* + 1);
       big_app1(*pp*);
       big_app(' ⊔ ');
       big_app1(*pp* + 1);
       if (*cat2* ≡ *semi*) *reduce*(*pp*, 2, *decl_head*, 0, 45);
       else {
         big_app(' ⊔ ');
         big_app1(*pp* + 2);
         reduce(*pp*, 3, *struct_head*, 0, 46);
       }
     }
     else if (*cat2* ≡ *colon*) *squash*(*pp* + 2, 1, *base*, 2, 47);
     else if (*cat2* ≠ *base*) {
       big_app1(*pp*);
       big_app(' ⊔ ');
       big_app1(*pp* + 1);
       reduce(*pp*, 2, *int_like*, −2, 48);
     }
   }
This code is used in section 110.

131.   ⟨ Cases for *struct_head* 131 ⟩ ≡
   if ((*cat1* ≡ *decl* ∨ *cat1* ≡ *stmt* ∨ *cat1* ≡ *function*) ∧ *cat2* ≡ *rbrace*) {
     big_app1(*pp*);
     big_app(*indent*);
     big_app(*force*);
     big_app1(*pp* + 1);
     big_app(*outdent*);
     big_app(*force*);
     big_app1(*pp* + 2);
     reduce(*pp*, 3, *int_like*, −2, 49);
   }
   else if (*cat1* ≡ *rbrace*) {
     big_app1(*pp*);
     app_str("\\,");
     big_app1(*pp* + 1);
     reduce(*pp*, 2, *int_like*, −2, 50);
   }
This code is used in section 110.

132.   ⟨ Cases for *fn_decl* 132 ⟩ ≡
    if (*cat1* ≡ *decl*) {
      big_app1 (*pp*);
      big_app (*force*);
      big_app1 (*pp* + 1);
      reduce (*pp*, 2, *fn_decl*, 0, 51);
    }
    else if (*cat1* ≡ *stmt*) {
      big_app1 (*pp*);
      app (*outdent*);
      app (*outdent*);
      big_app (*force*);
      big_app1 (*pp* + 1);
      reduce (*pp*, 2, *function*, −1, 52);
    }
This code is used in section 110.

133.   ⟨ Cases for *function* 133 ⟩ ≡
    if (*cat1* ≡ *function* ∨ *cat1* ≡ *decl* ∨ *cat1* ≡ *stmt*) {
      big_app1 (*pp*);
      big_app (*big_force*);
      big_app1 (*pp* + 1);
      reduce (*pp*, 2, *cat1*, −1, 53);
    }
This code is used in section 110.

134.   ⟨ Cases for *lbrace* 134 ⟩ ≡
    if (*cat1* ≡ *rbrace*) {
      big_app1 (*pp*);
      app ('\\');
      app (',');
      big_app1 (*pp* + 1);
      reduce (*pp*, 2, *stmt*, −1, 54);
    }
    else if ((*cat1* ≡ *stmt* ∨ *cat1* ≡ *decl* ∨ *cat1* ≡ *function*) ∧ *cat2* ≡ *rbrace*) {
      big_app (*force*);
      big_app1 (*pp*);
      big_app (*indent*);
      big_app (*force*);
      big_app1 (*pp* + 1);
      big_app (*force*);
      big_app (*backup*);
      big_app1 (*pp* + 2);
      big_app (*outdent*);
      big_app (*force*);
      reduce (*pp*, 3, *stmt*, −1, 55);
    }
    else if (*cat1* ≡ *exp*) {
      if (*cat2* ≡ *rbrace*) *squash* (*pp*, 3, *exp*, −2, 56);
      else if (*cat2* ≡ *comma* ∧ *cat3* ≡ *rbrace*) *squash* (*pp*, 4, *exp*, −2, 56);
    }
This code is used in section 110.

135.   ⟨ Cases for *if_like* 135 ⟩ ≡
  if (*cat1* ≡ *exp*) {
    big_app1(*pp*);
    big_app('␣');
    big_app1(*pp* + 1);
    reduce(*pp*, 2, *if_clause*, 0, 57);
  }
This code is used in section 110.

136.   ⟨ Cases for *else_like* 136 ⟩ ≡
  if (*cat1* ≡ *colon*) *squash*(*pp* + 1, 1, *base*, 1, 58);
  else if (*cat1* ≡ *lbrace*) *squash*(*pp*, 1, *else_head*, 0, 59);
  else if (*cat1* ≡ *stmt*) {
    big_app(*force*);
    big_app1(*pp*);
    big_app(*indent*);
    big_app(*break_space*);
    big_app1(*pp* + 1);
    big_app(*outdent*);
    big_app(*force*);
    reduce(*pp*, 2, *stmt*, −1, 60);
  }
This code is used in section 110.

137.   ⟨ Cases for *else_head* 137 ⟩ ≡
  if (*cat1* ≡ *stmt* ∨ *cat1* ≡ *exp*) {
    big_app(*force*);
    big_app1(*pp*);
    big_app(*break_space*);
    app(*noop*);
    big_app(*cancel*);
    big_app1(*pp* + 1);
    big_app(*force*);
    reduce(*pp*, 2, *stmt*, −1, 61);
  }
This code is used in section 110.

138. ⟨Cases for *if_clause* 138⟩ ≡
  if (*cat1* ≡ *lbrace*) *squash*(*pp*, 1, *if_head*, 0, 62);
  else if (*cat1* ≡ *stmt*) {
    if (*cat2* ≡ *else_like*) {
      big_app(*force*);
      big_app1(*pp*);
      big_app(*indent*);
      big_app(*break_space*);
      big_app1(*pp* + 1);
      big_app(*outdent*);
      big_app(*force*);
      big_app1(*pp* + 2);
      if (*cat3* ≡ *if_like*) {
        big_app('␣');
        big_app1(*pp* + 3);
        reduce(*pp*, 4, *if_like*, 0, 63);
      } **else** *reduce*(*pp*, 3, *else_like*, 0, 64);
    }
    else *squash*(*pp*, 1, *else_like*, 0, 65);
  }
This code is used in section 110.

139. ⟨Cases for *if_head* 139⟩ ≡
  if (*cat1* ≡ *stmt* ∨ *cat1* ≡ *exp*) {
    if (*cat2* ≡ *else_like*) {
      big_app(*force*);
      big_app1(*pp*);
      big_app(*break_space*);
      app(*noop*);
      big_app(*cancel*);
      big_app1(*pp* + 1);
      big_app(*force*);
      big_app1(*pp* + 2);
      if (*cat3* ≡ *if_like*) {
        big_app('␣');
        big_app1(*pp* + 3);
        reduce(*pp*, 4, *if_like*, 0, 66);
      } **else** *reduce*(*pp*, 3, *else_like*, 0, 67);
    }
    else *squash*(*pp*, 1, *else_head*, 0, 68);
  }
This code is used in section 110.

140. ⟨ Cases for *do_like* 140 ⟩ ≡
  if (*cat1* ≡ *stmt* ∧ *cat2* ≡ *else_like* ∧ *cat3* ≡ *semi*) {
    big_app1 (*pp*);
    big_app(*break_space*);
    app(*noop*);
    big_app(*cancel*);
    big_app1 (*pp* + 1);
    big_app(*cancel*);
    app(*noop*);
    big_app(*break_space*);
    big_app2 (*pp* + 2);
    reduce(*pp*, 4, *stmt*, −1, 69);
  }
This code is used in section 110.

141. ⟨ Cases for *case_like* 141 ⟩ ≡
  if (*cat1* ≡ *semi*) *squash*(*pp*, 2, *stmt*, −1, 70);
  else if (*cat1* ≡ *colon*) *squash*(*pp*, 2, *tag*, −1, 71);
  else if (*cat1* ≡ *exp*) {
    big_app1 (*pp*);
    big_app(' ⎵ ');
    big_app1 (*pp* + 1);
    reduce(*pp*, 2, *exp*, −2, 72);
  }
This code is used in section 110.

142. ⟨ Cases for *catch_like* 142 ⟩ ≡
  if (*cat1* ≡ *cast* ∨ *cat1* ≡ *exp*) {
    big_app2 (*pp*);
    big_app(*indent*);
    big_app(*indent*);
    reduce(*pp*, 2, *fn_decl*, 0, 73);
  }
This code is used in section 110.

143. ⟨ Cases for *tag* 143 ⟩ ≡
  if (*cat1* ≡ *tag*) {
    big_app1 (*pp*);
    big_app(*break_space*);
    big_app1 (*pp* + 1);
    reduce(*pp*, 2, *tag*, −1, 74);
  }
  else if (*cat1* ≡ *stmt* ∨ *cat1* ≡ *decl* ∨ *cat1* ≡ *function*) {
    big_app(*force*);
    big_app(*backup*);
    big_app1 (*pp*);
    big_app(*break_space*);
    big_app1 (*pp* + 1);
    reduce(*pp*, 2, *cat1* , −1, 75);
  }
This code is used in section 110.

144.   The user can decide at run-time whether short statements should be grouped together on the same line.

#define *force_lines* *flags*[`'f'`]   /* should each statement be on its own line? */

⟨ Cases for *stmt* 144 ⟩ ≡
  if (*cat1* ≡ *stmt* ∨ *cat1* ≡ *decl* ∨ *cat1* ≡ *function*) {
    big_app1(*pp*);
    if (*cat1* ≡ *function*) *big_app*(*big_force*);
    else if (*cat1* ≡ *decl*) *big_app*(*big_force*);
    else if (*force_lines*) *big_app*(*force*);
    else *big_app*(*break_space*);
    big_app1(*pp* + 1);
    reduce(*pp*, 2, *cat1*, −1, 76);
  }
This code is used in section 110.

145.   ⟨ Cases for *semi* 145 ⟩ ≡
  big_app(`'␣'`);
  big_app1(*pp*);
  reduce(*pp*, 1, *stmt*, −1, 77);
This code is used in section 110.

146.   ⟨ Cases for *lproc* 146 ⟩ ≡
  if (*cat1* ≡ *define_like*) *make_underlined*(*pp* + 2);
  if (*cat1* ≡ *else_like* ∨ *cat1* ≡ *if_like* ∨ *cat1* ≡ *define_like*) *squash*(*pp*, 2, *lproc*, 0, 78);
  else if (*cat1* ≡ *rproc*) {
    app(*inserted*);
    big_app2(*pp*);
    reduce(*pp*, 2, *insert*, −1, 79);
  }
  else if (*cat1* ≡ *exp* ∨ *cat1* ≡ *function*) {
    if (*cat2* ≡ *rproc*) {
      app(*inserted*);
      big_app1(*pp*);
      big_app(`'␣'`);
      big_app2(*pp* + 1);
      reduce(*pp*, 3, *insert*, −1, 80);
    }
    else if (*cat2* ≡ *exp* ∧ *cat3* ≡ *rproc* ∧ *cat1* ≡ *exp*) {
      app(*inserted*);
      big_app1(*pp*);
      big_app(`'␣'`);
      big_app1(*pp* + 1);
      app_str(`"␣\\5"`);
      big_app2(*pp* + 2);
      reduce(*pp*, 4, *insert*, −1, 80);
    }
  }
This code is used in section 110.

147. ⟨Cases for *section_scrap* 147⟩ ≡
  if (*cat1* ≡ *semi*) {
    big_app2(*pp*);
    big_app(*force*);
    reduce(*pp*, 2, *stmt*, −2, 81);
  }
  else *squash*(*pp*, 1, *exp*, −2, 82);
This code is used in section 110.

148. ⟨Cases for *insert* 148⟩ ≡
  if (*cat1*) *squash*(*pp*, 2, *cat1*, 0, 83);
This code is used in section 110.

149. ⟨Cases for *prelangle* 149⟩ ≡
  init_mathness ← *cur_mathness* ← *yes_math*;
  app('<');
  reduce(*pp*, 1, *binop*, −2, 84);
This code is used in section 110.

150. ⟨Cases for *prerangle* 150⟩ ≡
  init_mathness ← *cur_mathness* ← *yes_math*;
  app('>');
  reduce(*pp*, 1, *binop*, −2, 85);
This code is used in section 110.

151. ⟨Cases for *langle* 151⟩ ≡
  if (*cat1* ≡ *prerangle*) {
    big_app1(*pp*);
    app('\\');
    app(',');
    big_app1(*pp* + 1);
    reduce(*pp*, 2, *cast*, −1, 86);
  }
  else if (*cat1* ≡ *decl_head* ∨ *cat1* ≡ *int_like* ∨ *cat1* ≡ *exp*) {
    if (*cat2* ≡ *prerangle*) *squash*(*pp*, 3, *cast*, −1, 87);
    else if (*cat2* ≡ *comma*) {
      big_app3(*pp*);
      app(*opt*);
      app('9');
      reduce(*pp*, 3, *langle*, 0, 88);
    }
  }
This code is used in section 110.

152.   ⟨ Cases for *template_like* 152 ⟩ ≡
    if ($cat1 \equiv exp \land cat2 \equiv prelangle$) $squash(pp+2, 1, langle, 2, 89)$;
    else if ($cat1 \equiv exp \lor cat1 \equiv raw\_int$) {
      $big\_app1(pp)$;
      $big\_app(\text{'}\sqcup\text{'})$;
      $big\_app1(pp+1)$;
      $reduce(pp, 2, cat1, -2, 90)$;
    } **else** $squash(pp, 1, raw\_int, 0, 91)$;
This code is used in section 110.

153.   ⟨ Cases for *new_like* 153 ⟩ ≡
    if ($cat1 \equiv lpar \land cat2 \equiv exp \land cat3 \equiv rpar$) $squash(pp, 4, new\_like, 0, 92)$;
    else if ($cat1 \equiv cast$) {
      $big\_app1(pp)$;
      $big\_app(\text{'}\sqcup\text{'})$;
      $big\_app1(pp+1)$;
      $reduce(pp, 2, exp, -2, 93)$;
    }
    else if ($cat1 \neq lpar$) $squash(pp, 1, new\_exp, 0, 94)$;
This code is used in section 110.

154.   ⟨ Cases for *new_exp* 154 ⟩ ≡
    if ($cat1 \equiv int\_like \lor cat1 \equiv const\_like$) {
      $big\_app1(pp)$;
      $big\_app(\text{'}\sqcup\text{'})$;
      $big\_app1(pp+1)$;
      $reduce(pp, 2, new\_exp, 0, 95)$;
    }
    else if ($cat1 \equiv struct\_like \land (cat2 \equiv exp \lor cat2 \equiv int\_like)$) {
      $big\_app1(pp)$;
      $big\_app(\text{'}\sqcup\text{'})$;
      $big\_app1(pp+1)$;
      $big\_app(\text{'}\sqcup\text{'})$;
      $big\_app1(pp+2)$;
      $reduce(pp, 3, new\_exp, 0, 96)$;
    }
    else if ($cat1 \equiv raw\_ubin$) {
      $big\_app1(pp)$;
      $big\_app(\text{'\{'})$;
      $big\_app1(pp+1)$;
      $big\_app(\text{'\}'})$;
      $reduce(pp, 2, new\_exp, 0, 97)$;
    }
    else if ($cat1 \equiv lpar$) $squash(pp, 1, exp, -2, 98)$;
    else if ($cat1 \equiv exp$) {
      $big\_app1(pp)$;
      $big\_app(\text{'}\sqcup\text{'})$;
      $reduce(pp, 1, exp, -2, 98)$;
    }
    else if ($cat1 \neq raw\_int \land cat1 \neq struct\_like \land cat1 \neq colcol$) $squash(pp, 1, exp, -2, 99)$;
This code is used in section 110.

155. ⟨ Cases for *ftemplate* 155 ⟩ ≡
   if (*cat1* ≡ *prelangle*) *squash*(*pp* + 1, 1, *langle*, 1, 100);
   else *squash*(*pp*, 1, *exp*, −2, 101);
This code is used in section 110.

156. ⟨ Cases for *for_like* 156 ⟩ ≡
  if (*cat1* ≡ *exp*) {
    big_app1(*pp*);
    big_app('␣');
    big_app1(*pp* + 1);
    reduce(*pp*, 2, *else_like*, −2, 102);
  }
This code is used in section 110.

157. ⟨ Cases for *raw_ubin* 157 ⟩ ≡
  if (*cat1* ≡ *const_like*) {
    big_app2(*pp*);
    app_str("\\␣");
    reduce(*pp*, 2, *raw_ubin*, 0, 103);
  }
  else *squash*(*pp*, 1, *ubinop*, −2, 104);
This code is used in section 110.

158. ⟨ Cases for *const_like* 158 ⟩ ≡
  squash(*pp*, 1, *int_like*, −2, 105);
This code is used in section 110.

159. ⟨ Cases for *raw_int* 159 ⟩ ≡
   if (*cat1* ≡ *prelangle*) *squash*(*pp* + 1, 1, *langle*, 1, 106);
   else if (*cat1* ≡ *colcol*) *squash*(*pp*, 2, *colcol*, −1, 107);
   else if (*cat1* ≡ *cast*) *squash*(*pp*, 2, *raw_int*, 0, 108);
   else if (*cat1* ≡ *lpar*) *squash*(*pp*, 1, *exp*, −2, 109);
   else if (*cat1* ≠ *langle*) *squash*(*pp*, 1, *int_like*, −3, 110);
This code is used in section 110.

160.   ⟨ Cases for *operator_like* 160 ⟩ ≡
$\quad$ **if** ($cat1 \equiv binop \lor cat1 \equiv unop \lor cat1 \equiv ubinop$) {
$\quad\quad$ **if** ($cat2 \equiv binop$) **break**;
$\quad\quad$ *big_app1*(pp);
$\quad\quad$ *big_app*('{');
$\quad\quad$ *big_app1*($pp + 1$);
$\quad\quad$ *big_app*('}');
$\quad\quad$ *reduce*($pp, 2, exp, -2, 111$);
$\quad$ }
$\quad$ **else if** ($cat1 \equiv new\_like \lor cat1 \equiv delete\_like$) {
$\quad\quad$ *big_app1*(pp);
$\quad\quad$ *big_app*('␣');
$\quad\quad$ *big_app1*($pp + 1$);
$\quad\quad$ *reduce*($pp, 2, exp, -2, 112$);
$\quad$ }
$\quad$ **else if** ($cat1 \equiv comma$) *squash*($pp, 2, exp, -2, 113$);
$\quad$ **else if** ($cat1 \neq raw\_ubin$) *squash*($pp, 1, new\_exp, 0, 114$);
This code is used in section 110.

161.   ⟨ Cases for *typedef_like* 161 ⟩ ≡
$\quad$ **if** (($cat1 \equiv int\_like \lor cat1 \equiv cast$) $\land$ ($cat2 \equiv comma \lor cat2 \equiv semi$)) *squash*($pp + 1, 1, exp, -1, 115$);
$\quad$ **else if** ($cat1 \equiv int\_like$) {
$\quad\quad$ *big_app1*(pp);
$\quad\quad$ *big_app*('␣');
$\quad\quad$ *big_app1*($pp + 1$);
$\quad\quad$ *reduce*($pp, 2, typedef\_like, 0, 116$);
$\quad$ }
$\quad$ **else if** ($cat1 \equiv exp \land cat2 \neq lpar \land cat2 \neq exp \land cat2 \neq cast$) {
$\quad\quad$ *make_underlined*($pp + 1$);
$\quad\quad$ *make_reserved*($pp + 1$);
$\quad\quad$ *big_app1*(pp);
$\quad\quad$ *big_app*('␣');
$\quad\quad$ *big_app1*($pp + 1$);
$\quad\quad$ *reduce*($pp, 2, typedef\_like, 0, 117$);
$\quad$ }
$\quad$ **else if** ($cat1 \equiv comma$) {
$\quad\quad$ *big_app2*(pp);
$\quad\quad$ *big_app*('␣');
$\quad\quad$ *reduce*($pp, 2, typedef\_like, 0, 118$);
$\quad$ }
$\quad$ **else if** ($cat1 \equiv semi$) *squash*($pp, 2, decl, -1, 119$);
$\quad$ **else if** ($cat1 \equiv ubinop \land (cat2 \equiv ubinop \lor cat2 \equiv cast$)) {
$\quad\quad$ *big_app*('{');
$\quad\quad$ *big_app1*($pp + 1$);
$\quad\quad$ *big_app*('}');
$\quad\quad$ *big_app1*($pp + 2$);
$\quad\quad$ *reduce*($pp + 1, 2, cat2, 0, 120$);
$\quad$ }
This code is used in section 110.

162.   ⟨ Cases for *delete_like* 162 ⟩ ≡
  if (*cat1* ≡ *lpar* ∧ *cat2* ≡ *rpar*) {
    big_app2 (*pp*);
    app (' \\ ');
    app (' , ');
    big_app1 (*pp* + 2);
    reduce (*pp*, 3, *delete_like*, 0, 121);
  }
  else if (*cat1* ≡ *exp*) {
    big_app1 (*pp*);
    big_app (' ␣ ');
    big_app1 (*pp* + 1);
    reduce (*pp*, 2, *exp*, −2, 122);
  }
This code is used in section 110.

163.   ⟨ Cases for *question* 163 ⟩ ≡
  if (*cat1* ≡ *exp* ∧ (*cat2* ≡ *colon* ∨ *cat2* ≡ *base*)) {
    (*pp* + 2)→*mathness* ← 5 ∗ *yes_math*;   /∗ this colon should be in math mode ∗/
    squash (*pp*, 3, *binop*, −2, 123);
  }
This code is used in section 110.

164. Now here's the *reduce* procedure used in our code for productions.

The '*freeze_text*' macro is used to give official status to a token list. Before saying *freeze_text*, items are appended to the current token list, and we know that the eventual number of this token list will be the current value of *text_ptr*. But no list of that number really exists as yet, because no ending point for the current list has been stored in the *tok_start* array. After saying *freeze_text*, the old current token list becomes legitimate, and its number is the current value of *text_ptr* − 1 since *text_ptr* has been increased. The new current token list is empty and ready to be appended to. Note that *freeze_text* does not check to see that *text_ptr* hasn't gotten too large, since it is assumed that this test was done beforehand.

```
#define freeze_text  *(++text_ptr) ← tok_ptr
  void reduce(j, k, c, d, n)
      scrap_pointer j;
      eight_bits c;
      short k, d, n;
  {
    scrap_pointer i, i1;       /* pointers into scrap memory */
    j→cat ← c;
    j→trans ← text_ptr;
    j→mathness ← 4 * cur_mathness + init_mathness;
    freeze_text;
    if (k > 1) {
        for (i ← j + k, i1 ← j + 1; i ≤ lo_ptr; i++, i1++) {
          i1→cat ← i→cat;
          i1→trans ← i→trans;
          i1→mathness ← i→mathness;
        }
        lo_ptr ← lo_ptr − k + 1;
    }
    pp ← (pp + d < scrap_base ? scrap_base : pp + d);
    ⟨ Print a snapshot of the scrap list if debugging 169 ⟩;
    pp --;       /* we next say pp++ */
  }
```

165. Here's the *squash* procedure, which takes advantage of the simplification that occurs when k ≡ 1.

```
  void squash(j, k, c, d, n)
      scrap_pointer j;
      eight_bits c;
      short k, d, n;
  {
    scrap_pointer i;       /* pointers into scrap memory */
    if (k ≡ 1) {
        j→cat ← c;
        pp ← (pp + d < scrap_base ? scrap_base : pp + d);
        ⟨ Print a snapshot of the scrap list if debugging 169 ⟩;
        pp --;       /* we next say pp++ */
        return;
    }
    for (i ← j; i < j + k; i++) big_app1(i);
    reduce(j, k, c, d, n);
  }
```

166. And here now is the code that applies productions as long as possible. Before applying the production mechanism, we must make sure it has good input (at least four scraps, the length of the lhs of the longest rules), and that there is enough room in the memory arrays to hold the appended tokens and texts. Here we use a very conservative test; it's more important to make sure the program will still work if we change the production rules (within reason) than to squeeze the last bit of space from the memory arrays.

#define *safe_tok_incr* 20
#define *safe_text_incr* 10
#define *safe_scrap_incr* 10

⟨ Reduce the scraps using the productions until no more rules apply 166 ⟩ ≡
  while (1) {
    ⟨ Make sure the entries *pp* through *pp* + 3 of *cat* are defined 167 ⟩;
    if (*tok_ptr* + *safe_tok_incr* > *tok_mem_end*) {
      if (*tok_ptr* > *max_tok_ptr*) *max_tok_ptr* ← *tok_ptr*;
      overflow("token");
    }
    if (*text_ptr* + *safe_text_incr* > *tok_start_end*) {
      if (*text_ptr* > *max_text_ptr*) *max_text_ptr* ← *text_ptr*;
      overflow("text");
    }
    if (*pp* > *lo_ptr*) **break**;
    init_mathness ← *cur_mathness* ← *maybe_math*;
    ⟨ Match a production at *pp*, or increase *pp* if there is no match 110 ⟩;
  }
This code is used in section 170.

167. If we get to the end of the scrap list, category codes equal to zero are stored, since zero does not match anything in a production.

⟨ Make sure the entries *pp* through *pp* + 3 of *cat* are defined 167 ⟩ ≡
  if (*lo_ptr* < *pp* + 3) {
    while (*hi_ptr* ≤ *scrap_ptr* ∧ *lo_ptr* ≠ *pp* + 3) {
      (++*lo_ptr*)⁻cat ← *hi_ptr*⁻cat;
      lo_ptr⁻mathness ← (*hi_ptr*)⁻mathness;
      lo_ptr⁻trans ← (*hi_ptr* ++)⁻trans;
    }
    for (*i* ← *lo_ptr* + 1; *i* ≤ *pp* + 3; *i*++) *i*⁻cat ← 0;
  }
This code is used in section 166.

168. If CWEAVE is being run in debugging mode, the production numbers and current stack categories will be printed out when *tracing* is set to 2; a sequence of two or more irreducible scraps will be printed out when *tracing* is set to 1.

⟨ Global variables 17 ⟩ +≡
  int *tracing*;   /* can be used to show parsing details */

169. ⟨ Print a snapshot of the scrap list if debugging 169 ⟩ ≡
{
　　scrap_pointer k;　　　/* pointer into *scrap_info* */
　　if (*tracing* ≡ 2) {
　　printf ("\n%d:", n);
　　　　for (k ← *scrap_base*; k ≤ *lo_ptr*; k++) {
　　　　　if (k ≡ *pp*) *putxchar* ('*');
　　　　　else *putxchar* ('␣');
　　　　　if (k→*mathness* % 4 ≡ *yes_math*) *putchar* ('+');
　　　　　else if (k→*mathness* % 4 ≡ *no_math*) *putchar* ('-');
　　　　　print_cat (k→*cat*);
　　　　　if (k→*mathness* /4 ≡ *yes_math*) *putchar* ('+');
　　　　　else if (k→*mathness* /4 ≡ *no_math*) *putchar* ('-');
　　　　}
　　　　if (*hi_ptr* ≤ *scrap_ptr*) *printf* ("..."); 　　/* indicate that more is coming */
　　}
}

This code is used in sections 164 and 165.

170. The *translate* function assumes that scraps have been stored in positions *scrap_base* through *scrap_ptr* of *cat* and *trans*. It applies productions as much as possible. The result is a token list containing the translation of the given sequence of scraps.

After calling *translate*, we will have *text_ptr* + 3 ≤ *max_texts* and *tok_ptr* + 6 ≤ *max_toks*, so it will be possible to create up to three token lists with up to six tokens without checking for overflow. Before calling *translate*, we should have *text_ptr* < *max_texts* and *scrap_ptr* < *max_scraps*, since *translate* might add a new text and a new scrap before it checks for overflow.

text_pointer *translate* ( )　　　/* converts a sequence of scraps */
{
　　scrap_pointer i,　　/* index into *cat* */
　　j;　/* runs through final scraps */
　　pp ← *scrap_base*;
　　lo_ptr ← *pp* − 1;
　　hi_ptr ← *pp*;
　　⟨ If tracing, print an indication of where we are 173 ⟩;
　　⟨ Reduce the scraps using the productions until no more rules apply 166 ⟩;
　　⟨ Combine the irreducible scraps that remain 171 ⟩;
}

171.   If the initial sequence of scraps does not reduce to a single scrap, we concatenate the translations of all remaining scraps, separated by blank spaces, with dollar signs surrounding the translations of scraps where appropriate.

⟨ Combine the irreducible scraps that remain 171 ⟩ ≡
```
  {
    ⟨ If semi-tracing, show the irreducible scraps 172 ⟩;
    for (j ← scrap_base; j ≤ lo_ptr; j++) {
      if (j ≠ scrap_base)  app('␣');
      if (j→mathness % 4 ≡ yes_math)  app('$');
      app1(j);
      if (j→mathness /4 ≡ yes_math)  app('$');
      if (tok_ptr + 6 > tok_mem_end)  overflow("token");
    }
    freeze_text;
    return (text_ptr − 1);
  }
```
This code is used in section 170.

172.   ⟨ If semi-tracing, show the irreducible scraps 172 ⟩ ≡
```
  if (lo_ptr > scrap_base ∧ tracing ≡ 1) {
    printf("\nIrreducible␣scrap␣sequence␣in␣section␣%d:", section_count);
    mark_harmless;
    for (j ← scrap_base; j ≤ lo_ptr; j++) {
      printf("␣");
      print_cat(j→cat);
    }
  }
```
This code is used in section 171.

173.   ⟨ If tracing, print an indication of where we are 173 ⟩ ≡
```
  if (tracing ≡ 2) {
    printf("\nTracing␣after␣l.␣%d:\n", cur_line);
    mark_harmless;
    if (loc > buffer + 50) {
      printf("...");
      term_write(loc − 51, 51);
    }
    else  term_write(buffer, loc − buffer);
  }
```
This code is used in section 170.

174.   Initializing the scraps.   If we are going to use the powerful production mechanism just developed, we must get the scraps set up in the first place, given a C text. A table of the initial scraps corresponding to C tokens appeared above in the section on parsing; our goal now is to implement that table. We shall do this by implementing a subroutine called *C_parse* that is analogous to the *C_xref* routine used during phase one.

Like *C_xref*, the *C_parse* procedure starts with the current value of *next_control* and it uses the operation *next_control* ← *get_next*() repeatedly to read C text until encountering the next '|' or '/*', or until *next_control* ≥ *format_code*. The scraps corresponding to what it reads are appended into the *cat* and *trans* arrays, and *scrap_ptr* is advanced.

> **void** *C_parse*(*spec_ctrl*)   /* creates scraps from C tokens */
>   **eight_bits** *spec_ctrl*;
> {
>   **int** *count*;   /* characters remaining before string break */
>   **while** (*next_control* < *format_code* ∨ *next_control* ≡ *spec_ctrl*) {
>   ⟨ Append the scrap appropriate to *next_control* 176 ⟩;
>   *next_control* ← *get_next*();
>   **if** (*next_control* ≡ '|' ∨ *next_control* ≡ *begin_comment* ∨ *next_control* ≡ *begin_short_comment*)
>   **return**;
>   }
> }

175.   The following macro is used to append a scrap whose tokens have just been appended:

#define *app_scrap*(*c*, *b*)
>   {
>   (++*scrap_ptr*)→*cat* ← (*c*);
>   *scrap_ptr*→*trans* ← *text_ptr*;
>   *scrap_ptr*→*mathness* ← 5 * (*b*);   /* no no, yes yes, or maybe maybe */
>   *freeze_text*;
>   }

176. ⟨ Append the scrap appropriate to *next_control* 176 ⟩ ≡
⟨ Make sure that there is room for the new scraps, tokens, and texts 177 ⟩;
switch (*next_control*) {
case *section_name*: *app*(*section_flag* + (**int**)(*cur_section* − *name_dir*));
  app_scrap(*section_scrap*, *maybe_math*);
  app_scrap(*exp*, *yes_math*); **break**;
case *string*: **case** *constant*: **case** *verbatim*: ⟨ Append a string or constant 179 ⟩; **break**;
case *identifier*: *app_cur_id*(1); **break**;
case *TEX_string*: ⟨ Append a TEX string, without forming a scrap 180 ⟩; **break**;
case '/': **case** '.': *app*(*next_control*);
  app_scrap(*binop*, *yes_math*); **break**;
case '<': *app_str*("\\langle"); *app_scrap*(*prelangle*, *yes_math*); **break**;
case '>': *app_str*("\\rangle"); *app_scrap*(*prerangle*, *yes_math*); **break**;
case '=': *app_str*("\\K");
  app_scrap(*binop*, *yes_math*); **break**;
case '|': *app_str*("\\OR");
  app_scrap(*binop*, *yes_math*); **break**;
case '^': *app_str*("\\XOR");
  app_scrap(*binop*, *yes_math*); **break**;
case '%': *app_str*("\\MOD");
  app_scrap(*binop*, *yes_math*); **break**;
case '!': *app_str*("\\R");
  app_scrap(*unop*, *yes_math*); **break**;
case '~': *app_str*("\\CM");
  app_scrap(*unop*, *yes_math*); **break**;
case '+': **case** '-': *app*(*next_control*);
  app_scrap(*ubinop*, *yes_math*); **break**;
case '*': *app*(*next_control*);
  app_scrap(*raw_ubin*, *yes_math*); **break**;
case '&': *app_str*("\\AND");
  app_scrap(*raw_ubin*, *yes_math*); **break**;
case '?': *app_str*("\\?");
  app_scrap(*question*, *yes_math*); **break**;
case '#': *app_str*("\\#");
  app_scrap(*ubinop*, *yes_math*); **break**;
case *ignore*: **case** *xref_roman*: **case** *xref_wildcard*: **case** *xref_typewriter*: **case** *noop*: **break**;
case '(': **case** '[': *app*(*next_control*);
  app_scrap(*lpar*, *maybe_math*); **break**;
case ')': **case** ']': *app*(*next_control*);
  app_scrap(*rpar*, *maybe_math*); **break**;
case '{': *app_str*("\\{");
  app_scrap(*lbrace*, *yes_math*); **break**;
case '}': *app_str*("\\}");
  app_scrap(*rbrace*, *yes_math*); **break**;
case ',': *app*(',');
  app_scrap(*comma*, *yes_math*); **break**;
case ';': *app*(';');
  app_scrap(*semi*, *maybe_math*); **break**;
case ':': *app*(':');
  app_scrap(*colon*, *no_math*); **break**;
⟨ Cases involving nonstandard characters 178 ⟩
case *thin_space*: *app_str*("\\,");

$app\_scrap(insert, maybe\_math)$; **break**;
case $math\_break$: $app(opt)$;
  $app\_str(\texttt{"0"})$;
  $app\_scrap(insert, maybe\_math)$; **break**;
case $line\_break$: $app(force)$;
  $app\_scrap(insert, no\_math)$; **break**;
case $left\_preproc$: $app(force)$;
  $app(preproc\_line)$;
  $app\_str(\texttt{"\\\#"})$;
  $app\_scrap(lproc, no\_math)$; **break**;
case $right\_preproc$: $app(force)$;
  $app\_scrap(rproc, no\_math)$; **break**;
case big_line_break: $app(big\_force)$;
  $app\_scrap(insert, no\_math)$; **break**;
case no_line_break: $app(big\_cancel)$;
  $app(noop)$;
  $app(break\_space)$;
  $app(noop)$;
  $app(big\_cancel)$;
  $app\_scrap(insert, no\_math)$; **break**;
case $pseudo\_semi$: $app\_scrap(semi, maybe\_math)$; **break**;
case $macro\_arg\_open$: $app\_scrap(begin\_arg, maybe\_math)$; **break**;
case $macro\_arg\_close$: $app\_scrap(end\_arg, maybe\_math)$; **break**;
case $join$: $app\_str(\texttt{"\\\\J"})$;
  $app\_scrap(insert, no\_math)$; **break**;
case $output\_defs\_code$: $app(force)$;
  $app\_str(\texttt{"\\\\ATH"})$;
  $app(force)$;
  $app\_scrap(insert, no\_math)$; **break**;
default: $app(inserted)$;
  $app(next\_control)$;
  $app\_scrap(insert, maybe\_math)$; **break**;
}

This code is used in section 174.

177. ⟨ Make sure that there is room for the new scraps, tokens, and texts 177 ⟩ ≡
  if $(scrap\_ptr + safe\_scrap\_incr > scrap\_info\_end \lor tok\_ptr + safe\_tok\_incr > tok\_mem\_end$
          $\lor\ text\_ptr + safe\_text\_incr > tok\_start\_end)$ {
    if $(scrap\_ptr > max\_scr\_ptr)\ max\_scr\_ptr \leftarrow scrap\_ptr$;
    if $(tok\_ptr > max\_tok\_ptr)\ max\_tok\_ptr \leftarrow tok\_ptr$;
    if $(text\_ptr > max\_text\_ptr)\ max\_text\_ptr \leftarrow text\_ptr$;
    $overflow(\texttt{"scrap/token/text"})$;
  }

This code is used in sections 176 and 184.

178.   Some nonstandard characters may have entered CWEAVE by means of standard ones. They are converted to TEX control sequences so that it is possible to keep CWEAVE from outputting unusual **char** codes.

⟨ Cases involving nonstandard characters 178 ⟩ ≡

case *not_eq*: *app_str*("\\I"); *app_scrap*(*binop*, *yes_math*); **break**;

case *lt_eq*: *app_str*("\\Z"); *app_scrap*(*binop*, *yes_math*); **break**;

case *gt_eq*: *app_str*("\\G"); *app_scrap*(*binop*, *yes_math*); **break**;

case *eq_eq*: *app_str*("\\E"); *app_scrap*(*binop*, *yes_math*); **break**;

case *and_and*: *app_str*("\\W"); *app_scrap*(*binop*, *yes_math*); **break**;

case *or_or*: *app_str*("\\V"); *app_scrap*(*binop*, *yes_math*); **break**;

case *plus_plus*: *app_str*("\\PP"); *app_scrap*(*unop*, *yes_math*); **break**;

case *minus_minus*: *app_str*("\\MM"); *app_scrap*(*unop*, *yes_math*); **break**;

case *minus_gt*: *app_str*("\\MG"); *app_scrap*(*binop*, *yes_math*); **break**;

case *gt_gt*: *app_str*("\\GG"); *app_scrap*(*binop*, *yes_math*); **break**;

case *lt_lt*: *app_str*("\\LL"); *app_scrap*(*binop*, *yes_math*); **break**;

case *dot_dot_dot*: *app_str*("\\,\\ldots\\,"); *app_scrap*(*raw_int*, *yes_math*); **break**;

case *colon_colon*: *app_str*("\\DC"); *app_scrap*(*colcol*, *maybe_math*); **break**;

case *period_ast*: *app_str*("\\PA"); *app_scrap*(*binop*, *yes_math*); **break**;

case *minus_gt_ast*: *app_str*("\\MGA"); *app_scrap*(*binop*, *yes_math*); **break**;

This code is used in section 176.

179. The following code must use *app_tok* instead of *app* in order to protect against overflow. Note that *tok_ptr* + 1 ≤ *max_toks* after *app_tok* has been used, so another *app* is legitimate before testing again.

Many of the special characters in a string must be prefixed by '\' so that TEX will print them properly.

⟨ Append a string or constant 179 ⟩ ≡
  count ← −1;
  if (*next_control* ≡ *constant*) *app_str*("\\T{");
  else if (*next_control* ≡ *string*) {
    count ← 20;
    app_str("\\.{");
  }
  else *app_str*("\\vb{");
  while (*id_first* < *id_loc*) {
    if (*count* ≡ 0) {   /* insert a discretionary break in a long string */
      app_str("}\\)\\.{");
      count ← 20;
    }
    if ((**eight_bits**)(∗*id_first*) > °*177*) {
      app_tok(*quoted_char*);
      app_tok((**eight_bits**)(∗*id_first* ++));
    }
    else {
      switch (∗*id_first*) {
      case '␣': **case** '\\': **case** '#': **case** '%': **case** '$': **case** '^': **case** '{': **case** '}': **case** '~':
        case '&': **case** '_': *app*('\\');
        break;
      case '@':
        if (∗(*id_first* + 1) ≡ '@') *id_first* ++;
        else *err_print*("! Double @ should be used in strings");
      }
      app_tok(∗*id_first* ++);
    }
    count −−;
  }
  app('}');
  app_scrap(*exp*, *maybe_math*);
This code is used in section 176.

180. We do not make the TEX string into a scrap, because there is no telling what the user will be putting into it; instead we leave it open, to be picked up by the next scrap. If it comes at the end of a section, it will be made into a scrap when *finish_C* is called.

There's a known bug here, in cases where an adjacent scrap is *prelangle* or *prerangle*. Then the TEX string can disappear when the \langle or \rangle becomes < or >. For example, if the user writes |x<@ty@>|, the TEX string \hbox{y} eventually becomes part of an *insert* scrap, which is combined with a *prelangle* scrap and eventually lost. The best way to work around this bug is probably to enclose the @t...@> in @[...@] so that the TEX string is treated as an expression.

⟨ Append a TEX string, without forming a scrap 180 ⟩ ≡
  app_str("\\hbox{");
  while (*id_first* < *id_loc*)
    if ((**eight_bits**)(*∗id_first*) > °*177*) {
      app_tok(*quoted_char*);
      app_tok((**eight_bits**)(*∗id_first* ++));
    }
    else {
      if (*∗id_first* ≡ '@') *id_first* ++;
      app_tok(*∗id_first* ++);
    }
  app('}');

This code is used in section 176.

181. The function *app_cur_id* appends the current identifier to the token list; it also builds a new scrap if *scrapping* ≡ 1.

⟨ Predeclaration of procedures 2 ⟩ +≡
  void *app_cur_id*( );

182. **void** *app_cur_id*(*scrapping*)
    boolean *scrapping*;   /∗ are we making this into a scrap? ∗/
{
  name_pointer *p* ← *id_lookup*(*id_first*, *id_loc*, *normal*);
  if (*p*→*ilk* ≤ *custom*) {   /∗ not a reserved word ∗/
    app(*id_flag* + (**int**)(*p* − *name_dir*));
    if (*scrapping*)
      app_scrap(*p*→*ilk* ≡ *func_template* ? *ftemplate* : *exp*, *p*→*ilk* ≡ *custom* ? *yes_math* : *maybe_math*);
  }
  else {
    app(*res_flag* + (**int**)(*p* − *name_dir*));
    if (*scrapping*) {
      if (*p*→*ilk* ≡ *alfop*) *app_scrap*(*ubinop*, *yes_math*);
      else *app_scrap*(*p*→*ilk*, *maybe_math*);
    }
  }
}

183. When the '|' that introduces C text is sensed, a call on *C_translate* will return a pointer to the TeX translation of that text. If scraps exist in *scrap_info*, they are unaffected by this translation process.

text_pointer *C_translate*( )
{
  text_pointer *p*;   /∗ points to the translation ∗/
  scrap_pointer *save_base*;   /∗ holds original value of *scrap_base* ∗/

  save_base ← *scrap_base*;
  scrap_base ← *scrap_ptr* + 1;
  C_parse(*section_name*);   /∗ get the scraps together ∗/
  if (*next_control* ≠ '|') *err_print*("!␣Missing␣'|'␣after␣C␣text");
  app_tok(*cancel*);
  app_scrap(*insert*, *maybe_math*);   /∗ place a *cancel* token as a final "comment" ∗/
  p ← *translate*( );   /∗ make the translation ∗/
  if (*scrap_ptr* > *max_scr_ptr*) *max_scr_ptr* ← *scrap_ptr*;
  scrap_ptr ← *scrap_base* − 1;
  scrap_base ← *save_base*;   /∗ scrap the scraps ∗/
  return (*p*);
}

184.   The *outer_parse* routine is to *C_parse* as *outer_xref* is to *C_xref*: It constructs a sequence of scraps for C text until *next_control* $\geq$ *format_code*. Thus, it takes care of embedded comments.

The token list created from within '| ... |' brackets is output as an argument to \PB, if the user has invoked CWEAVE with the +e flag. Although cwebmac ignores \PB, other macro packages might use it to localize the special meaning of the macros that mark up program text.

#**define** *make_pb* *flags*['e']

  void *outer_parse*( )   /* makes scraps from C tokens and comments */
  {
    int *bal*;   /* brace level in comment */
    text_pointer *p*, *q*;   /* partial comments */
    while (*next_control* < *format_code*)
      if (*next_control* $\neq$ *begin_comment* $\wedge$ *next_control* $\neq$ *begin_short_comment*) *C_parse*(*ignore*);
      else {
        boolean *is_long_comment* $\leftarrow$ (*next_control* $\equiv$ *begin_comment*);
        ⟨ Make sure that there is room for the new scraps, tokens, and texts 177 ⟩;
        app(*cancel*);
        app(*inserted*);
        if (*is_long_comment*) *app_str*("\\C{");
        else *app_str*("\\SHC{");
        bal $\leftarrow$ *copy_comment*(*is_long_comment*, 1);
        next_control $\leftarrow$ *ignore*;
        while (*bal* > 0) {
          p $\leftarrow$ *text_ptr*;
          freeze_text;
          q $\leftarrow$ *C_translate*( );   /* at this point we have *tok_ptr* + 6 $\leq$ *max_toks* */
          app(*tok_flag* + (**int**)(*p* − *tok_start*));
          if (*make_pb*) *app_str*("\\PB{");
          app(*inner_tok_flag* + (**int**)(*q* − *tok_start*));
          if (*make_pb*) *app_tok*('}');
          if (*next_control* $\equiv$ '|') {
            bal $\leftarrow$ *copy_comment*(*is_long_comment*, *bal*);
            next_control $\leftarrow$ *ignore*;
          }
          else *bal* $\leftarrow$ 0;   /* an error has been reported */
        }
        app(*force*);
        app_scrap(*insert*, *no_math*);   /* the full comment becomes a scrap */
      }
  }

185. Output of tokens.   So far our programs have only built up multi-layered token lists in CWEAVE's internal memory; we have to figure out how to get them into the desired final form. The job of converting token lists to characters in the TEX output file is not difficult, although it is an implicitly recursive process. Four main considerations had to be kept in mind when this part of CWEAVE was designed. (a) There are two modes of output: *outer* mode, which translates tokens like *force* into line-breaking control sequences, and *inner* mode, which ignores them except that blank spaces take the place of line breaks. (b) The *cancel* instruction applies to adjacent token or tokens that are output, and this cuts across levels of recursion since '*cancel*' occurs at the beginning or end of a token list on one level. (c) The TEX output file will be semi-readable if line breaks are inserted after the result of tokens like *break_space* and *force*. (d) The final line break should be suppressed, and there should be no *force* token output immediately after '\Y\B'.

186.   The output process uses a stack to keep track of what is going on at different "levels" as the token lists are being written out. Entries on this stack have three parts:

    end_field is the *tok_mem* location where the token list of a particular level will end;

    tok_field is the *tok_mem* location from which the next token on a particular level will be read;

    mode_field is the current mode, either *inner* or *outer*.

The current values of these quantities are referred to quite frequently, so they are stored in a separate place instead of in the *stack* array. We call the current values *cur_end*, *cur_tok*, and *cur_mode*.

    The global variable *stack_ptr* tells how many levels of output are currently in progress. The end of output occurs when an *end_translation* token is found, so the stack is never empty except when we first begin the output process.

#define *inner*   0   /* value of *mode* for C texts within TEX texts */
#define *outer*   1   /* value of *mode* for C texts in sections */
⟨ Typedef declarations 18 ⟩ +≡
  typedef int mode;
  typedef struct {
    token_pointer *end_field*;   /* ending location of token list */
    token_pointer *tok_field*;   /* present location within token list */
    boolean *mode_field*;   /* interpretation of control tokens */
  } **output_state**;
  typedef output_state *stack_pointer;

187.   **#define** *cur_end*   *cur_state.end_field*   /* current ending location in *tok_mem* */
#define *cur_tok*   *cur_state.tok_field*   /* location of next output token in *tok_mem* */
#define *cur_mode*   *cur_state.mode_field*   /* current mode of interpretation */
#define *init_stack*   *stack_ptr* ← *stack*; *cur_mode* ← *outer*   /* initialize the stack */
⟨ Global variables 17 ⟩ +≡
  output_state *cur_state*;   /* *cur_end*, *cur_tok*, *cur_mode* */
  output_state *stack*[*stack_size*];   /* info for non-current levels */
  stack_pointer *stack_ptr*;   /* first unused location in the output state stack */
  stack_pointer *stack_end* ← *stack* + *stack_size* − 1;   /* end of *stack* */
  stack_pointer *max_stack_ptr*;   /* largest value assumed by *stack_ptr* */

188.   ⟨ Set initial values 20 ⟩ +≡
  max_stack_ptr ← *stack*;

189.   To insert token-list p into the output, the *push_level* subroutine is called; it saves the old level of output and gets a new one going. The value of *cur_mode* is not changed.

```
void push_level(p)          /* suspends the current level */
    text_pointer p;
{
    if (stack_ptr ≡ stack_end) overflow("stack");
    if (stack_ptr > stack) {        /* save current state */
        stack_ptr→end_field ← cur_end;
        stack_ptr→tok_field ← cur_tok;
        stack_ptr→mode_field ← cur_mode;
    }
    stack_ptr ++;
    if (stack_ptr > max_stack_ptr) max_stack_ptr ← stack_ptr;
    cur_tok ← *p;
    cur_end ← *(p + 1);
}
```

190.   Conversely, the *pop_level* routine restores the conditions that were in force when the current level was begun. This subroutine will never be called when $stack\_ptr \equiv 1$.

```
void pop_level()
{
    cur_end ← (-- stack_ptr)→end_field;
    cur_tok ← stack_ptr→tok_field;
    cur_mode ← stack_ptr→mode_field;
}
```

191.   The *get_output* function returns the next byte of output that is not a reference to a token list. It returns the values *identifier* or *res_word* or *section_code* if the next token is to be an identifier (typeset in italics), a reserved word (typeset in boldface), or a section name (typeset by a complex routine that might generate additional levels of output). In these cases *cur_name* points to the identifier or section name in question.

⟨ Global variables 17 ⟩ +≡
    name_pointer *cur_name*;

192.   **#define** *res_word* °*201*   /* returned by *get_output* for reserved words */
#define *section_code* °*200*   /* returned by *get_output* for section names */
  eight_bits *get_output*( )   /* returns the next token of output */
  {
    sixteen_bits *a*;   /* current item read from *tok_mem* */
  restart:
    while (*cur_tok* ≡ *cur_end*) *pop_level*( );
    a ← *(*cur_tok*++);
    if (*a* ≥ °*400*) {
      cur_name ← *a* % *id_flag* + *name_dir*;
      switch (*a*/*id_flag*) {
      case 2: **return** (*res_word*);   /* *a* ≡ *res_flag* + *cur_name* */
      case 3: **return** (*section_code*);   /* *a* ≡ *section_flag* + *cur_name* */
      case 4: *push_level*(*a* % *id_flag* + *tok_start*);
        goto *restart*;   /* *a* ≡ *tok_flag* + *cur_name* */
      case 5: *push_level*(*a* % *id_flag* + *tok_start*);
        cur_mode ← *inner*;
        goto *restart*;   /* *a* ≡ *inner_tok_flag* + *cur_name* */
      default: **return** (*identifier*);   /* *a* ≡ *id_flag* + *cur_name* */
      }
    }
    return (*a*);
  }

193.   The real work associated with token output is done by *make_output*. This procedure appends an *end_translation* token to the current token list, and then it repeatedly calls *get_output* and feeds characters to the output buffer until reaching the *end_translation* sentinel. It is possible for *make_output* to be called recursively, since a section name may include embedded C text; however, the depth of recursion never exceeds one level, since section names cannot be inside of section names.

A procedure called *output_C* does the scanning, translation, and output of C text within '| . . . |' brackets, and this procedure uses *make_output* to output the current token list. Thus, the recursive call of *make_output* actually occurs when *make_output* calls *output_C* while outputting the name of a section.

```
void output_C()      /* outputs the current token list */
{
  token_pointer save_tok_ptr;
  text_pointer save_text_ptr;
  sixteen_bits save_next_control;      /* values to be restored */
  text_pointer p;      /* translation of the C text */

  save_tok_ptr ← tok_ptr;
  save_text_ptr ← text_ptr;
  save_next_control ← next_control;
  next_control ← ignore;
  p ← C_translate();
  app(inner_tok_flag + (int)(p − tok_start));
  if (make_pb) {
    out_str("\\PB{");
    make_output();
    out('}');
  } else make_output();      /* output the list */
  if (text_ptr > max_text_ptr) max_text_ptr ← text_ptr;
  if (tok_ptr > max_tok_ptr) max_tok_ptr ← tok_ptr;
  text_ptr ← save_text_ptr;
  tok_ptr ← save_tok_ptr;      /* forget the tokens */
  next_control ← save_next_control;      /* restore next_control to original state */
}
```

194.   Here is **CWEAVE**'s major output handler.

⟨ Predeclaration of procedures 2 ⟩ +≡
```
  void make_output();
```

195.   **void** *make_output*( )   /* outputs the equivalents of tokens */
  {
    eight_bits *a*,   /* current output byte */
    b;   /* next output byte */
    int *c*;   /* count of *indent* and *outdent* tokens */
    char *scratch*[*longest_name*];   /* scratch area for section names */
    char **k*, **k_limit*;   /* indices into *scratch* */
    char **j*;   /* index into *buffer* */
    char **p*;   /* index into *byte_mem* */
    char *delim*;   /* first and last character of string being copied */
    char **save_loc*, **save_limit*;   /* *loc* and *limit* to be restored */
    name_pointer *cur_section_name*;   /* name of section being output */
    boolean *save_mode*;   /* value of *cur_mode* before a sequence of breaks */
    app(*end_translation*);   /* append a sentinel */
    freeze_text;
    push_level(*text_ptr* − 1);
    while (1) {
      a ← *get_output*( );
    reswitch:
      switch (*a*) {
      case *end_translation*: **return**;
      case *identifier*: **case** *res_word*: ⟨Output an identifier 196⟩;
        break;
      case *section_code*: ⟨Output a section name 200⟩;
        break;
      case *math_rel*: *out_str*("\\MRL{");
      case *noop*: **case** *inserted*: **break**;
      case *cancel*: **case** *big_cancel*: *c* ← 0;
        b ← *a*;
        while (1) {
          a ← *get_output*( );
          if (*a* ≡ *inserted*) **continue**;
          if ((*a* < *indent* ∧ ¬(*b* ≡ *big_cancel* ∧ *a* ≡ '␣')) ∨ *a* > *big_force*) **break**;
          if (*a* ≡ *indent*) *c*++;
          else if (*a* ≡ *outdent*) *c*−−;
          else if (*a* ≡ *opt*) *a* ← *get_output*( );
        }
        ⟨Output saved *indent* or *outdent* tokens 199⟩;
        goto *reswitch*;
      case *indent*: **case** *outdent*: **case** *opt*: **case** *backup*: **case** *break_space*: **case** *force*: **case** *big_force*:
        case *preproc_line*:
        ⟨Output a control, look ahead in case of line breaks, possibly **goto** *reswitch* 197⟩;
        break;
      case *quoted_char*: *out*(*(*cur_tok*++));
      case *qualifier*: **break**;
      default: *out*(*a*);   /* otherwise *a* is an ordinary character */
      }
    }
  }

196.   An identifier of length one does not have to be enclosed in braces, and it looks slightly better if set in a math-italic font instead of a (slightly narrower) text-italic font. Thus we output '\|a' but '\\{aa}'.

⟨ Output an identifier 196 ⟩ ≡
  out(`'\\'`);
  if (*a* ≡ *identifier*) {
    if (*cur_name*→*ilk* ≡ *custom* ∧ ¬*doing_format*) {
    custom_out:
      for (*p* ← *cur_name*→*byte_start*; *p* < (*cur_name* + 1)→*byte_start*; *p*++)
        out(∗*p* ≡ `'_'` ? `'x'` : ∗*p* ≡ `'$'` ? `'X'` : ∗*p*);
      break;
    }
    else if (*is_tiny*(*cur_name*)) *out*(`'|'`)
    else {
      delim ← `'.'`;
      for (*p* ← *cur_name*→*byte_start*; *p* < (*cur_name* + 1)→*byte_start*; *p*++)
        if (*xislower*(∗*p*)) {   /∗ not entirely uppercase ∗/
          delim ← `'\\'`;
          break;
        }
      out(*delim*);
    }
  } **else if** (*cur_name*→*ilk* ≡ *alfop*) {
    out(`'X'`);
    goto *custom_out*;
  } **else** *out*(`'&'`);   /∗ *a* ≡ *res_word* ∗/
  if (*is_tiny*(*cur_name*)) {
    if (*isxalpha*((*cur_name*→*byte_start*)[0])) *out*(`'\\'`);
    out((*cur_name*→*byte_start*)[0]);
  }
  else *out_name*(*cur_name*, 1);

This code is used in section 195.

197.   The current mode does not affect the behavior of **CWEAVE**'s output routine except when we are outputting control tokens.

⟨ Output a control, look ahead in case of line breaks, possibly **goto** *reswitch* 197 ⟩ ≡
  if (*a* < *break_space* ∨ *a* ≡ *preproc_line*) {
    if (*cur_mode* ≡ *outer*) {
      out(`'\\'`);
      out(*a* − *cancel* + `'0'`);
      if (*a* ≡ *opt*) {
        b ← *get_output*();   /∗ *opt* is followed by a digit ∗/
        if (*b* ≠ `'0'` ∨ *force_lines* ≡ 0) *out*(*b*)
        else *out_str*(`"{-1}"`);   /∗ *force_lines* encourages more @| breaks ∗/
      }
    }
    else if (*a* ≡ *opt*) *b* ← *get_output*();   /∗ ignore digit following *opt* ∗/
  }
  else ⟨ Look ahead for strongest line break, **goto** *reswitch* 198 ⟩

This code is used in section 195.

198.   If several of the tokens *break_space*, *force*, *big_force* occur in a row, possibly mixed with blank spaces (which are ignored), the largest one is used. A line break also occurs in the output file, except at the very end of the translation. The very first line break is suppressed (i.e., a line break that follows '\Y\B').

⟨ Look ahead for strongest line break, **goto** *reswitch* 198 ⟩ ≡

```
{
    b ← a;
    save_mode ← cur_mode;
    c ← 0;
    while (1) {
        a ← get_output( );
        if (a ≡ inserted) continue;
        if (a ≡ cancel ∨ a ≡ big_cancel) {
            ⟨ Output saved indent or outdent tokens 199 ⟩;
            goto reswitch;        /* cancel overrides everything */
        }
        if ((a ≠ '␣' ∧ a < indent) ∨ a ≡ backup ∨ a > big_force) {
            if (save_mode ≡ outer) {
                if (out_ptr > out_buf + 3 ∧ strncmp(out_ptr − 3, "\\Y\\B", 4) ≡ 0) goto reswitch;
                ⟨ Output saved indent or outdent tokens 199 ⟩;
                out('\\');
                out(b − cancel + '0');
                if (a ≠ end_translation) finish_line( );
            }
            else if (a ≠ end_translation ∧ cur_mode ≡ inner) out('␣');
            goto reswitch;
        }
        if (a ≡ indent) c++;
        else if (a ≡ outdent) c−−;
        else if (a ≡ opt) a ← get_output( );
        else if (a > b) b ← a;        /* if a ≡ '␣' we have a < b */
    }
}
```
This code is used in section 197.

199.   ⟨ Output saved *indent* or *outdent* tokens 199 ⟩ ≡
```
    for ( ; c > 0; c−−) out_str("\\1");
    for ( ; c < 0; c++) out_str("\\2");
```
This code is used in sections 195 and 198.

200.   The remaining part of *make_output* is somewhat more complicated. When we output a section name, we may need to enter the parsing and translation routines, since the name may contain C code embedded in | ... | constructions. This C code is placed at the end of the active input buffer and the translation process uses the end of the active *tok_mem* area.

⟨ Output a section name 200 ⟩ ≡

```
{
    out_str("\\X");
    cur_xref ← (xref_pointer) cur_name→xref;
    if (cur_xref→num ≡ file_flag) {
        an_output ← 1;
        cur_xref ← cur_xref→xlink;
    }
    else  an_output ← 0;
    if (cur_xref→num ≥ def_flag) {
        out_section(cur_xref→num − def_flag);
        if (phase ≡ 3) {
            cur_xref ← cur_xref→xlink;
            while (cur_xref→num ≥ def_flag) {
                out_str(",␣");
                out_section(cur_xref→num − def_flag);
                cur_xref ← cur_xref→xlink;
            }
        }
    }
    else  out('0');      /* output the section number, or zero if it was undefined */
    out(':');
    if (an_output)  out_str("\\.{");
    ⟨ Output the text of the section name 201 ⟩;
    if (an_output)  out_str("␣}");
    out_str("\\X");
}
```

This code is used in section 195.

201. ⟨Output the text of the section name 201⟩ ≡
sprint_section_name(*scratch*, *cur_name*);
$k \leftarrow scratch$;
$k\_limit \leftarrow scratch + strlen(scratch)$;
$cur\_section\_name \leftarrow cur\_name$; **while** $(k < k\_limit)$ { $b \leftarrow *(k{+}{+})$;
if $(b \equiv \text{'\@'})$ ⟨Skip next character, give error if not '@' 202⟩;
if (*an_output*)
  switch (b) {
  case '␣': **case** '\\': **case** '#': **case** '%': **case** '$': **case** '^': **case** '{': **case** '}': **case** '~':
    case '&': **case** '_': *out*('\\');   /* falls through */
  default: *out*(*b*);
  }
 else if $(b \neq \text{'|'})$ *out*(*b*)
 else {
  ⟨Copy the C text into the *buffer* array 203⟩;
  $save\_loc \leftarrow loc$;
  $save\_limit \leftarrow limit$;
  $loc \leftarrow limit + 2$;
  $limit \leftarrow j + 1$;
  $*limit \leftarrow \text{'|'}$;
  output_C( );
  $loc \leftarrow save\_loc$;
  $limit \leftarrow save\_limit$;
 }
}
This code is used in section 200.

202. ⟨Skip next character, give error if not '@' 202⟩ ≡
 if $(*k{+}{+} \neq \text{'\@'})$ {
  printf("\n!␣Illegal␣control␣code␣in␣section␣name:␣<");
  print_section_name(*cur_section_name*);
  printf(">␣");
  mark_error;
 }
This code is used in section 201.

203.   The C text enclosed in | ... | should not contain '|' characters, except within strings. We put a '|' at the front of the buffer, so that an error message that displays the whole buffer will look a little bit sensible. The variable *delim* is zero outside of strings, otherwise it equals the delimiter that began the string being copied.

⟨ Copy the C text into the *buffer* array 203 ⟩ ≡
```
  j ← limit + 1;
  *j ← '|';
  delim ← 0; while (1) {
  if (k ≥ k_limit) {
    printf("\n!␣C␣text␣in␣section␣name␣didn't␣end:␣<");
    print_section_name(cur_section_name);
    printf(">␣");
    mark_error;
    break;
  }
  b ← *(k++); if (b ≡ '@' ∨ (b ≡ '\\' ∧ delim ≠ 0)) ⟨ Copy a quoted character into the buffer 204 ⟩
  else {
    if (b ≡ '\'' ∨ b ≡ '"')
      if (delim ≡ 0) delim ← b;
      else if (delim ≡ b) delim ← 0;
    if (b ≠ '|' ∨ delim ≠ 0) {
      if (j > buffer + long_buf_size − 3) overflow("buffer");
      *(++j) ← b;
    }
    else break;
  }
  }
```
This code is used in section 201.

204.   ⟨ Copy a quoted character into the buffer 204 ⟩ ≡
```
  {
    if (j > buffer + long_buf_size − 4) overflow("buffer");
    *(++j) ← b;
    *(++j) ← *(k++);
  }
```
This code is used in section 203.

205. Phase two processing. We have assembled enough pieces of the puzzle in order to be ready to specify the processing in CWEAVE's main pass over the source file. Phase two is analogous to phase one, except that more work is involved because we must actually output the TeX material instead of merely looking at the CWEB specifications.

⟨ Predeclaration of procedures 2 ⟩ +≡
  void *phase_two*( );

206. **void** *phase_two*( )
  {
    reset_input( );
    if (*show_progress*) *printf*("\nWriting␣the␣output␣file...");
    section_count ← 0;
    format_visible ← 1;
    copy_limbo( );
    finish_line( );
    flush_buffer(*out_buf*, 0, 0);   /∗ insert a blank line, it looks nice ∗/
    while (¬*input_has_ended*) ⟨ Translate the current section 208 ⟩;
  }

207. The output file will contain the control sequence \Y between non-null sections of a section, e.g., between the TeX and definition parts if both are nonempty. This puts a little white space between the parts when they are printed. However, we don't want \Y to occur between two definitions within a single section. The variables *out_line* or *out_ptr* will change if a section is non-null, so the following macros 'save_position' and 'emit_space_if_needed' are able to handle the situation:

#define *save_position* *save_line* ← *out_line*; *save_place* ← *out_ptr*
#define *emit_space_if_needed*
        if (*save_line* ≠ *out_line* ∨ *save_place* ≠ *out_ptr*) *out_str*("\\Y");
        space_checked ← 1

⟨ Global variables 17 ⟩ +≡
  int *save_line*;   /∗ former value of *out_line* ∗/
  char ∗*save_place*;   /∗ former value of *out_ptr* ∗/
  int *sec_depth*;   /∗ the integer, if any, following @∗ ∗/
  boolean *space_checked*;   /∗ have we done *emit_space_if_needed*? ∗/
  boolean *format_visible*;   /∗ should the next format declaration be output? ∗/
  boolean *doing_format* ← 0;   /∗ are we outputting a format declaration? ∗/
  boolean *group_found* ← 0;   /∗ has a starred section occurred? ∗/

208. ⟨ Translate the current section 208 ⟩ ≡
  {
    section_count ++;
    ⟨ Output the code for the beginning of a new section 209 ⟩;
    save_position;
    ⟨ Translate the TeX part of the current section 210 ⟩;
    ⟨ Translate the definition part of the current section 211 ⟩;
    ⟨ Translate the C part of the current section 217 ⟩;
    ⟨ Show cross-references to this section 220 ⟩;
    ⟨ Output the code for the end of a section 224 ⟩;
  }
This code is used in section 206.

209. Sections beginning with the CWEB control sequence '@␣' start in the output with the TEX control sequence '\M', followed by the section number. Similarly, '@*' sections lead to the control sequence '\N'. In this case there's an additional parameter, representing one plus the specified depth, immediately after the \N. If the section has changed, we put * just after the section number.

⟨ Output the code for the beginning of a new section 209 ⟩ ≡
```
    if (*(loc − 1) ≠ '*') out_str("\\M");
    else {
        while (*loc ≡ '␣') loc++;
        if (*loc ≡ '*') {       /* "top" level */
            sec_depth ← −1;
            loc++;
        }
        else {
            for (sec_depth ← 0; xisdigit(*loc); loc++) sec_depth ← sec_depth * 10 + (*loc) − '0';
        }
        while (*loc ≡ '␣') loc++;       /* remove spaces before group title */
        group_found ← 1;
        out_str("\\N");
        { char s[32]; sprintf(s, "{%d}", sec_depth + 1); out_str(s); }
        if (show_progress) printf("*%d", section_count);
        update_terminal;       /* print a progress report */
    }
    out_str("{");
    out_section(section_count);
    out_str("}");
```
This code is used in section 208.

210. In the TEX part of a section, we simply copy the source text, except that index entries are not copied and C text within | ... | is translated.

⟨ Translate the TEX part of the current section 210 ⟩ ≡
```
    do {
        next_control ← copy_TEX();
        switch (next_control) {
        case '|': init_stack;
            output_C();
            break;
        case '@': out('@');
            break;
        case TEX_string: case noop: case xref_roman: case xref_wildcard: case xref_typewriter:
            case section_name: loc −= 2;
            next_control ← get_next();       /* skip to @> */
            if (next_control ≡ TEX_string) err_print("! TeX string should be in C text only");
            break;
        case thin_space: case math_break: case ord: case line_break: case big_line_break:
            case no_line_break: case join: case pseudo_semi: case macro_arg_open: case macro_arg_close:
            case output_defs_code: err_print("! You can't do that in TeX text");
            break;
        }
    } while (next_control < format_code);
```
This code is used in section 208.

211. When we get to the following code we have $next\_control \geq format\_code$, and the token memory is in its initial empty state.

⟨ Translate the definition part of the current section 211 ⟩ ≡
  $space\_checked \leftarrow 0$;
  while ($next\_control \leq definition$) {   /* $format\_code$ or $definition$ */
    $init\_stack$;
    if ($next\_control \equiv definition$) ⟨ Start a macro definition 214 ⟩
    else ⟨ Start a format definition 215 ⟩;
    $outer\_parse(\,)$;
    $finish\_C(format\_visible)$;
    $format\_visible \leftarrow 1$;
    $doing\_format \leftarrow 0$;
  }
This code is used in section 208.

212. The $finish\_C$ procedure outputs the translation of the current scraps, preceded by the control sequence '\B' and followed by the control sequence '\par'. It also restores the token and scrap memories to their initial empty state.

A $force$ token is appended to the current scraps before translation takes place, so that the translation will normally end with \6 or \7 (the TeX macros for $force$ and big_force). This \6 or \7 is replaced by the concluding \par or by \Y\par.

⟨ Predeclaration of procedures 2 ⟩ +≡
  void $finish\_C(\,)$;

213. **void** $finish\_C(visible)$ /* finishes a definition or a C part */
    boolean $visible$;   /* nonzero if we should produce TeX output */
  {
    text_pointer p;   /* translation of the scraps */
    if ($visible$) {
      $out\_str("\backslash\backslash B")$;
      $app\_tok(force)$;
      $app\_scrap(insert, no\_math)$;
      $p \leftarrow translate(\,)$;
      $app(tok\_flag + (\textbf{int})(p - tok\_start))$;
      $make\_output(\,)$;   /* output the list */
      if ($out\_ptr > out\_buf + 1$)
        if ($*(out\_ptr - 1) \equiv '\backslash\backslash'$)
          if ($*out\_ptr \equiv '6'$) $out\_ptr \mathrel{-}= 2$;
          else if ($*out\_ptr \equiv '7'$) $*out\_ptr \leftarrow 'Y'$;
      $out\_str("\backslash\backslash par")$;
      $finish\_line(\,)$;
    }
    if ($text\_ptr > max\_text\_ptr$) $max\_text\_ptr \leftarrow text\_ptr$;
    if ($tok\_ptr > max\_tok\_ptr$) $max\_tok\_ptr \leftarrow tok\_ptr$;
    if ($scrap\_ptr > max\_scr\_ptr$) $max\_scr\_ptr \leftarrow scrap\_ptr$;
    $tok\_ptr \leftarrow tok\_mem + 1$;
    $text\_ptr \leftarrow tok\_start + 1$;
    $scrap\_ptr \leftarrow scrap\_info$;   /* forget the tokens and the scraps */
  }

214.   Keeping in line with the conventions of the C preprocessor (and otherwise contrary to the rules of
CWEB) we distinguish here between the case that '(' immediately follows an identifier and the case that
the two are separated by a space. In the latter case, and if the identifier is not followed by '(' at all,
the replacement text starts immediately after the identifier. In the former case, it starts after we scan the
matching ')'.

⟨ Start a macro definition 214 ⟩ ≡

```
{
    if (save_line ≠ out_line ∨ save_place ≠ out_ptr ∨ space_checked) app(backup);
    if (¬space_checked) {
        emit_space_if_needed;
        save_position;
    }
    app_str("\\D");      /* this will produce 'define ' */
    if ((next_control ← get_next()) ≠ identifier) err_print("!␣Improper␣macro␣definition");
    else {
        app('$');
        app_cur_id(0);
        if (*loc ≡ '(')
        reswitch:
            switch (next_control ← get_next()) {
            case '(': case ',': app(next_control);
                goto reswitch;
            case identifier: app_cur_id(0);
                goto reswitch;
            case ')': app(next_control);
                next_control ← get_next();
                break;
            default: err_print("!␣Improper␣macro␣definition");
                break;
            }
        else next_control ← get_next();
        app_str("$␣");
        app(break_space);
        app_scrap(dead, no_math);       /* scrap won't take part in the parsing */
    }
}
```

This code is used in section 211.

215.   ⟨ Start a format definition 215 ⟩ ≡
  {
      $doing\_format \leftarrow 1$;
      if $(*(loc - 1) \equiv \texttt{'s'} \lor *(loc - 1) \equiv \texttt{'S'})$ $format\_visible \leftarrow 0$;
      if $(\neg space\_checked)$ {
        $emit\_space\_if\_needed$;
        $save\_position$;
      }
      $app\_str(\texttt{"\\\\F"})$;   /∗ this will produce '**format** ' ∗/
      $next\_control \leftarrow get\_next(\,)$;
      if $(next\_control \equiv identifier)$ {
        $app(id\_flag + (\textbf{int})(id\_lookup(id\_first, id\_loc, normal) - name\_dir))$;
        $app(\texttt{'\textvisiblespace'})$;
        $app(break\_space)$;   /∗ this is syntactically separate from what follows ∗/
        $next\_control \leftarrow get\_next(\,)$;
        if $(next\_control \equiv identifier)$ {
          $app(id\_flag + (\textbf{int})(id\_lookup(id\_first, id\_loc, normal) - name\_dir))$;
          $app\_scrap(exp, maybe\_math)$;
          $app\_scrap(semi, maybe\_math)$;
          $next\_control \leftarrow get\_next(\,)$;
        }
      }
      if $(scrap\_ptr \neq scrap\_info + 2)$ $err\_print(\texttt{"!\textvisiblespace Improper\textvisiblespace format\textvisiblespace definition"})$;
  }
This code is used in section 211.

216.   Finally, when the TeX and definition parts have been treated, we have $next\_control \geq begin\_C$. We will make the global variable $this\_section$ point to the current section name, if it has a name.
⟨ Global variables 17 ⟩ +≡
  name_pointer $this\_section$;   /∗ the current section name, or zero ∗/

217.   ⟨ Translate the C part of the current section 217 ⟩ ≡
  $this\_section \leftarrow name\_dir$;
  if $(next\_control \leq section\_name)$ {
    $emit\_space\_if\_needed$;
    $init\_stack$;
    if $(next\_control \equiv begin\_C)$ $next\_control \leftarrow get\_next(\,)$;
    else {
      $this\_section \leftarrow cur\_section$;
      ⟨ Check that '=' or '==' follows this section name, and emit the scraps to start the section
          definition 218 ⟩;
    }
    while $(next\_control \leq section\_name)$ {
      $outer\_parse(\,)$;
      ⟨ Emit the scrap for a section name if present 219 ⟩;
    }
    $finish\_C(1)$;
  }
This code is used in section 208.

218.   The title of the section and an $\equiv$ or $+\equiv$ are made into a scrap that should not take part in the parsing.

$\langle$ Check that '=' or '==' follows this section name, and emit the scraps to start the section definition 218 $\rangle \equiv$
    do $next\_control \leftarrow get\_next(\ )$; **while** $(next\_control \equiv \text{'+'})$;   /* allow optional '+=' */
    if $(next\_control \neq \text{'='} \wedge next\_control \neq eq\_eq)$
       $err\_print(\texttt{"!}_\sqcup\texttt{You}_\sqcup\texttt{need}_\sqcup\texttt{an}_\sqcup\texttt{=sign}_\sqcup\texttt{after}_\sqcup\texttt{the}_\sqcup\texttt{section}_\sqcup\texttt{name"})$;
    else $next\_control \leftarrow get\_next(\ )$;
    if $(out\_ptr > out\_buf + 1 \wedge *out\_ptr \equiv \text{'Y'} \wedge *(out\_ptr - 1) \equiv \text{'}\backslash\backslash\text{'})$ $app(backup)$;
       /* the section name will be flush left */
    $app(section\_flag + (\textbf{int})(this\_section - name\_dir))$;
    $cur\_xref \leftarrow (\textbf{xref\_pointer}) \ this\_section \rightarrow xref$;
    if $(cur\_xref \rightarrow num \equiv file\_flag)$ $cur\_xref \leftarrow cur\_xref \rightarrow xlink$;
    $app\_str(\texttt{"\${}\}"})$;
    if $(cur\_xref \rightarrow num \neq section\_count + def\_flag)$ {
       $app\_str(\texttt{"\\\\mathrel+"})$;   /* section name is multiply defined */
       $this\_section \leftarrow name\_dir$;   /* so we won't give cross-reference info here */
    }
    $app\_str(\texttt{"\\\\E"})$;   /* output an equivalence sign */
    $app\_str(\texttt{"\{}\$"})$;
    $app(force)$;
    $app\_scrap(dead, no\_math)$;   /* this forces a line break unless '@+' follows */
This code is used in section 217.

219. $\langle$ Emit the scrap for a section name if present 219 $\rangle \equiv$
    if $(next\_control < section\_name)$ {
       $err\_print(\texttt{"!}_\sqcup\texttt{You}_\sqcup\texttt{can't}_\sqcup\texttt{do}_\sqcup\texttt{that}_\sqcup\texttt{in}_\sqcup\texttt{C}_\sqcup\texttt{text"})$;
       $next\_control \leftarrow get\_next(\ )$;
    }
    else if $(next\_control \equiv section\_name)$ {
       $app(section\_flag + (\textbf{int})(cur\_section - name\_dir))$;
       $app\_scrap(section\_scrap, maybe\_math)$;
       $next\_control \leftarrow get\_next(\ )$;
    }
This code is used in section 217.

220.   Cross references relating to a named section are given after the section ends.

$\langle$ Show cross-references to this section 220 $\rangle \equiv$
    if $(this\_section > name\_dir)$ {
       $cur\_xref \leftarrow (\textbf{xref\_pointer}) \ this\_section \rightarrow xref$;
       if $(cur\_xref \rightarrow num \equiv file\_flag)$ {
          $an\_output \leftarrow 1$;
          $cur\_xref \leftarrow cur\_xref \rightarrow xlink$;
       }
       else $an\_output \leftarrow 0$;
       if $(cur\_xref \rightarrow num > def\_flag)$ $cur\_xref \leftarrow cur\_xref \rightarrow xlink$;   /* bypass current section number */
       $footnote(def\_flag)$;
       $footnote(cite\_flag)$;
       $footnote(0)$;
    }
This code is used in section 208.

221. The *footnote* procedure gives cross-reference information about multiply defined section names (if the *flag* parameter is *def_flag*), or about references to a section name (if *flag* ≡ *cite_flag*), or to its uses (if *flag* ≡ 0). It assumes that *cur_xref* points to the first cross-reference entry of interest, and it leaves *cur_xref* pointing to the first element not printed. Typical outputs: '\A101.'; '\Us 370\ET1009.'; '\As 8, 27*\ETs64.'.

Note that the output of **CWEAVE** is not English-specific; users may supply new definitions for the macros \A, \As, etc.

⟨ Predeclaration of procedures 2 ⟩ +≡
    void *footnote* ( );

222.   **void** *footnote* (*flag*)   /∗ outputs section cross-references ∗/
    sixteen_bits *flag*;
  {
    xref_pointer *q*;   /∗ cross-reference pointer variable ∗/
    if (*cur_xref*→*num* ≤ *flag*) **return**;
    finish_line ( );
    out ('\\');
    out (*flag* ≡ 0 ? 'U' : *flag* ≡ *cite_flag* ? 'Q' : 'A');
    ⟨ Output all the section numbers on the reference list *cur_xref* 223 ⟩;
    out ('.');
  }

223. The following code distinguishes three cases, according as the number of cross-references is one, two, or more than two. Variable *q* points to the first cross-reference, and the last link is a zero.

⟨ Output all the section numbers on the reference list *cur_xref* 223 ⟩ ≡
  q ← *cur_xref*;
  if (*q*→*xlink*→*num* > *flag*) *out* ('s');   /∗ plural ∗/
  while (1) {
    out_section (*cur_xref*→*num* − *flag*);
    cur_xref ← *cur_xref*→*xlink*;   /∗ point to the next cross-reference to output ∗/
    if (*cur_xref*→*num* ≤ *flag*) **break**;
    if (*cur_xref*→*xlink*→*num* > *flag*) *out_str* (",␣");   /∗ not the last ∗/
    else {
      out_str ("\\ET");   /∗ the last ∗/
      if (*cur_xref* ≠ *q*→*xlink*) *out* ('s');   /∗ the last of more than two ∗/
    }
  }
This code is used in section 222.

224.   ⟨ Output the code for the end of a section 224 ⟩ ≡
  out_str ("\\fi");
  finish_line ( );
  flush_buffer (*out_buf*, 0, 0);   /∗ insert a blank line, it looks nice ∗/
This code is used in section 208.

225.   Phase three processing.   We are nearly finished! CWEAVE's only remaining task is to write out the index, after sorting the identifiers and index entries.

If the user has set the *no_xref* flag (the -x option on the command line), just finish off the page, omitting the index, section name list, and table of contents.

⟨ Predeclaration of procedures 2 ⟩ +≡
　　void *phase_three* ( );

226.   void *phase_three* ( )
　　{
　　　if (*no_xref*) {
　　　　finish_line ( );
　　　　out_str ("\\end");
　　　　finish_line ( );
　　　}
　　　else {
　　　　phase ← 3;
　　　　if (*show_progress*) *printf* ("\nWriting␣the␣index...");
　　　　finish_line ( );
　　　　if ((*idx_file* ← *fopen*(*idx_file_name*, "w")) ≡ Λ)
　　　　　fatal ("!␣Cannot␣open␣index␣file␣", *idx_file_name*);
　　　　if (*change_exists*) {
　　　　　⟨ Tell about changed sections 228 ⟩;
　　　　　finish_line ( );
　　　　　finish_line ( );
　　　　}
　　　　out_str ("\\inx");
　　　　finish_line ( );
　　　　active_file ← *idx_file*;　　　/* change active file to the index file */
　　　　⟨ Do the first pass of sorting 230 ⟩;
　　　　⟨ Sort and output the index 239 ⟩;
　　　　finish_line ( );
　　　　fclose(*active_file*);　　　/* finished with *idx_file* */
　　　　active_file ← *tex_file*;　　　/* switch back to *tex_file* for a tic */
　　　　out_str ("\\fin");
　　　　finish_line ( );
　　　　if ((*scn_file* ← *fopen*(*scn_file_name*, "w")) ≡ Λ)
　　　　　fatal ("!␣Cannot␣open␣section␣file␣", *scn_file_name*);
　　　　active_file ← *scn_file*;　　　/* change active file to section listing file */
　　　　⟨ Output all the section names 248 ⟩;
　　　　finish_line ( );
　　　　fclose(*active_file*);　　　/* finished with *scn_file* */
　　　　active_file ← *tex_file*;
　　　　if (*group_found*) *out_str* ("\\con"); **else** *out_str* ("\\end");
　　　　finish_line ( );
　　　　fclose(*active_file*);
　　　}
　　　if (*show_happiness*) *printf* ("\nDone.");
　　　check_complete ( );　　　/* was all of the change file used? */
　　}

227.   Just before the index comes a list of all the changed sections, including the index section itself.

⟨ Global variables 17 ⟩ +≡
 sixteen_bits $k\_section$;   /∗ runs through the sections ∗/

228.   ⟨ Tell about changed sections 228 ⟩ ≡
  {   /∗ remember that the index is already marked as changed ∗/
   $k\_section \leftarrow 0$;
   while ($\neg changed\_section[++k\_section]$) ;
   $out\_str("\backslash\backslash\mathbf{ch}_\sqcup")$;
   $out\_section(k\_section)$;
   while ($k\_section < section\_count$) {
    while ($\neg changed\_section[++k\_section]$) ;
    $out\_str(",_\sqcup")$;
    $out\_section(k\_section)$;
   }
   $out('.')$;
  }
This code is used in section 226.

229.   A left-to-right radix sorting method is used, since this makes it easy to adjust the collating sequence and since the running time will be at worst proportional to the total length of all entries in the index. We put the identifiers into 102 different lists based on their first characters. (Uppercase letters are put into the same list as the corresponding lowercase letters, since we want to have '$t < TeX < \mathbf{to}$'.) The list for character c begins at location $bucket[c]$ and continues through the $blink$ array.

⟨ Global variables 17 ⟩ +≡
 name_pointer $bucket[256]$;
 name_pointer $next\_name$;   /∗ successor of cur_name when sorting ∗/
 name_pointer $blink[max\_names]$;   /∗ links in the buckets ∗/

230.   To begin the sorting, we go through all the hash lists and put each entry having a nonempty cross-reference list into the proper bucket.

⟨ Do the first pass of sorting 230 ⟩ ≡
  {
   int c;
   for ($c \leftarrow 0$; $c \leq 255$; $c{+}{+}$) $bucket[c] \leftarrow \Lambda$;
   for ($h \leftarrow hash$; $h \leq hash\_end$; $h{+}{+}$) {
    $next\_name \leftarrow {*}h$;
    while ($next\_name$) {
     $cur\_name \leftarrow next\_name$;
     $next\_name \leftarrow cur\_name{\rightarrow}link$;
     if ($cur\_name{\rightarrow}xref \neq (\mathbf{char} *) xmem$) {
      $c \leftarrow (\mathbf{eight\_bits})((cur\_name{\rightarrow}byte\_start)[0])$;
      if ($xisupper(c)$) $c \leftarrow tolower(c)$;
      $blink[cur\_name - name\_dir] \leftarrow bucket[c]$;
      $bucket[c] \leftarrow cur\_name$;
     }
    }
   }
  }
This code is used in section 226.

231.   During the sorting phase we shall use the *cat* and *trans* arrays from CWEAVE's parsing algorithm and rename them *depth* and *head*. They now represent a stack of identifier lists for all the index entries that have not yet been output. The variable *sort_ptr* tells how many such lists are present; the lists are output in reverse order (first *sort_ptr*, then *sort_ptr* − 1, etc.). The *j*th list starts at *head*[*j*], and if the first *k* characters of all entries on this list are known to be equal we have $depth[j] \equiv k$.

232.   ⟨ Rest of *trans_plus* union 232 ⟩ ≡
  name_pointer *Head*;

This code is used in section 103.

233.   **#define** *depth*   *cat*   /* reclaims memory that is no longer needed for parsing */
#define *head*   *trans_plus.Head*   /* ditto */
  format *sort_pointer*   *int*
#define **sort_pointer** **scrap_pointer**   /* ditto */
#define *sort_ptr*   *scrap_ptr*   /* ditto */
#define *max_sorts*   *max_scraps*   /* ditto */
⟨ Global variables 17 ⟩ +≡
  eight_bits *cur_depth*;   /* depth of current buckets */
  char **cur_byte*;   /* index into *byte_mem* */
  sixteen_bits *cur_val*;   /* current cross-reference number */
  sort_pointer *max_sort_ptr*;   /* largest value of *sort_ptr* */

234.   ⟨ Set initial values 20 ⟩ +≡
  max_sort_ptr ← *scrap_info*;

235.   The desired alphabetic order is specified by the *collate* array; namely, *collate*[0] < *collate*[1] < ⋯ < *collate*[100].
⟨ Global variables 17 ⟩ +≡
  eight_bits *collate*[102 + 128];   /* collation order */

236.   We use the order null $<$ ␣ $<$ other characters $<$ _ $<$ A $=$ a $< \cdots <$ Z $=$ z $<$ 0 $< \cdots <$ 9. Warning: The collation mapping needs to be changed if ASCII code is not being used.

We initialize *collate* by copying a few characters at a time, because some C compilers choke on long strings.

⟨ Set initial values 20 ⟩ +≡
  collate[0] ← 0;
  strcpy(*collate* + 1, "␣\1\2\3\4\5\6\7\10\11\12\13\14\15\16\17");   /* 16 characters + 1 = 17 */
  strcpy(*collate* + 17, "\20\21\22\23\24\25\26\27\30\31\32\33\34\35\36\37");
    /* 16 characters + 17 = 33 */
  strcpy(*collate* + 33, "!\42#$%&'()*+,-./:;<=>?@[\\]^'{|}~_");   /* 32 characters + 33 = 65 */
  strcpy(*collate* + 65, "abcdefghijklmnopqrstuvwxyz0123456789");
    /* (26 + 10) characters + 65 = 101 */
  strcpy(*collate* + 101, "\200\201\202\203\204\205\206\207\210\211\212\213\214\215\216\217");
    /* 16 characters + 101 = 117 */
  strcpy(*collate* + 117, "\220\221\222\223\224\225\226\227\230\231\232\233\234\235\236\237");
    /* 16 characters + 117 = 133 */
  strcpy(*collate* + 133, "\240\241\242\243\244\245\246\247\250\251\252\253\254\255\256\257");
    /* 16 characters + 133 = 149 */
  strcpy(*collate* + 149, "\260\261\262\263\264\265\266\267\270\271\272\273\274\275\276\277");
    /* 16 characters + 149 = 165 */
  strcpy(*collate* + 165, "\300\301\302\303\304\305\306\307\310\311\312\313\314\315\316\317");
    /* 16 characters + 165 = 181 */
  strcpy(*collate* + 181, "\320\321\322\323\324\325\326\327\330\331\332\333\334\335\336\337");
    /* 16 characters + 181 = 197 */
  strcpy(*collate* + 197, "\340\341\342\343\344\345\346\347\350\351\352\353\354\355\356\357");
    /* 16 characters + 197 = 213 */
  strcpy(*collate* + 213, "\360\361\362\363\364\365\366\367\370\371\372\373\374\375\376\377");
    /* 16 characters + 213 = 229 */

237.   Procedure *unbucket* goes through the buckets and adds nonempty lists to the stack, using the collating sequence specified in the *collate* array. The parameter to *unbucket* tells the current depth in the buckets. Any two sequences that agree in their first 255 character positions are regarded as identical.

#define *infinity* 255   /* ∞ (approximately) */

⟨ Predeclaration of procedures 2 ⟩ +≡
  void *unbucket*( );

238.   **void** *unbucket*(d)   /* empties buckets having depth d */
      eight_bits d;
  {
    int c;   /* index into *bucket*; cannot be a simple **char** because of sign comparison below */
    for ($c ←$ 100 + 128; $c ≥$ 0; c—)
      if (*bucket*[*collate*[c]]) {
        if (*sort_ptr* $≥$ *scrap_info_end*) *overflow*("sorting");
        sort_ptr ++;
        if (*sort_ptr* $>$ *max_sort_ptr*) *max_sort_ptr* ← *sort_ptr*;
        if ($c ≡$ 0) *sort_ptr→depth* ← *infinity*;
        else *sort_ptr→depth* ← d;
        sort_ptr→head ← *bucket*[*collate*[c]];
        bucket[*collate*[c]] ← Λ;
      }
  }

239. ⟨ Sort and output the index 239 ⟩ ≡

  $sort\_ptr \leftarrow scrap\_info$;

  $unbucket(1)$;

  while $(sort\_ptr > scrap\_info)$ {

    $cur\_depth \leftarrow sort\_ptr{\rightarrow}depth$;

    if $(blink[sort\_ptr{\rightarrow}head - name\_dir] \equiv 0 \lor cur\_depth \equiv infinity)$

      ⟨ Output index entries for the list at $sort\_ptr$ 241 ⟩

    else ⟨ Split the list at $sort\_ptr$ into further lists 240 ⟩;

  }

This code is used in section 226.

240. ⟨ Split the list at $sort\_ptr$ into further lists 240 ⟩ ≡

  {

    eight_bits c;

    $next\_name \leftarrow sort\_ptr{\rightarrow}head$;

    do {

      $cur\_name \leftarrow next\_name$;

      $next\_name \leftarrow blink[cur\_name - name\_dir]$;

      $cur\_byte \leftarrow cur\_name{\rightarrow}byte\_start + cur\_depth$;

      if $(cur\_byte \equiv (cur\_name + 1){\rightarrow}byte\_start)$ $c \leftarrow 0$;   /* hit end of the name */

      else {

        $c \leftarrow$ (**eight_bits**) $*cur\_byte$;

        if $(xisupper(c))$ $c \leftarrow tolower(c)$;

      }

      $blink[cur\_name - name\_dir] \leftarrow bucket[c]$;

      $bucket[c] \leftarrow cur\_name$;

    } **while** $(next\_name)$;

    $-\!\!-sort\_ptr$;

    $unbucket(cur\_depth + 1)$;

  }

This code is used in section 239.

241. ⟨ Output index entries for the list at $sort\_ptr$ 241 ⟩ ≡

  {

    $cur\_name \leftarrow sort\_ptr{\rightarrow}head$;

    do {

      $out\_str(\texttt{"\textbackslash\textbackslash I"})$;

      ⟨ Output the name at cur_name 242 ⟩;

      ⟨ Output the cross-references at cur_name 243 ⟩;

      $cur\_name \leftarrow blink[cur\_name - name\_dir]$;

    } **while** (cur_name);

    $-\!\!-sort\_ptr$;

  }

This code is used in section 239.

242.   ⟨ Output the name at *cur_name* 242 ⟩ ≡
  switch (*cur_name→ilk*) {
  case *normal*: **case** *func_template*:
    if (*is_tiny*(*cur_name*)) *out_str*("\\|");
    else {
      char **j*;
      for (*j* ← *cur_name→byte_start*; *j* < (*cur_name* + 1)*→byte_start*; *j*++)
        if (*xislower*(**j*)) **goto** *lowcase*;
      out_str("\\.");
      break;
    lowcase: *out_str*("\\\\");
    }
    break;
  case *wildcard*: *out_str*("\\9"); **goto** *not_an_identifier*;
  case *typewriter*: *out_str*("\\.");
  case *roman*: *not_an_identifier*: *out_name*(*cur_name*, 0);
    goto *name_done*;
  case *custom*:
    {
      char **j*;
      out_str("$\\");
      for (*j* ← *cur_name→byte_start*; *j* < (*cur_name* + 1)*→byte_start*; *j*++)
        out(**j* ≡ '_' ? 'x' : **j* ≡ '$' ? 'X' : **j*);
      out('$');
      goto *name_done*;
    }
  default: *out_str*("\\&");
  }
  out_name(*cur_name*, 1);
name_done:
This code is used in section 241.

243.   Section numbers that are to be underlined are enclosed in '\[...]'.
⟨ Output the cross-references at *cur_name* 243 ⟩ ≡
  ⟨ Invert the cross-reference list at *cur_name*, making *cur_xref* the head 245 ⟩;
  do {
    out_str(",␣");
    cur_val ← *cur_xref→num*;
    if (*cur_val* < *def_flag*) *out_section*(*cur_val*);
    else {
      out_str("\\[");
      out_section(*cur_val* − *def_flag*);
      out(']');
    }
    cur_xref ← *cur_xref→xlink*;
  } **while** (*cur_xref* ≠ *xmem*);
  out('.');
  finish_line( );
This code is used in section 241.

244.   List inversion is best thought of as popping elements off one stack and pushing them onto another. In this case *cur_xref* will be the head of the stack that we push things onto.

⟨ Global variables 17 ⟩ +≡
 xref_pointer *next_xref*, *this_xref*; /* pointer variables for rearranging a list */

245.   ⟨ Invert the cross-reference list at *cur_name*, making *cur_xref* the head 245 ⟩ ≡
 this_xref ← (**xref_pointer**) *cur_name→xref*;
 cur_xref ← *xmem*;
 do {
  next_xref ← *this_xref→xlink*;
  this_xref→xlink ← *cur_xref*;
  cur_xref ← *this_xref*;
  this_xref ← *next_xref*;
 } **while** (*this_xref* ≠ *xmem*);
This code is used in section 243.

246.   The following recursive procedure walks through the tree of section names and prints them.

⟨ Predeclaration of procedures 2 ⟩ +≡
 void *section_print* ( );

247.   **void** *section_print* (*p*) /* print all section names in subtree *p* */
   name_pointer *p*;
 {
  if (*p*) {
   section_print (*p→llink*);
   out_str ("\\I");
   tok_ptr ← *tok_mem* + 1;
   text_ptr ← *tok_start* + 1;
   scrap_ptr ← *scrap_info*;
   init_stack;
   app (*p* − *name_dir* + *section_flag*);
   make_output ( );
   footnote (*cite_flag*);
   footnote (0); /* *cur_xref* was set by *make_output* */
   finish_line ( );
   section_print (*p→rlink*);
  }
 }

248.   ⟨ Output all the section names 248 ⟩ ≡
 section_print (*root*)
This code is used in section 226.

249. Because on some systems the difference between two pointers is a **long** rather than an **int**, we use %ld to print these quantities.

   void *print_stats*( )
   {
     printf ("\nMemory␣usage␣statistics:\n");
     printf ("%ld␣names␣(out␣of␣%ld)\n", (**long**)(*name_ptr* − *name_dir*), (**long**) *max_names*);
     printf ("%ld␣cross-references␣(out␣of␣%ld)\n", (**long**)(*xref_ptr* − *xmem*), (**long**) *max_refs*);
     printf ("%ld␣bytes␣(out␣of␣%ld)\n", (**long**)(*byte_ptr* − *byte_mem*), (**long**) *max_bytes*);
     printf ("Parsing:\n");
     printf ("%ld␣scraps␣(out␣of␣%ld)\n", (**long**)(*max_scr_ptr* − *scrap_info*), (**long**) *max_scraps*);
     printf ("%ld␣texts␣(out␣of␣%ld)\n", (**long**)(*max_text_ptr* − *tok_start*), (**long**) *max_texts*);
     printf ("%ld␣tokens␣(out␣of␣%ld)\n", (**long**)(*max_tok_ptr* − *tok_mem*), (**long**) *max_toks*);
     printf ("%ld␣levels␣(out␣of␣%ld)\n", (**long**)(*max_stack_ptr* − *stack*), (**long**) *stack_size*);
     printf ("Sorting:\n");
     printf ("%ld␣levels␣(out␣of␣%ld)\n", (**long**)(*max_sort_ptr* − *scrap_info*), (**long**) *max_scraps*);
   }

250. Index.   If you have read and understood the code for Phase III above, you know what is in this index and how it got here. All sections in which an identifier is used are listed with that identifier, except that reserved words are indexed only when they appear in format definitions, and the appearances of identifiers in section names are not indexed. Underlined entries correspond to where the identifier was declared. Error messages, control sequences put into the output, and a few other things like "recursion" are indexed here too.

app_scrap: <u>175</u>, 176, 178, 179, 182, 183, 184, 213, 214, 215, 218, 219.

app_str: <u>109</u>, 131, 146, 157, 176, 178, 179, 180, 184, 214, 215, 218.

app_tok: <u>91</u>, 92, 94, 95, 109, 179, 180, 183, 184, 213.

append_xref: <u>21</u>, 22, 23, 116.

app1: <u>108</u>, 171.

argc: 3, <u>13</u>.

argv: 3, <u>13</u>, <u>113</u>.

ASCII code dependencies: 7, 30, 236.

av: <u>3</u>, 13.

b: <u>78</u>, <u>102</u>, <u>195</u>.

backup: <u>100</u>, 102, 107, 134, 143, 195, 198, 214, 218.

bal: <u>65</u>, <u>92</u>, 93, 95, <u>184</u>.

banner: <u>1</u>, 3.

base: <u>97</u>, 98, 102, 110, 117, 129, 130, 136, 163.

begin_arg: <u>97</u>, 98, 101, 102, 110, 176.

begin_C: <u>30</u>, 32, 72, 216, 217.

begin_comment: <u>30</u>, 46, 63, 65, 174, 184.

begin_short_comment: <u>30</u>, 46, 63, 65, 174, 184.

big_app: 108, <u>109</u>, 117, 118, 120, 121, 122, 123, 124, 127, 128, 129, 130, 131, 132, 133, 134, 135, 136, 137, 138, 139, 140, 141, 142, 143, 144, 145, 146, 147, 152, 153, 154, 156, 160, 161, 162.

big_app1: 108, <u>109</u>, 117, 118, 120, 121, 122, 123, 124, 127, 128, 129, 130, 131, 132, 133, 134, 135, 136, 137, 138, 139, 140, 141, 143, 144, 145, 146, 151, 152, 153, 154, 156, 160, 161, 162, 165.

big_app2: <u>108</u>, 117, 118, 127, 129, 140, 142, 146, 147, 157, 161, 162.

big_app3: <u>108</u>, 118, 151.

big_app4: <u>108</u>.

big_cancel: <u>100</u>, 101, 107, 109, 176, 195, 198.

big_force: <u>100</u>, 101, 102, 107, 109, 128, 133, 144, 176, 195, 198, 212.

big_line_break: <u>30</u>, 32, 176, 210.

binop: 96, <u>97</u>, 98, 101, 102, 110, 117, 120, 121, 124, 127, 149, 150, 160, 163, 176, 178.

blink: <u>229</u>, 230, 239, 240, 241.

boolean: <u>5</u>, 11, 12, 13, 17, 41, 43, 65, 73, 78, 87, 92, 182, 184, 186, 195, 207, 213.

break_out: 81, 82, <u>83</u>, <u>84</u>.

break_space: <u>100</u>, 101, 102, 107, 136, 137, 138, 139, 140, 143, 144, 176, 185, 195, 197, 198, 214, 215.

bucket: <u>229</u>, 230, 238, 240.

buf_size: <u>4</u>.

buffer: <u>8</u>, 40, 48, 49, 53, 79, 92, 173, 195, 203, 204.

buffer_end: <u>8</u>, 44.

bug, known: 180.

byte_mem: <u>9</u>, 24, 87, 195, 233, 249.

byte_mem_end: <u>9</u>.

byte_ptr: <u>9</u>, 249.

byte_start: <u>9</u>, 21, 27, 37, 68, 87, 196, 230, 240, 242.

C: <u>102</u>.

c: <u>32</u>, <u>35</u>, <u>40</u>, <u>88</u>, <u>90</u>, <u>92</u>, <u>99</u>, <u>164</u>, <u>165</u>, <u>195</u>, <u>230</u>, <u>238</u>, <u>240</u>.

`C text...didn't end`: 203.

C_file: 11, <u>14</u>.

C_file_name: <u>11</u>.

c_line_write: <u>78</u>.

C_parse: <u>174</u>, 183, 184.

C_printf: <u>14</u>.

C_putc: <u>14</u>.

C_translate: <u>183</u>, 184, 193.

C_xref: <u>62</u>, <u>63</u>, 64, 65, 66, 174, 184.

cancel: <u>100</u>, 101, 102, 107, 137, 139, 140, 183, 184, 185, 195, 197, 198.

`Cannot open index file`: 226.

`Cannot open section file`: 226.

carryover: <u>78</u>.

case_found: <u>111</u>.

case_like: <u>16</u>, 28, 98, 101, 102, 110, 111, 117.

cast: 96, <u>97</u>, 98, 102, 110, 117, 118, 120, 123, 127, 142, 151, 153, 159, 161.

cat: <u>103</u>, 108, 110, 112, 164, 165, 167, 169, 170, 172, 174, 175, 231, 233.

cat_index: <u>97</u>, 98.

cat_name: <u>97</u>, 98, 99.

catch_like: <u>16</u>, 28, 98, 101, 102, 110.

cat1: <u>110</u>, 117, 118, 119, 120, 121, 122, 123, 124, 125, 126, 127, 128, 129, 130, 131, 132, 133, 134, 135, 136, 137, 138, 139, 140, 141, 142, 143, 144, 146, 147, 148, 151, 152, 153, 154, 155, 156, 157, 159, 160, 161, 162, 163.

cat2: <u>110</u>, 117, 118, 120, 124, 127, 129, 130, 131, 134, 138, 139, 140, 146, 151, 152, 153, 154, 160, 161, 162, 163.

cat3: <u>110</u>, 117, 127, 134, 138, 139, 140, 146, 153.

ccode: <u>31</u>, 32, 33, 35, 36, 37, 50, 54, 88, 90.

change_exists: <u>17</u>, 60, 61, 226.

change_file: <u>11</u>.

change_file_name: <u>11</u>.

change_line: <u>11</u>.

change_pending: <u>12</u>.

changed_section: <u>12</u>, 17, 60, 61, 86, 228.

changing: <u>11</u>, 61.

check_complete: <u>11</u>, 226.

chunk_marker: <u>9</u>.

cite_flag: 18, <u>20</u>, 22, 63, 75, 220, 221, 222, 247.

colcol: <u>97</u>, 98, 101, 102, 110, 126, 154, 159, 178.

collate: <u>235</u>, 236, 237, 238.

colon: <u>97</u>, 98, 101, 102, 117, 124, 125, 127, 130, 136, 141, 163, 176.

format_code: 30, 32, 35, 62, 63, 64, 65, 66, 69, 88, 174, 184, 210, 211.

format_visible: 206, 207, 211, 215.

found: 102, 113, 117.

fprintf: 14, 78.

freeze_text: 164, 171, 175, 184, 195.

ftemplate: 97, 98, 101, 102, 110, 182.

func_template: 16, 28, 182, 242.

function: 97, 98, 102, 110, 128, 131, 132, 133, 134, 143, 144, 146.

fwrite: 14, 78.

get_line: 11, 35, 36, 40, 45, 49, 53, 79, 88, 90, 92.

get_next: 37, 39, 40, 41, 58, 63, 66, 69, 70, 71, 72, 88, 174, 210, 214, 215, 217, 218, 219.

get_output: 191, 192, 193, 195, 197, 198.

group_found: 207, 209, 226.

gt_eq: 7, 46, 178.

gt_gt: 7, 46, 178.

h: 9.

harmless_message: 10.

hash: 9, 230.

hash_end: 9, 230.

hash_pointer: 9.

hash_size: 4.

Head: 232, 233.

head: 231, 233, 238, 239, 240, 241.

hi_ptr: 103, 104, 112, 167, 169, 170.

high-bit character handling: 39, 100, 179, 180, 235, 236, 238.

history: 10.

i: 102, 164, 165, 170.

id_first: 7, 37, 47, 48, 49, 56, 57, 63, 66, 67, 70, 71, 179, 180, 182, 215.

id_flag: 106, 111, 112, 113, 182, 192, 215.

id_loc: 7, 37, 47, 48, 49, 56, 57, 63, 66, 67, 70, 71, 179, 180, 182, 215.

id_lookup: 9, 27, 28, 37, 63, 66, 70, 71, 182, 215.

identifier: 37, 47, 62, 63, 66, 70, 71, 88, 176, 191, 192, 195, 196, 214, 215.

idx_file: 11, 14, 226.

idx_file_name: 11, 226.

if_clause: 97, 98, 102, 110, 135.

if_head: 97, 98, 102, 110, 138.

if_like: 16, 28, 98, 101, 102, 110, 138, 139, 146.

ignore: 30, 62, 65, 176, 184, 193.

ilk: 16, 21, 27, 70, 71, 111, 112, 182, 196, 242.

Ilk: 9, 16.

Illegal control code...: 202.

Illegal use of @...: 94.

Improper format definition: 215.

Improper macro definition: 214.

in: 102.

include_depth: 11.

indent: 100, 102, 107, 117, 127, 131, 134, 136, 138, 142, 195, 198.

infinity: 237, 238, 239.

init_mathness: 108, 109, 149, 150, 164, 166.

init_node: 27.

init_p: 27.

init_stack: 187, 210, 211, 217, 247.

inner: 185, 186, 192, 198.

inner_tok_flag: 106, 111, 184, 192, 193.

Input ended in mid-comment: 92.

Input ended in middle of string: 49.

Input ended in section name: 53.

input_has_ended: 11, 34, 60, 206.

insert: 97, 98, 101, 102, 110, 146, 176, 180, 183, 184, 213.

inserted: 100, 107, 111, 146, 176, 184, 195, 198.

int_like: 16, 28, 96, 97, 98, 101, 102, 110, 117, 118, 119, 120, 124, 125, 126, 127, 129, 130, 131, 151, 154, 158, 159, 161.

Irreducible scrap sequence...: 172.

is_long_comment: 65, 92, 184.

is_tiny: 21, 196, 242.

isalpha: 8, 38, 47.

isdigit: 8, 38, 47.

ishigh: 39, 40, 47, 92.

islower: 8.

isspace: 8.

isupper: 8.

isxalpha: 39, 40, 47, 87, 196.

isxdigit: 8.

i1: 164.

j: 78, 106, 111, 164, 165, 170, 195, 242.

join: 30, 32, 176, 210.

k: 51, 79, 84, 87, 102, 164, 165, 169, 195.

k_end: 87.

k_limit: 195, 201, 203.

k_section: 227, 228.

l: 27.

langle: 97, 98, 102, 110, 151, 152, 155, 159.

lbrace: 96, 97, 98, 101, 102, 110, 117, 127, 129, 130, 136, 138, 176.

left_preproc: 41, 42, 176.

length: 9, 27.

lhs: 68, 70, 71.

lhs_not_simple: 110.

limit: 8, 29, 35, 36, 40, 45, 46, 49, 53, 56, 57, 79, 88, 90, 92, 195, 201, 203.

line: 11.

Line had to be broken: 85.

line_break: 30, 32, 176, 210.

line_length: 4, 77.

scrap_base: 103, <u>104</u>, 105, 164, 165, 169, 170, 171, 172, 183.

scrap_info: 103, <u>104</u>, 105, 169, 183, 213, 215, 234, 239, 247, 249.

scrap_info_end: <u>104</u>, 177, 238.

scrap_pointer: 103, 104, 109, 112, 113, 164, 165, 169, 170, 183, 233.

scrap_ptr: 103, <u>104</u>, 105, 112, 167, 169, 170, 174, 175, 177, 183, 213, 215, 233, 247.

scrapping: 181, <u>182</u>.

scratch: <u>195</u>, 201.

sec_depth: <u>207</u>, 209.

Section name didn't end: 54.

Section name too long: 53.

section_check: <u>74</u>, <u>75</u>, 76.

section_code: 191, <u>192</u>, 195.

section_count: <u>12</u>, 17, 21, 22, 60, 61, 115, 172, 206, 208, 209, 218, 228.

section_flag: <u>106</u>, 111, 176, 192, 218, 219, 247.

section_lookup: <u>9</u>, 51, 52.

section_name: <u>30</u>, 32, 37, 50, 51, 62, 63, 65, 66, 72, 176, 183, 210, 217, 219.

section_print: <u>246</u>, <u>247</u>, 248.

section_scrap: <u>97</u>, 98, 101, 102, 110, 176, 219.

section_text: <u>7</u>, 37, 48, 49, 51, 52, 53.

section_text_end: <u>7</u>, 49, 53.

section_xref_switch: 18, <u>19</u>, 20, 22, 63, 72.

semi: <u>97</u>, 98, 101, 102, 110, 117, 122, 124, 127, 130, 140, 141, 147, 161, 176, 215.

set_file_flag: <u>23</u>, 72.

sharp_include_line: 40, <u>43</u>, 44, 45.

show_banner: 3, <u>13</u>.

show_happiness: <u>13</u>, 226.

show_progress: <u>13</u>, 61, 206, 209, 226.

sixteen_bits: <u>12</u>, 18, 19, 21, 24, 86, 106, 111, 112, 115, 192, 193, 222, 227, 233.

sizeof_like: <u>16</u>, 28, 98, 101, 102, 110.

skip_comment: 88.

skip_limbo: <u>34</u>, <u>35</u>, 60, 88.

skip_restricted: 35, 50, <u>55</u>, <u>56</u>, 88.

skip_TEX: <u>36</u>, 66, 88.

sort_pointer: <u>233</u>.

sort_ptr: 231, <u>233</u>, 238, 239, 240, 241.

space_checked: <u>207</u>, 211, 214, 215.

spec_ctrl: 62, 63, <u>174</u>.

special string characters: 179.

spotless: <u>10</u>.

sprint_section_name: <u>9</u>, 201.

sprintf: 86, 209.

squash: 108, 110, 117, 118, 119, 122, 123, 124, 125, 126, 127, 130, 134, 136, 138, 139, 141,

146, 147, 148, 151, 152, 153, 154, 155, 157, 158, 159, 160, 161, 163, <u>165</u>.

src: <u>67</u>.

stack: 186, <u>187</u>, 188, 189, 249.

stack_end: <u>187</u>, 189.

stack_pointer: <u>186</u>, 187.

stack_ptr: 186, <u>187</u>, 189, 190.

stack_size: <u>4</u>, 187, 249.

stdout: 14, 106.

stmt: <u>97</u>, 98, 102, 110, 117, 118, 128, 131, 132, 133, 134, 136, 137, 138, 139, 140, 141, 143, 144, 145, 147.

strcmp: <u>2</u>.

strcpy: <u>2</u>, 98, 236.

string: <u>37</u>, 49, 176, 179.

String didn't end: 49.

String too long: 49.

strlen: <u>2</u>, 201.

strncmp: <u>2</u>, 27, 44, 51, 198.

strncpy: <u>2</u>, 78.

struct_head: <u>97</u>, 98, 102, 110, 130.

struct_like: <u>16</u>, 28, 98, 101, 102, 110, 124, 154.

t: <u>27</u>.

tag: <u>97</u>, 98, 102, 110, 117, 125, 141, 143.

template_like: <u>16</u>, 28, 98, 101, 102, 110.

term_write: 9, <u>14</u>, 49, 53, 85, 173.

TeX string should be...: 210.

tex_file: 11, <u>14</u>, 80, 226.

tex_file_name: <u>11</u>.

tex_new_line: <u>78</u>.

tex_printf: <u>78</u>, 80.

tex_putc: <u>78</u>.

TEX_string: <u>30</u>, 32, 37, 50, 176, 210.

text_pointer: <u>24</u>, 25, 103, 106, 111, 170, 183, 184, 189, 193, 213.

text_ptr: <u>25</u>, 26, 106, 111, 164, 166, 170, 171, 175, 177, 184, 193, 195, 213, 247.

thin_space: <u>30</u>, 32, 176, 210.

this_section: <u>216</u>, 217, 218, 220.

this_xref: <u>244</u>, 245.

time: <u>102</u>.

tok_field: <u>186</u>, 187, 189, 190.

tok_flag: <u>106</u>, 108, 109, 111, 184, 192, 213.

tok_loc: <u>112</u>, 113.

tok_mem: 25, 26, <u>106</u>, 108, 186, 187, 192, 200, 213, 247, 249.

tok_mem_end: <u>25</u>, 91, 166, 171, 177.

tok_ptr: <u>25</u>, 26, 91, 92, 94, 108, 164, 166, 170, 171, 177, 179, 184, 193, 213, 247.

tok_start: 24, <u>25</u>, 26, 103, 108, 109, 111, 164, 184, 192, 193, 213, 247, 249.

tok_start_end: <u>25</u>, 166, 177.

⟨ Append a TEX string, without forming a scrap 180 ⟩   Used in section 176.

⟨ Append a string or constant 179 ⟩   Used in section 176.

⟨ Append the scrap appropriate to *next_control* 176 ⟩   Used in section 174.

⟨ Cases for *base* 129 ⟩   Used in section 110.

⟨ Cases for *binop* 121 ⟩   Used in section 110.

⟨ Cases for *case_like* 141 ⟩   Used in section 110.

⟨ Cases for *cast* 122 ⟩   Used in section 110.

⟨ Cases for *catch_like* 142 ⟩   Used in section 110.

⟨ Cases for *colcol* 126 ⟩   Used in section 110.

⟨ Cases for *const_like* 158 ⟩   Used in section 110.

⟨ Cases for *decl_head* 127 ⟩   Used in section 110.

⟨ Cases for *decl* 128 ⟩   Used in section 110.

⟨ Cases for *delete_like* 162 ⟩   Used in section 110.

⟨ Cases for *do_like* 140 ⟩   Used in section 110.

⟨ Cases for *else_head* 137 ⟩   Used in section 110.

⟨ Cases for *else_like* 136 ⟩   Used in section 110.

⟨ Cases for *exp* 117 ⟩   Used in section 110.

⟨ Cases for *fn_decl* 132 ⟩   Used in section 110.

⟨ Cases for *for_like* 156 ⟩   Used in section 110.

⟨ Cases for *ftemplate* 155 ⟩   Used in section 110.

⟨ Cases for *function* 133 ⟩   Used in section 110.

⟨ Cases for *if_clause* 138 ⟩   Used in section 110.

⟨ Cases for *if_head* 139 ⟩   Used in section 110.

⟨ Cases for *if_like* 135 ⟩   Used in section 110.

⟨ Cases for *insert* 148 ⟩   Used in section 110.

⟨ Cases for *int_like* 124 ⟩   Used in section 110.

⟨ Cases for *langle* 151 ⟩   Used in section 110.

⟨ Cases for *lbrace* 134 ⟩   Used in section 110.

⟨ Cases for *lpar* 118 ⟩   Used in section 110.

⟨ Cases for *lproc* 146 ⟩   Used in section 110.

⟨ Cases for *new_exp* 154 ⟩   Used in section 110.

⟨ Cases for *new_like* 153 ⟩   Used in section 110.

⟨ Cases for *operator_like* 160 ⟩   Used in section 110.

⟨ Cases for *prelangle* 149 ⟩   Used in section 110.

⟨ Cases for *prerangle* 150 ⟩   Used in section 110.

⟨ Cases for *public_like* 125 ⟩   Used in section 110.

⟨ Cases for *question* 163 ⟩   Used in section 110.

⟨ Cases for *raw_int* 159 ⟩   Used in section 110.

⟨ Cases for *raw_ubin* 157 ⟩   Used in section 110.

⟨ Cases for *section_scrap* 147 ⟩   Used in section 110.

⟨ Cases for *semi* 145 ⟩   Used in section 110.

⟨ Cases for *sizeof_like* 123 ⟩   Used in section 110.

⟨ Cases for *stmt* 144 ⟩   Used in section 110.

⟨ Cases for *struct_head* 131 ⟩   Used in section 110.

⟨ Cases for *struct_like* 130 ⟩   Used in section 110.

⟨ Cases for *tag* 143 ⟩   Used in section 110.

⟨ Cases for *template_like* 152 ⟩   Used in section 110.

⟨ Cases for *typedef_like* 161 ⟩   Used in section 110.

⟨ Cases for *ubinop* 120 ⟩   Used in section 110.

⟨ Cases for *unop* 119 ⟩   Used in section 110.

⟨ Cases involving nonstandard characters 178 ⟩   Used in section 176.

⟨ Check for end of comment 93 ⟩   Used in section 92.

⟨Check if next token is **include** 44⟩   Used in section 42.

⟨Check if we're at the end of a preprocessor command 45⟩   Used in section 40.

⟨Check that '=' or '==' follows this section name, and emit the scraps to start the section definition 218⟩   Used in section 217.

⟨Clear *bal* and **return** 95⟩   Used in section 92.

⟨Combine the irreducible scraps that remain 171⟩   Used in section 170.

⟨Common code for CWEAVE and CTANGLE 5, 7, 8, 9, 10, 11, 12, 13, 14, 15⟩   Used in section 1.

⟨Compress two-symbol operator 46⟩   Used in section 40.

⟨Copy a quoted character into the buffer 204⟩   Used in section 203.

⟨Copy special things when $c \equiv$ '@', '\\' 94⟩   Used in section 92.

⟨Copy the C text into the *buffer* array 203⟩   Used in section 201.

⟨Do the first pass of sorting 230⟩   Used in section 226.

⟨Emit the scrap for a section name if present 219⟩   Used in section 217.

⟨Get a constant 48⟩   Used in section 40.

⟨Get a string 49⟩   Used in sections 40 and 50.

⟨Get an identifier 47⟩   Used in section 40.

⟨Get control code and possible section name 50⟩   Used in section 40.

⟨Global variables 17, 19, 25, 31, 37, 41, 43, 58, 68, 73, 77, 97, 104, 108, 168, 187, 191, 207, 216, 227, 229, 233, 235, 244⟩   Used in section 1.

⟨If end of name or erroneous control code, **break** 54⟩   Used in section 53.

⟨If semi-tracing, show the irreducible scraps 172⟩   Used in section 171.

⟨If tracing, print an indication of where we are 173⟩   Used in section 170.

⟨Include files 6, 38⟩   Used in section 1.

⟨Insert new cross-reference at q, not at beginning of list 116⟩   Used in section 115.

⟨Invert the cross-reference list at *cur_name*, making *cur_xref* the head 245⟩   Used in section 243.

⟨Look ahead for strongest line break, **goto** *reswitch* 198⟩   Used in section 197.

⟨Make sure that there is room for the new scraps, tokens, and texts 177⟩   Used in sections 176 and 184.

⟨Make sure the entries *pp* through $pp + 3$ of *cat* are defined 167⟩   Used in section 166.

⟨Match a production at *pp*, or increase *pp* if there is no match 110⟩   Used in section 166.

⟨Output a control, look ahead in case of line breaks, possibly **goto** *reswitch* 197⟩   Used in section 195.

⟨Output a section name 200⟩   Used in section 195.

⟨Output all the section names 248⟩   Used in section 226.

⟨Output all the section numbers on the reference list *cur_xref* 223⟩   Used in section 222.

⟨Output an identifier 196⟩   Used in section 195.

⟨Output index entries for the list at *sort_ptr* 241⟩   Used in section 239.

⟨Output saved *indent* or *outdent* tokens 199⟩   Used in sections 195 and 198.

⟨Output the code for the beginning of a new section 209⟩   Used in section 208.

⟨Output the code for the end of a section 224⟩   Used in section 208.

⟨Output the cross-references at *cur_name* 243⟩   Used in section 241.

⟨Output the name at *cur_name* 242⟩   Used in section 241.

⟨Output the text of the section name 201⟩   Used in section 200.

⟨Predeclaration of procedures 2, 34, 39, 55, 59, 62, 64, 74, 83, 91, 114, 181, 194, 205, 212, 221, 225, 237, 246⟩   Used in section 1.

⟨Print a snapshot of the scrap list if debugging 169⟩   Used in sections 164 and 165.

⟨Print error messages about unused or undefined section names 76⟩   Used in section 60.

⟨Print token r in symbolic form 107⟩   Used in section 106.

⟨Print warning message, break the line, **return** 85⟩   Used in section 84.

⟨Process a format definition 70⟩   Used in section 69.

⟨Process simple format in limbo 71⟩   Used in section 35.

⟨Put section name into *section_text* 53⟩   Used in section 51.

⟨Raise preprocessor flag 42⟩   Used in section 40.

⟨Reduce the scraps using the productions until no more rules apply 166⟩   Used in section 170.

⟨ Replace `"@@"` by `"@"` 67 ⟩   Used in sections 63 and 66.

⟨ Rest of *trans_plus* union 232 ⟩   Used in section 103.

⟨ Scan a verbatim string 57 ⟩   Used in section 50.

⟨ Scan the section name and make *cur_section* point to it 51 ⟩   Used in section 50.

⟨ Set initial values 20, 26, 32, 52, 80, 82, 98, 105, 188, 234, 236 ⟩   Used in section 3.

⟨ Show cross-references to this section 220 ⟩   Used in section 208.

⟨ Skip next character, give error if not '@' 202 ⟩   Used in section 201.

⟨ Sort and output the index 239 ⟩   Used in section 226.

⟨ Special control codes for debugging 33 ⟩   Used in section 32.

⟨ Split the list at *sort_ptr* into further lists 240 ⟩   Used in section 239.

⟨ Start a format definition 215 ⟩   Used in section 211.

⟨ Start a macro definition 214 ⟩   Used in section 211.

⟨ Store all the reserved words 28 ⟩   Used in section 3.

⟨ Store cross-reference data for the current section 61 ⟩   Used in section 60.

⟨ Store cross-references in the C part of a section 72 ⟩   Used in section 61.

⟨ Store cross-references in the TEX part of a section 66 ⟩   Used in section 61.

⟨ Store cross-references in the definition part of a section 69 ⟩   Used in section 61.

⟨ Tell about changed sections 228 ⟩   Used in section 226.

⟨ Translate the C part of the current section 217 ⟩   Used in section 208.

⟨ Translate the TEX part of the current section 210 ⟩   Used in section 208.

⟨ Translate the current section 208 ⟩   Used in section 206.

⟨ Translate the definition part of the current section 211 ⟩   Used in section 208.

⟨ Typedef declarations 18, 24, 103, 186 ⟩   Used in section 1.